CONTEMPLATING SUICIDE

Suicide is devastating. It is an assault on our ideas of what living is about. In *Contemplating Suicide*, Gavin Fairbairn takes a fresh look at suicidal self harm. His view is distinctive in emphasising the intentions that a person has in acting, rather than external facts.

Fairbairn constructs a natural history of suicidal self harm and examines some of the ethical issues it raises. He sets his philosophical reflections against a background of experience in the caring professions and uses a storytelling approach in offering a critique of the current language of self harm. He offers cogent reasons for abandoning the mindless use of terms such as *attempted suicide* and *parasuicide*, and introduces a number of new terms including *cosmic roulette*, which he uses to describe a family of human acts in which people gamble with their lives.

By elaborating a richer model of suicidal self harm than most philosophers and practitioners of caring professions currently inhabit, Fairbairn makes a significant contribution to the development of understanding in this area.

Gavin Fairbairn worked in psychiatric social work and special education before taking up his present post at the North East Wales Institute of Higher Education, where he teaches education. He has published widely on the ethics of the caring professions, including medicine, nursing, social work and special education.

SOCIAL ETHICS AND POLICY SERIES
Edited by Anthony Dyson and John Harris
Centre for Social Ethics and Policy,
University of Manchester

CONTEMPLATING SUICIDE

The language and ethics of self harm

Gavin J. Fairbairn

London and New York

First published 1995
by Routledge
11 New Fetter Lane, London EC4P 4EE

Simultaneously published in the USA and Canada
by Routledge
29 West 35th Street, New York, NY 10001

Typeset in Garamond by LaserScript, Mitcham, Surrey
Printed and bound in Great Britain by
Mackays of Chatham PLC, Chatham, Kent

British Library Cataloguing in Publication Data
A catalogue record for this book is available from the British Library

Library of Congress Cataloging in Publication Data
A catalog record for this book has been requested

ISBN 0–415–10605–2 (hbk)
ISBN 0–415–10606–0 (pbk)

By death a person ceases to be involved in interpersonal relationships and he becomes a Thing which his fellow men bury in the ground. The act by which a person turns himself into a Thing is called suicide.

(Chapman, 1970, p. 161)

CONTENTS

PREFACE AND
ACKNOWLEDGEMENTS

> I have heard of . . . a post-war writer who, after having finished
> his first book, committed suicide to attract attention to his
> work. Attention was in fact attracted, but the book was judged
> no good.
>
> (Camus, The Myth of Sisyphus, p. 14)

Human life is a composite history made up of real and imagined
stories and this is reflected in the approach I have taken in writing
this book. At times, it is atypical as a work of either conceptual or
applied philosophy. This is due, in part, to its mixed parentage – it
is born out of a commitment to both moral philosophy and practical
caring; despite its philosophical nature, it makes much use of realistic case material drawn from both my own experience and from
the shared experience of others. At other times it is typical of the
work of applied moral philosophers in making use of hypothetical
examples. This brings me to its godparent – the practice of storytelling; a wide range of examples are explored through this medium.
It is with reference to such examples that we can begin to think
about individual cases, to become sensitive to what was actually
going on.

A number of people have given me support and help in a variety
of ways during the time that I have been thinking of suicide and I
wish to express my gratitude to them. First I wish to acknowledge
the support of John Harris whose interest in my work has helped me
to maintain the conviction that I have something to say. I am also
grateful to a number of friends and colleagues who gave support in
various ways while I was writing my PhD on this topic and also a
chapter for a book edited by others (Fairbairn, 1992d and Fairbairn,
1991b), including Suzy Braye, Heather Draper, Faith Fairbairn, Thomas
Fairbairn, David Francey, Sharon Grimes, Richard Lindley, Dennis

Rowley, Martin Stafford, and Mary West. Susan Fairbairn, in this as in most of my work, deserves particular thanks; though she seldom agrees with what I have to say she often helps me to say it better. I am grateful also for my friends Kathy Galloway and Miller Mair whose quite separate ideas about storytelling led me to view storytelling as a respectable underpinning for my work, even though their influence is not so obvious in these pages as it might have been. One group of my students at NEWI, Cartrefle, deserve thanks for the time that they came to me expressing concern about my welfare saying, 'It's just that whatever topic we are talking about – aesthetics, the nature of education, equality, the primary school curriculum or whatever – you seem to end up talking about suicide. We just wanted to know that you weren't depressed or anything.' Finally I want to express my gratitude to the staff of the Open Access Centre at NEWI, Cartrefle: David Mosford, Mark Williams and Sandra Pegum, to whom I owe my development of that most valuable of late twentieth century skills: wordprocessing.

Though I hope that *Contemplating Suicide* will attract some attention, I do not intend to suicide in order to see that it does. I do, however, wish to dedicate it to someone. It is dedicated, with my love, to Susan with whom I have faced the fire, the flood and the ice, and with whom I have shared and am sharing the joys and sorrows of parenthood.

Gavin J. Fairbairn
Dumfries
September 1994

A NOTE ABOUT
LANGUAGE AND STYLE

At times I have written in a personal way, owning experiences as having happened to me and bringing them to bear upon the subject matter with which I am dealing. Other parts of my personal experience, for reasons of confidentiality, I have written about in a more impersonal style, attributing them to imaginary characters. Referring to first hand experiences, whether of myself or others, is perhaps unusual in a philosophical book. However, I hope that doing so has helped me to guard against the possibility of falling into the trap of writing philosophically in a way that fails really to connect with what matters to those whose lives and work bring them into contact with the human phenomena and dilemmas with which I am concerned. I have, however, tried to avoid simply gossiping about personal experience; when real cases are referred to they are used in making points with more general application.

At other times I use the device, beloved of the majority of moral philosophers who deal in similar areas, of invoking hypothetical, sometimes rather far fetched, examples; I hope it is obvious from the context when I am doing this rather than using real case studies. The use of stories which are successively modified in order to make points is arguably the principal tool of the applied moral philosopher. It is interesting to note its relationship to other disciplines including psychodrama, where it relates closely to the use of techniques such as role play (Moreno, 1948), and theology, where it relates to the spiritual exercises devised by St Ignatius (Fleming, 1980) and also to more recent work about ways of developing understanding of Biblical events (Galloway, 1988).

GENDER SPECIFIC LANGUAGE

It is common nowadays for writers to avoid the exclusive use of the masculine pronouns to indicate their awareness that there are 'shes' as well as 'hes' in the world. One way of doing this is to make sure that they use personal pronouns, for example 'she', 'he' or 'her', only when a specific person is being discussed and that, when they do so, they accurately match the pronouns used to the sex of the individual in question. Another possibility is to use the plural forms 'they', 'their' and 'them' in place of singular personal pronouns. I find the second of these two practices stylistically offensive. The first would be a difficult convention for me to adopt because I often use hypothetical examples.

As a way of trying to avoid the exclusive use of male pronouns I have, however, adopted a convention which I think is quite successful (Fairbairn and Winch, 1991). Where possible, I use masculine pronouns when I am referring to clients or patients, or where the person in question is a self harmer or a suicide. Where the individual is a professional or an intervener in another's self harm or suicide, I have tried to use feminine pronouns. Exceptions to this convention sometimes occur when I am discussing actual cases, where to adopt the convention would be to mis-sex someone, or where to stick with the convention would cause confusion, and also where I am discussing examples raised by others, where to stick to my convention might again cause confusion by mis-sexing a character. No doubt this convention is not entirely satisfactory. A person from another planet (if there are any) reading this book might gain the impression not only that most suicides are male rather than female, which is probably true, but also that most suicide gesturers, cosmic gamblers and other suicidal self harmers are male rather than female, which is probably false. However, since I am committed not only to the idea that there are both 'shes' and 'hes' in the world, but also to the belief that each is as important as the other, I believe it is right to avoid the exclusive use of male pronouns in spite of the danger of being thought illogical by, for example, Martians. The danger of being thought sexist by, for example, feminists, is for me far more scary.

OTHER PROBLEMS WITH LANGUAGE

In mapping out the conceptual territory inhabited by suicide and related forms of self harm, I will be introducing both new terms, and modifications to the use of existing terms. Since existing terms are often inadequate in arguing for the changes I wish to make, at times I have found myself using terms that I have not yet introduced, before I have set out the reasons for their introduction. Rather than solving this problem by introducing a glossary of terms at the outset, I introduce terms when necessary, revisiting and clarifying them when appropriate.

The poverty of our language for discussing suicidal self harm has created other terminological problems for me in discussing the phenomena with which I deal in this book. Though I distinguish between suicide and various self harming activities such as *gestures at suicide* and *cosmic roulette*, for the sake of brevity I sometimes use the common language. For example, at times I refer to a range of self harming acts that resemble suicide, using the expression *suicidal behaviour* though many such acts are not aimed at death. Similarly I sometimes refer to *suiciders* when it would be more accurate (though more long-winded) to refer to 'people who suicide or gesture at suicide or who otherwise deliberately act in self injurious ways that could conceivably end in their deaths'. The term *suicider* I thus use generically in situations where it is equivocal whether a person who has acted in a self harming way, wishes or wished to die and intends or intended to bring about his death. The term *suicide*, when used to refer to people, I have tried to reserve for occasions when it has been decided that a person did act thus, as in the statement, 'The fact that he drank a cup of paraquat, slit his throat and then having put his head in a plastic bag which he secured with an elastic band, he jumped from the top of a fifty storey block, leaves it in little doubt that he was a suicide.'

Another problem that has arisen for me in formulating my ideas is that I make frequent reference to others who discuss the same phenomena using different terms or using the same, or similar, terms in different ways. It is always difficult to cite other writers who use different terms to discuss the same topic, and perhaps even more difficult when they use the same terms but with different meanings. As a result of this, when discussing the work of others, I sometimes use terms in ways that seem inconsistent with the meanings I have stipulated for them. For example, I sometimes use 'suicide' when 'suicider', according to my account, would be more accurate.

1

SUICIDE, LANGUAGE AND ETHICS

An introduction

> The man who kills a man, kills a man. The man who kills himself, kills all men; as far as he is concerned he wipes out the world.
>
> (G.K. Chesterton, cited in Holland, 1969, p. 82)

> Every two hours someone in Britain commits suicide. Translated on to a global scale, an estimated one thousand people a day take their own lives or nearly one a minute.
>
> (Wertheimer, 1991, p. 1)

People harm themselves for a variety of reasons and in a variety of ways and sometimes their self harm results in death. Of course not all of the harm that people cause themselves is deliberate. For example, the harm a person causes himself by overeating or by smoking tobacco, is unlikely to be wished for and aimed at. Nevertheless intentional self harm is very common. Some is aimed at achieving the death of the self harmer and some that is not, may look as if it was.

So some intentional self harm that could end in death, does not have death as its aim. In spite of this, when the protagonist ends up dead, it is most often referred to as *suicide*, the act of intentional and intended, wished-for self destruction. Or at least this is the tendency if the circumstances suggest that the person may have been attempting to kill himself. When a person ends up alive, after acting in a similar way, it is common to talk in terms of *attempted suicide*, even when there is little evidence that death was his intention.

This book is a study of suicide and other varieties of suicidal self harm. However, it is neither a medical study nor a psychological study; nor is it a sociological study. Although it makes reference to the work of those who come into contact with suicidal self harm through their professional and voluntary work, it is neither a critique of practice nor a guidebook for action. Rather it is a philosophical study. It is concerned both with the development of a new way of thinking about suicidal self harm that recognises its complexity as a phenomenon, and with some of the ethical issues that suicidal self harm throws up. My view of suicide is distinctive in not emphasising external facts: the presence or absence of a corpse, along with evidence that the person who has become a corpse intended by some act of his own to do so; it focuses on inward rather than outward events and facts. Unlike murder, or the scoring of goals in football, the definitions of both of which have external facts as their main criteria, suicide is defined by reference to internal facts about intentions.

Much of the book is devoted to an attempt to construct a natural history of suicidal self harm. It is my hope that elaborating a richer model of suicidal self harm than most philosophers and most practitioners of caring professions that come in contact with suicidal behaviour currently inhabit, might contribute to the development of understanding in this area. Among other things, developing a richer model of suicidal self harm may help to reduce the possibility that those who come across what look like self harming acts should think in a simplistic way about them, and thus misidentify them. For example, it may make it less likely that they will believe, or act as if they believe, that familiarity with the physical facts of the matter – the actions of the suicider – is always, or nearly always, sufficient to justify a definite conclusion about the nature of his self harming act.

Acts, actions and suicidal self harm

When I take a pen and write my name on a piece of paper, the sequence of actions that I perform can constitute a variety of different acts depending on the context in which I do so and the piece of paper on which I write. For example, I may be validating an execution, pledging money to a cause in which I have been persuaded to believe, or agreeing to make regular payments to a bank in relation to a loan that the manager has agreed to advance to me. In a similar way the action or sequence of actions that a person performs in causing himself serious harm can constitute a variety of acts. Consider, for example, Debbie and Paula, each of whom set fire to herself.

Debbie had a long history of 'suicide attempts' and of self abuse including the ingestion of non-therapeutic dosages of prescribed medication and the infliction of minor wounds on her arms and legs. She had spent several periods in a psychiatric hospital as an informal patient. During one of these she had an argument with the ward sister, towards the end of which she lit a match and held it close to her nightdress saying that she was going to kill herself.

Paula's family was in turmoil because of problems that her son was experiencing. As a result they were receiving regular help from community psychiatric services. Though she herself had received treatment for depression many years before, Paula was receiving none at present. One day she went to the newsagent's and bought a cigarette lighter though she didn't smoke. The following day she went to a garage and bought a petrol can and a gallon of petrol though she didn't drive. The next day, after lunch with her family, she went out into the garden shed, poured the petrol over her clothes and set fire to herself. She died some hours later. After her death a note was found in her desk apologising for having been a bad mother.

Paula planned what she was going to do with great care and took several days to gather together the materials necessary to burn herself to death. Her act was probably suicide; she seems to have wanted to be dead, planned her death carefully and succeeded in bringing it about. By contrast, Debbie acted on impulse, without thinking about the likely outcome. Though she intentionally lit the match that set her nightdress alight causing her injuries, and indeed intended to set her nightdress alight, she was surprised when it caught fire so violently that despite the proximity of help, she suffered 30 per cent burns. Debbie probably did not intend to die. Her act was stupid but not suicidal; it is probably best thought of as an aggressive gesture, aimed at the ward sister rather than at herself. Even if she had died, Debbie would not have been a suicide.[1]

In distinguishing between the 'actions' Debbie and Paula performed and the 'acts' they represented, I am drawing on a distinction made by Harré and Secord (1972) though there is an important difference between the way in which they think of this distinction and the way in which I construe it. Whereas by their account, the act enacted by way of a given action or action sequence depends upon the context in which it is performed, I think the nature of acts depends also on the intention with which the actions, or action sequences that comprise them, are performed. Following a description of the action sequence that comprises the act of marriage for gypsies, Harré and Secord write:

> Reference to inner states is of no help . . . for one can leap over the fire joyfully, resentfully, fearfully, nervously, unintentionally, unwillingly, unwittingly, drunk or sober etc., etc., and still find oneself married. Compare the variety of inner states to the accompaniment of which one may buy something at an auction, where a careless movement, if it has a certain meaning to the auctioneer may land you with a Vermeer that you can ill afford.
>
> (p. 163)

Most acts depend for their meaning on the context in which they are performed; it is this that allows Harré and Secord to make their amusing observation about the dangers of auction sale rooms. But while buying at an auction, becoming married, scoring goals, etc., are acts that gain their meaning in performance, this is not true of all acts. For example, the act of promising, acts of religious devotion and the act of suicide depend upon something happening with a certain intention in mind. In each case the agent's intention in acting makes his act different from what it would have been had he behaved in the same way but with a different intention.

A priest who recites the words of the eucharistic prayer and distributes the bread and wine while thinking about his Sunday dinner, does not celebrate the eucharist any more than a tape recorder that 'recited' the words would, though interestingly enough his flock, using his citation as a focus, may do so. The person who swears faithfully that he will never divulge a secret shared by a friend, does not promise (even though he may say that he does) unless his intention is always to keep the secret. And a suicide is not a suicide because of what a person does, or where he does it, or how he ends up; it is a suicide because of the intention with which he does it.

What act is represented by *these* actions on the part of *this* individual?

The same action or action sequence can represent more than one act at the same time. Consider, for example, the meeting of two heads of state on an official occasion. They shake hands warmly because as well as acting in their official capacities, they happen to like one another rather a lot and are hence pleased to meet again. If they make their warm handshaking *look vigorous* for the sake of the film crews transmitting the event to the world, their handshake constitutes several acts – the official greeting, the genuine meeting of friends and a theatrical performance designed to convince others of their good intentions towards one another.

So the same action can at the same time constitute several acts. Sometimes also it may be construed as representing different acts by different people. Consider, for example, a woman who greets her husband's best friend warmly as he enters their home before a dinner party. Her husband might construe her actions as representing a warm and kindly greeting to someone she hasn't seen in ages, while both she and her husband's friend see them for what they really are – a deliciously warm, because illicit, greeting to her lover, whom she hasn't seen for twenty-four hours.

Sometimes people set out to deceive others by their actions, intending that they should be viewed as one act when in fact they are another. The dinner party wife suppressed her feelings so that her act in greeting her guest looked kindly rather than passionate; and the husband who tries to persuade his wife that his holding hands with the pretty young woman she saw him with in the café was really the sealing of a business contract, tries to persuade her that his act was honourable rather than a sign of infidelity. Or consider two people holidaying in the same Florida hotel who have met, apparently by chance, but actually because one of them, in the best tradition of Hollywood movies, has set things up so that their meeting is inevitable. The one who has staged their 'chance' meeting has designs on the other and spends the evening flattering and wooing and generally setting the scene for a 'romantic' and intimate encounter. The other, romantically wooed and flattered, and melting with the passion that such wooing and flattery can produce, is persuaded after more flattery to 'have a nightcap' in his new acquaintance's suite. In this situation a seducer has used all available means to get another into bed. The seduced individual for his part construed his new lover's flattery as genuine and honourable interest; he has construed his companion's act – which is in truth not what it seems to be for s/he is acting the romantic while being a scoundrel – as a genuine expression of interest in him as a person. His companion's act is one of seduction; the flattery was designed to ensnare him. When he wakes up alone the next morning to discover that his lover of the night before has checked out of the hotel, he realises that rather than having been swept off his feet in the spirit of all true romance, he has been used, abused and discarded. As a result he will probably reconstrue his lover's actions as an act of despicable deceit.

The examples of deception that I have given are examples of what we might call dishonourable deception. But some deception is honourable. Consider an actor on the stage who gives the impression that he is overcome with despair at the news that someone has died – what is his act? From the point of view of a member of the audience, it looks like an act of despair; however, the fact that the 'tender act' in question is happening on stage allows the audience to recognise it for what it is, a piece of play-acting. Harré and Secord discuss the range of acts that it is possible to simulate:

> some episodes are made up of the genuine performance of the actions constituting the act–action structure of the episode, while in other episodes the very same actions may be only a mock or simulated performance. In this way there can be real marriages, and simulated marriages on the stage, real murders and simulated murders in a TV serial.
>
> (p. 13)

And there can be simulated suicides – which I call gestured suicides – that are enacted in the everyday world.[2] In the case of simulated murders or marriages or even suicides, which take place in the theatre, in the movies, or on TV, the context in which it takes place tells us when a given act is a simulation and when it is the real thing. In real life on the other hand, it may be difficult to tell when a suicide is simulated because the cues that would tell us that what we were witness to was a simulation in each of the other cases is, in life, missing. The job of deciding what kind of act an apparent 'suicide' represents, such as is carried out in a legal setting by coroners, and in situations of practical care by professionals such as doctors, nurses and social workers, involves detective work of a complex kind, drawing together information from the individual's past, from his friends, relatives and associates, witnesses to his last actions if there are any, and any empirical evidence from the scene that might be available.

Deciding whether an act was aimed at death

Suicide, the act of deliberate, intentional and wished-for self destruction, may be performed via a wide range of self harming actions including overdosing on drugs, cutting one's throat or wrists, putting one's head in a gas oven, leaping from a building or running in front of a fast moving train or car. Perhaps more importantly, the same self harming action may represent a number of different acts depending on the intentions of the actor. Does a person who takes an overdose of pills intend to kill himself, to end up alive, or to take a gamble on life? Each of these, by my account, would constitute a different act. But as I have already shown, it is not just the physical intentions that a self harmer has that can change the nature of his act; his social and personal intentions are also important in determining the nature of the act he performs.

In coming to a decision about what act is performed (or what acts are performed) by a person who self harms, it will thus be necessary to consider not only whether he intended to end up alive or dead, but what personal and social intentions motivated him when he acted. An act of suicide performed via the action of taking a fatal overdose could at the same time represent the act of communicating to the world that one's life is so bad that one would prefer to be dead, and the act of blaming or punishing a loved one for some real or imagined hurt. And an act of gestured suicide performed via the action of taking a non-fatal overdose could constitute a similar range of acts. However, the question of whether a person who self harms suicidally intended by his actions to achieve his death, remains of primary importance.

The ways that we think about (and act in relation to) the self harm that an individual causes himself will depend both upon the act that we take it to represent, and our view of such acts. It is thus important to come to some decision about the nature of a self harmer's act whether he ended up dead or alive. If alive it is important in order that sensible and helpful action can be taken to do what is best for the individual and those who care about him; if dead it is important in order that those who cared for the person might be able to have the peace that comes from knowing, as far as is possible, the way in which someone they loved or cared for died.

No one can tell with certainty whether a person who has survived serious self inflicted harm intended to live or to die. Nor is it possible to tell in relation to one who dies as the result of such harm whether he intended to die or to live; certainly his ending up dead or alive will not be a sure indication of his intention. However, there is no doubt that some people who take apparently suicidal action have no intention of dying. Perhaps especially in the case of drug overdose, it is possible to miscalculate and to end up dead rather than the object of caring attention, though sometimes, like Frances who I discuss in Chapter 7, a person might both be the object of caring attention for a while and end up dead. More importantly from a practical point of view, an individual who has carried out an intentional self harming which has not led to his death, may actually have intended to kill himself. So it is important to decide what a suicidal self harmer's physical intentions were in order that decisions can be made about how he should be treated, what would be helpful to him and what, for example, might decrease the chances that he will act in similar ways in the future.

What should count as convincing evidence that someone who has died or who is likely to die, as the result of an intentional act, intended to die? The apparently objective evidence provided by a suicide note may not give a foolproof means of deciding the intentions of a suicidal self harmer. Decisions about whether a 'suicide note' is an honest attempt to communicate the intentions of the individual who wrote it are difficult, since the individual who has written it may have had something other than straightforward intentions in doing so. He may have intended only to induce in others the belief that he intended to kill himself and his 'suicide note' might thus be nothing more than part of an elaborate suicide gesture.

Consider, for example, the following case.

Joseph had been a nurse for many years but was in hospital awaiting major surgery; he was anxious and depressed about his future. One evening the night sister found him unconscious and bleeding from the neck; he had taken an overdose of pain killers and had cut his throat; by his bedside was a note saying that he had taken his life because he couldn't cope with more medical treatment.

From the fact that he cut his throat and took an overdose that could have killed him, we might conclude that Joseph hoped to ensure his swift and certain demise. However, when we consider that he had worked as a nurse and hence was aware of the likelihood that he would be discovered, and that the wound he had caused himself was of a relatively trivial nature, things seem much less clear. The fact that the morning after his self harming actions, many of Joseph's friends and colleagues received dramatic letters beginning 'By the time you receive this letter I will be dead' and giving a gory description of what he intended to do, suggests that perhaps his intention was to attract attention rather than to achieve his death. Whether this is true or not is beside the point. It remains the case that his suicide note did not announce his death. The fact that he left a note saying that he intended suicide, proves only that he intended to inform people that death was his aim, and not that it *was* his aim.

The method for self harming that a person who acts in what looks like a suicidal way chooses, is sometimes thought important in making a decision about whether he should be considered a suicide. Discussing the methods self harmers choose, Curran *et al.* (1980) write:

> some of them are nearly always associated with serious intent to die, and rarely with attention seeking or other non-serious attempts. These are fire arms, hanging, drowning, jumping from heights, swallowing caustics or acids and, especially recently, the use of paraquat and similar weed killers.
>
> (p. 201)

By contrast some self harming actions, such as cutting the wrists transversely and overdosing on prescribed medication, are much less likely to end in death and are much less likely to be about the attempt to achieve death. As a result of these differences in the likelihood that different methods will end in death, those who adopt methods with a high risk of death are likely to be thought of as unequivocally having had the intention to die. On the other hand, those who adopt methods from which rescue is more probable, are more likely to be thought of as play-acting, or gesturing, or crying for help, or gambling, or submitting themselves to trial by ordeal, or as dying as the result of a tragic accident or mistake.

However, though there may be some correlation between what a person does and his intention – for example, a man does not leap from a skyscraper with a plastic bag over his head having recently ingested a large quantity of sleeping pills and slit his wrists, with the idea in mind that he may be saved – a simple correlation cannot be made between method and intention.

Even if what he does involves, or seems to involve, acting in a way that is very likely to end with him dead, a self harmer may not intend to die. For example, he may die as the result of an accident while threatening or gesturing suicide. A person could fall accidentally from a multi-storey building while threatening to do so, though he had no intention of carrying out his threat; or he may intentionally close his finger on the trigger of a loaded gun that he believed to be empty, or accidentally close it on the trigger of a gun that he knew to be loaded but did not intend to use. Or in a deliberate but spontaneous act, he could do something that ended his life having given no thought to its result, because he was so overcome with grief or with upset at another person, that for a time rational thought was beyond him. On the other hand, even if a person's death results from what looks like an accident, it may have been intended to bring death; for example, a person who is knocked down by an articulated lorry as he steps out from behind a parked bus, may have been waiting until a suitably large vehicle approached before he drifted, apparently dreamily, into the road.

So the method used is not a reliable indicator of suicidal intention. To some extent the methods that people use to self harm will depend upon availability. As a result the act of a person who self harms using a method that has a high likelihood of a fatal outcome in a place where that method of self harming is readily available, may well be different from that of one who uses the same method in a place where this method is not readily available. In a country with a modern health service and freely available medical care, the incidence of drug overdosing is likely to be higher than in a country where such societally sanctioned poisons are not readily available; where firearms are a common household item, we might expect an increase in the rate of suicidal self harmings involving weapons; and since a higher percentage of suicidal acts involving firearms lead to death than suicidal acts involving prescribed drugs, we would expect to see higher rates of fatal self harm in countries where firearms are more frequently used. At first sight it might seem that people in such countries must be more suicidal. However, it could less dramatically simply be the case that because of availability, they more frequently use highly dangerous means in order to gesture suicide or gamble with life and death, and by miscalculation, accident or bad luck, end up dead rather than alive.

Curran *et al.* (1980) suggest that the circumstances in which a self harming takes place will also give an indication of the intention of the individual. Certainly the place in which the self harm was performed and whether it was apparently planned or impulsive, will offer clues about the protagonist's motivation and intentions in acting as he did. Where the chances were high that an individual would be found before death, it seems less likely that he intended to die. On the other hand, where a person has taken his fatal action in a place and at a time that make it unlikely that he will be discovered, say in the middle of a deserted moor late at night, it seems much more likely that the intention was death.

Misidentifying and mislabelling suicidal self harm of different kinds

Partly as a result of the difficulties in telling what an individual intends by what he does, suicide and other varieties of suicidal self harm are often misidentified.

Where death has occurred

Some suicides will mistakenly be labelled as death by misadventure or accident, while some actions that end in death but were not aimed at achieving it, may be viewed as suicide. One reason that mistakes occur in deciding on the nature of the suicidal acts that people perform is that most often it is difficult to decide what the intention of a person was in acting. Another reason is that the model of suicidal self harm that is embraced by most people is narrow and relatively unelaborated. As a result there is a tendency to jump to conclusions without giving proper attention to the complexity of the human persons whose lives they are assessing and in relation to whom they will be acting.

At times there may be some reticence about deciding that a death was a suicide even where it was publicly and dramatically achieved. Where suicide seems possible or even plausible, and yet, as often happens in coroners' courts, it is decided that there is insufficient evidence to conclude that the protagonist's act was a suicide, its nature is brought into question. But coroners' courts do not necessarily come to the correct conclusions and some coroners may be rather unwilling to reach suicide verdicts. As a result they may not conclude that a death was suicide even where independent witnesses

11

have testified to the apparently intentional nature of the deceased person's actions in procuring his death. Verdicts other than suicide are thus likely unless there is a considerable accumulation of other evidence, such as a previous history of such behaviour and/or a suicide note, to suggest that the person intended to die, and in some cases may be delivered even if there is.

Why should coroners be unwilling to deliver suicide verdicts? One reason might be that they might wish to protect family and friends from trauma. Wertheimer (1991) concurs with this view: 'they will seek to protect relatives from what is sometimes considered to be a distressing and unwelcome verdict' (p. 2). Trauma might be caused to relatives and others who cared for the deceased, in two ways. First of all, knowing that someone they cared for killed himself, could create feelings of guilt should they conclude that they could have noticed that something was amiss and taken steps to prevent the suicidal act occurring. A second way in which trauma might be caused relates to the fact that though it is no longer a legal offence,[3] suicide still carries considerable stigma in the public imagination. To have their relative's or friend's death labelled as a suicide might, for this reason, cause distress to the family and friends of a self harmer.

Another and perhaps more common reason that a benevolent coroner might choose to decide that a given death was not the result of a suicide, might be that in the case of death by suicide, families are unlikely to be able to benefit from insurance policies covering the deceased person's life. A coroner who delivered a verdict that she believed to be false could thus be involved in cheating an insurance company out of money; perhaps for this reason no coroner would ever do such a thing.

Where death has not occurred

Where death has not occurred, mistakes can also be made in identifying the nature of a suicidal act. Writing in the context of a discussion of his study into self poisoning in Edinburgh in the early 1960s, Kessel (1965) addresses the possibility that a failed suicide may be misidentified; he writes:

Some instances when an elderly person is overcome by carbon monoxide are accidents, and sympathetic physicians, to spare patients or their relatives unnecessary distress, often feel disposed to fall in with this explanation when it is proffered. Such stories should not be accepted without thorough inquiries. In our experience coal-gas poisoning does not often turn out to be accidental. It is no kindness to a patient to discharge him home with his depression undisclosed and untreated and the circumstances all too ripe for a repeat performance.

(p. 15)

Kessel is drawing attention to the possibility that a person who has acted suicidally with the intention of arranging his death may be harmed by the apparent kindness of those who, out of sympathy, fail to investigate his act thoroughly, because by doing so they may pave the way for another attempt on his life. This is not the only harm that may come to a person as a result of mistakes made in identifying the true nature of his suicidally self harming act. For example, those who rather than attempting suicide unsuccessfully, feign it successfully, may be harmed by having their gesture at suicide treated as if it were an attempt deliberately to bring death, because treating their act as the real thing may encourage them to adopt similar means of influencing the world in the future, perhaps increasing the possibility of death by mistake or even by design.

Developing a richer model of suicide and suicidal self harm

People are not unitary beings and at any time they may have a range of barely formed possibilities for intentional action, each of which may issue for them in acts in the world with which others will have to interact. In the case of suicidal self harm, these others are faced with the problem of deciding which of the possible intentional acts that the self harmer may have been performing, is enacted by the scene from his life story in which they are co-actors. A simple and uncluttered model of such acts makes for easy decision making both about their nature and about the response that would be most appropriate from others. For example, if a psychiatrist embraces a model of suicidal self harm that allows her to assume that whenever she comes into contact with someone who has acted in a way that may have been intended to bring about his death, her patient must be depressed and therefore in need of psychiatric treatment, she has an easy guide to the action she should take. That action, of course, will vary according to the clinical stance she adopts in these matters,

13

whether, for example, she leans towards psychotherapy or towards chemical treatment for depression; nevertheless the view that all who act in serious self harming ways must have intended to die and must therefore be depressed, is a sure guide to action.

However, the fact that a decision is made easier by having an impoverished model does not mean that this model is a good one, nor that the decisions that its adherents make are right or even helpful. A richer model of suicidal self harm and a vocabulary in which to discuss it, would both help us to distinguish between self harmings of different kinds and allow more helpful discussions about, and reactions to, those who self harm in life threatening or apparently life threatening, ways. In this book I begin to develop such a model.

Suicide is devastating. It is an assault on our ideas of what living is about. In attempting to outline a new way of thinking about it and about other self harmings that end or may end in death, or that look as if they might do so or may have done so,[4] I emphasise the intentions that the protagonist had in acting, rather than the consequences that follow from his actions. I am particularly concerned to make some observations about the nature of self harming acts that are not aimed at death though they may have been contrived to resemble suicide and may thus be confused with it.

In Chapter 2, I discuss, in general terms, some of the ways in which a person might kill himself though I do not offer specific advice to those who have suicide in mind. In Chapters 3 to 9, I discuss the nature of, and relationship between, suicide and a range of related phenomena. In Chapter 10, I engage in some philosophical archaeology, reopening famous cases from the past. And in Chapters 11 to 14, I discuss some of the moral questions that suicide and self harm raise in relation to the question of whether and when it is permissible to intervene in the suicidal acts of others.

NOTES

1   Some years later Debbie died as the result of severe burns after setting fire to herself in a public place. The fact that she ended up burning herself to death suggests the question of whether perhaps even on this occasion, she actually intended to kill herself. We cannot know what was in her mind as she struck the match. However, her own account of the incident was that though she intended to set her nightie alight she did not expect it to catch fire in the violent way that it did, and so I think we are justified in thinking of it as something other than suicide.

2 I discuss what I mean by 'suicide gesture' in Chapter 7 where, in elaborating the conceptual apparatus in terms of which we might think about suicide and suicidal self harm, I also introduce a number of other terms, including 'cosmic roulette'.

3 Since the Suicide Act, 1961, it has not been a criminal offence to commit, or attempt to commit, suicide in the UK. However, the Act provides that 'a person who aids, abets, counsels or procures the suicide of another or an attempt by another to commit suicide, shall be liable on conviction . . . to a term not exceeding 14 years' (Brazier, 1987). It is interesting to speculate on the reason for the difference between the way in which suicide and assisted suicide are viewed legally; how could it be wrong to assist another to do what it is not wrong for that other to do or to attempt to do, himself? Underlying this apparent oddity in the law is perhaps the fear that those who apparently 'aid, abet, counsel or procure the suicide of another', may be doing so for corrupt reasons, for example, for personal gain rather than for beneficent reasons. At the limit the fear might be that someone who seems to have assisted another to die by actually delivering the death blow, might in fact have been engaged in the attempt to achieve the death of that other in a way that to my mind would make her a murderer rather than a suicide aider, abetter, counsellor or procurer.

4 I am not concerned to discuss self harm of a minor kind at any length. For example, I will not consider self mutilation by scratching oneself with sharp objects, tearing out one's hair, head banging and so on, even though some of those who kill themselves may have engaged in such self harming activities earlier.

15

2

MORALS AND MEANS

In this chapter I address two questions: How might one suicide? and Is suicide OK?

HOW MIGHT ONE SUICIDE?

Although I will be examining some of the ways in which one might kill oneself, it is not my intention to offer guidance to those who wish to achieve their deaths. Such advice is available elsewhere and it is no part of my project to compete with suicide experts in offering advice to would-be suicidal self killers. What I want to do is to make some general observations about the different varieties of act that can be used by suicides in attempting to arrange their deaths.

Actions, omissions and putting oneself in the way of anticipated events

The most obvious variety of suicide act involves the suicide actively bringing harm to himself. However, suicide may also be achieved by the direct action of another, by the omissions to act of either the suicide or another and by the suicide's putting himself in the way of events that he expects and intends to kill him. I want to say a little about each of these.

Suicide by actions

It is clear that a person can suicide through an action or actions of his own. For example, he can do this by slitting his throat, drinking a potion calculated to poison him, inhaling noxious gas, jumping

16

from a high place, blowing out his brains with a high calibre weapon, or hanging himself from a rope.

What is less obvious, perhaps, is that a person could suicide through another's actions; for example, by asking, begging, coercing or ordering another person to kill him. Since she performs the fatal act, we might think of this other as the agent of the suicide's destruction in an act of assisted suicide. However, since he commissioned her to perform the fatal act, the suicide would still in a sense be the agent of his own death, though it was another's hand and not his that held the gun or administered the injection, for example. Provided that the person who administered the fatal hurt had benevolent intentions, that, for example, she had not been plotting to murder him, she might be thought of simply as an extension of the suicide in achieving his death.[1] However, if she had entertained murderous wishes towards him before he asked her to help him to die, her act, while comprising suicide for the person who died, could from her point of view be murder.

A suicide could also use another to achieve his purpose without that other being aware of what was going on. For example, he could leap in front of a train or juggernaut that she was driving. Or he could arrange things such that he came between a marksman and her target by standing up on a firing range just as she was letting off a round of rapid fire.

Suicide by omission

Though suicide is most often thought of as resulting from something that a person does, it may be achieved by refraining from action just as easily as it can by acting; and so some deaths that occur as the result of omissions, whether of the protagonist or of some other person, should also be thought of as suicides.

Where the omission is the suicide's, there are at least two possibilities: refraining from doing something to his body that needs to be done if he is to survive, and refraining from acting so as to avoid harm that will prove fatal. An example of the first would be where the suicide achieved his death by refraining from eating or drinking, or from carrying out some life preserving procedure such as injecting insulin. An example of the second might be where, finding himself by chance in a dangerous situation, he arranged his death by refraining from taking avoiding action such as leaping out of the way of an oncoming bus.

Suicide by the omission of another person may also take two forms. First of all, an individual could suicide through the omission of another to administer treatment that was necessary to preserve his life. For example, he could suicide by asking, begging, coercing or ordering this other to refrain from injecting him with a life preserving drug or from setting up a blood transfusion. In these cases though the omissions that cause the harm are omissions by others to act upon the suicide, they are omissions that he has commissioned by his refusal to consent to treatment. Many people would assume that a decision to refuse life saving treatment must result from irrationality and would hence refuse to believe that a person could suicide in this way. However, it is possible to imagine circumstances in which it would seem perfectly reasonable that a person should choose to die rather than suffer now to gain a prize, even the prize of continued and healthy life, in the future. Such people may be viewed as forfeiting life in order to avoid unbearable pain, and their acts are thus related to, though distinct from, voluntary and requested euthanasia. They have carried out a cost-benefit analysis (however sketchy and hypothetical) in relation to their treatment and likely prognosis, and decided that the cost does not justify the benefit.

Secondly, it would be possible for a person to suicide by arranging that others failed to prevent his being harmed by an external source, though examples of this are more difficult to think of. A possible, though far fetched, example would be where the would-be suicide happens (luckily from his perspective) to be in a building when it catches fire; if he begged the firemen to leave him to burn because he'd rather be dead anyway, and they complied with his wish, then we could say that he had suicided by their omission to save him from the fire. Another, perhaps more plausible example might be where a soldier, dreadfully wounded and terrified of the life he would face in the future given his injuries, asked his comrades to leave him to die on the battlefield rather than carrying him with them as they retreated.

Self harming by putting oneself in the way of anticipated events

There is, I think, a third kind of self harming act by which a person may suicide. An individual could intend his death and arrange it by manipulating a situation so that he was killed by an anticipated event. For example, he could walk, inadequately clothed, into the hills, on a day when he was anticipating a snowstorm to occur, expecting that he would die as a result; or he could set out to sea in a beautiful (but small) pea green boat on a day when gales were forecast, expecting to be drowned in the storm that he anticipated. In such cases it would seem odd to say that he killed himself; it would even seem odd to say that his omission to wear appropriate clothes or to ensure that his boat was able to withstand the conditions he was likely to meet, killed him. Though a person who died in such circumstances will have died because of something that he did, his action will not have killed him, rather he will have suicided by putting himself in the way of an event that would do the killing for him. Of course he could just as easily have arranged his death by omission, by *allowing* himself to be killed by the event in question, if, say, he happened to be out in his pea green boat when the storm unexpectedly (and fortunately given his plans to end it all) appeared on the horizon, and rather than turning for shore he continued to read his *Sunday Times* and drink claret.

Rather than saying, in such cases, that the suicide killed himself or even that his omission killed him, we would naturally say that the event in the way of which he has put himself – the storm or whatever – killed him. However, it killed him because he wanted it to do so and arranged that it would; this is why Captain Oates may have committed suicide despite what Holland (1969) and others have to say.[2]

IS SUICIDE OK?

If suicide is allowed then everything is allowed. If anything is not allowed then suicide is not allowed. This throws light on the nature of ethics, for suicide is, so to speak, the elementary sin.

(Wittgenstein, 1961, *Notebooks 1914–16*)

If suicide be criminal, it must be a transgression of our duty either to God, our neighbour, or ourselves.

(Hume, 1784)

In suicide a person both kills and is killed; does he necessarily cause himself harm by doing so and if he does, is he necessarily wrong to do so? If he could kill himself without thereby causing himself harm, does this mean that doing so would necessarily be OK? Or could there be other reasons, aside from the harm he could cause himself, why a person should not suicide? Questions like these would have to be examined in order to give a comprehensive answer to the question of whether suicide is morally acceptable.

My main concern in this book is to map out some of the conceptual territory of suicide and suicidal self harm, a discussion of which I think has some practical relevance as well as being of considerable interest philosophically speaking. A study of the morality of suicide interests me less because it seems to me to have less practical importance,[3] and so I do not intend to offer a comprehensive review of the reasons that might be advanced for considering suicide to be morally permissible or impermissible. However, I would like briefly to venture into this moral territory by addressing the question 'Is suicide OK?' and also the question of whether, even if it is, it is an act that we should perform just because death would suit us, or whether there should be constraints upon suicidal behaviour, relating, for example, to the effects it might have on others.

Killing people is usually considered to be harmful because life is held to be a good thing and depriving a person of a good thing is generally thought to harm him. It is for this reason that except in particular circumstances, such as self defence, or war, intentionally killing a person is usually thought to be morally wrong. In spite of this, killing may sometimes be beneficial rather than harmful and in certain cases of this kind I believe that killing another will be morally right. For example, if a person suffering from a terminal illness is in intolerable pain or distress which cannot be alleviated without the use of treatment that will render him unconscious or non-autonomous, I believe it would be right to kill him if he asked to be killed and wrong not to do so. I believe that to refuse to kill another person in such circumstances could be construed as *deathmaking*, to use Wolfensberger's term (Wolfensberger, 1987), because it forces a person to endure a life that for him is worse than death.[4] This does not mean that I believe that we should always kill those who would benefit from being killed. For example, I believe it would be wrong to kill a person for whom death would be a benefit, if he would rather put up with a dreadful life than die.[5]

It would be unusual to think of suicide as arising from wicked intentions. Even those who believe that suicide is wrong are more likely to think that the suicide is somehow misguided and does not realise that what he is doing is sinful. A person could kill himself with wicked intentions, however, if he intended that others should suffer as a result of his death. For example, by killing himself a person could aim to harm another or others by upsetting them, making them feel guilty and so on; this, I think, is probably quite common.

Suicide is a significant step to undertake and so are all of the various species of self harming act which are not aimed at death. Not only are such acts significant for the agent who performs them; they are significant also for friends, relations, workmates and anyone else who has some degree of engagement with the agent or who might become bound up with him as a result of his act. It therefore seems to me that suicide and other self harmings will not be undertaken lightly by those who are responsible in the sense of having regard for the effects that their acts will have on others.

So is suicide OK?

Sometimes suicide is question-beggingly referred to as 'self murder'. Since murder is killing from bad intentions, it is, I think, better and less emotive to think in terms of 'intentional self killing' because to think of suicide as self murder clearly pre-empts the question of whether it is morally right or wrong.

I think we are entitled to decide what to do with our lives. I think this even if our lives, both biological and biographical, are the gifts of God. If life is the gift of God, then she may reasonably expect us to treat it respectfully, to use it well and to give it up gracefully when the time is right. But I do not think she can expect us to hold on to it when it has no meaning for us any longer or it is unbearably painful to do so. Suicide may, but of course need not, amount to squandering the gift of life; but so may many ways of living the life which we have. Indeed, as I suggest in Chapter 6, it could be argued that at least some suicides might be a celebration of life.

However, although I think suicide is morally acceptable in itself, because our lives are our own and we can choose what to do with them, there will most often be important reasons why it is to be avoided. When they are dead most suicides will be discovered by others who will be affected by this experience, often adversely, and sometimes for ever. Most if not all of those with whom a suicide has had close contact, including members of the caring professions and neighbours as well as relatives, colleagues and friends, and even those of less close acquaintance such as shopkeepers and postmen, are likely to be shocked and upset by his death. Friends and relatives may be affected in a lifelong way. The suicide may even, if he is sufficiently thoughtless about the well being of others, or perhaps if his intention is wicked, and involves deliberately harming them, involve others in his dying; for example, he could do this by jumping in front of a train or car, setting fire to himself in public, or leaping from a building.

I was thus at first inclined to believe that where suicide is morally wrong, it is morally wrong because of the adverse effects it has; on the other hand, I believed that if no one is adversely affected, suicide is not offensive or morally wrong. I thought that the extent to which a particular suicide is harmful to others and the extent to which it was intended to harm, would suggest how morally acceptable it is. On reflection, however, it seems obvious that suicide could be morally wrong even if it harms no one, because very often it takes a cavalier approach to the possibility of harm coming to others.

Morally, the suicide might be compared with a driver who has been drinking. He may get home without meeting with any vigilant traffic police or being involved in any incidents with other road users; or he may be involved in an accident in which an innocent pedestrian is killed; but it seems clear that in both cases he has acted equally badly. The fact that he does not kill or even hurt anyone else on the way home does not make him less immoral for failing to take due care, though it does mean that he will not be charged with manslaughter because moral luck, we might say, is on his side.

If a drunk driver causes an accident or kills a pedestrian the consequences may be serious; for one thing, if he is caught, he will be prosecuted and may well receive a significant punishment; in this case lady luck has not smiled on him. If he gets home without being stopped by the police and without being involved in any incidents, the absence of serious consequences following from his drunken drive (such as a pile-up on the motorway or a body in the morgue) means that he will be charged with nothing. But whether he is caught by the police or gets home without incident, his reprehensible status as a drunken driver is unchanged. Those who drive while incapable of doing so safely because they have been drinking are guilty not only of the legal offence of drunk driving but of a careless disregard for the welfare of others. Being fortunate enough to avoid hitting anyone does not absolve from guilt a driver who has been drinking. Of course, not all of those who drink and drive are unconcerned about the possible consequences; many who do so will take particular care because they are aware of the possibility or likelihood that their abilities as drivers will be impaired as a result of drinking. Nevertheless they show, by driving after drinking, that they are more concerned with gratifying their desire to drink without the inconvenience of having to walk or catch a cab, than they are with the welfare of those they might meet while driving.

Let me return to suicide. Where harm does come to others as a result, the question of whether suicide is wrong does not depend upon whether the harm in question was intended. Intended harm isn't necessarily more harmful than unintended harm and neither is it necessarily more important in judging character.

Jack could intend to harm several others by suiciding but fail to harm any of them. For example, the people he intended to harm may have been killed in an accident before hearing of his death. Or he may have misjudged the extent to which they would be upset by his death; indeed they might be glad, rather than sad, to hear of it. For example, if Jack 's reason for suiciding was because he wanted to punish his wife and his best friend for having had an affair, his plan would backfire if, rather than being upset, they were deliriously happy at the news of his death because it gave them the freedom to go off together.

However, even if Jack failed to harm those he intended to harm, he might have harmed others who he had no intention of harming; indeed most suicides will harm others, whether they intend to do so or not, because others will become unwittingly or unwillingly involved in their self destructive acts. Consider, for example, a person who hangs himself in a public park intending no more than to end his dismal life. He might cause an unsuspecting passer-by who discovers his body to have recurrent nightmares; he might upset the young police constable who is charged with cutting him down; and he might upset the girl in the office who secretly loved him though he did nothing to win her affection. I am inclined to believe that this suicide is both causally and morally responsible for the hurt caused to these others though he did not plan and intend to inflict it.

It seems unlikely to me that there are many suicides in which no one is harmed. Killing oneself without one's death and/or dying having an effect on others would be a difficult business, especially for those who meet with others on a daily basis and will hence be missed. If a suicide doesn't want to be found and is concerned enough to make sure that he isn't found, he will take precautions about the time, place and method of his suicide, to ensure that he isn't. At least he will do this unless he lacks the wherewithal to work this out. So the number of cases in which an individual could kill himself without affecting others is likely to be small. An example would be that of a solitary person who left behind nobody who would miss him or be sad about his disappearance, who washed down a large overdose with a glass of paraquat, cut his wrists and jumped into a disused and isolated mineshaft.

Some people might argue that I am being a bit tough on those who suicide or who think of suiciding. They would argue that any effects the suicide has on others are incidental to his purpose. Since everyone is entitled to take his own life, the argument would go, taking it is no more a matter for moral condemnation than, say, leaving a lover or telling one's student that she cannot write acceptable English. Both things might cause hurt, the argument would continue, but the fact that hurt will be caused to one's lover does not remove one's entitlement to leave her; the fact that telling one's student that she is a bad essay writer does not remove one's entitlement (in this case, it might be argued, one's duty) to do so; and the fact that one's death will cause pain and anguish to others does not mean that one is not entitled to suicide.

But I am not saying that the suicide does not have the right to take his life, only that by doing so he may, and in most cases will, hurt others and that if he does he will be morally responsible for the hurt they suffer and may be blamed for hurting them. As a result it seems appropriate to me that those who suffer as survivors of a suicide should, among all the other feelings that they are likely to experience, feel anger; causing them to experience such anger is, of course, another way that the suicide can hurt others even after he is dead. Not everyone would share this point of view. In particular those who embrace a rather romantic view of suicide or whose empathic understanding for those who suicide outweighs their empathy for those who are affected by suicide, might believe that suicide always results from the simple desire of an individual to flee from a life that for him is unbearable, and hence that anger towards those who suicide, whether successfuly or unsuccessfully, is inappropriate.

Human care for suicides rather than for those upon whom suicide is an assault, may result in quite odd views at times. For example, though he demonstrates sensitivity not only towards suicides but also towards those who suffer as a result of suicide, Glover (1977) thinks it is inappropriate and unhelpful to reproach those who attempt suicide unsuccessfully. He writes:

> To suggest that some act of suicide may be morally wrong is not to advocate that those who make failed 'attempts' ought to be responded to with condemnation or reproach: it is obvious that the last thing that is helpful is any pressure of this kind.
>
> (p. 175)

If an act that is morally wrong is not one which should be met with moral reproach, what kind of act should be met with such reproach? Consider what this statement would sound like if we substituted 'murder' for 'suicide'. Doesn't the fact that an act is morally wrong mean that it should be met with reproach? If an act of suicide should not be met with moral reproach this must mean that it is an act that is not morally culpable for some reason. The most likely reason for this, it seems to me, would be that the individual who made the suicide 'attempt' was for some reason not considered responsible for his actions at the time. And if that was the case, perhaps his act was not one of 'suicide', considered as the autonomous attempt intentionally to bring about one's death. Glover is right to be concerned that where it is possible, a person who has attempted to end his life should be given help to deal with the problems that may have led to his attempt; but this does not mean that angry feelings must be kept from him. It might even be the case that for at least some of those who attempt to end their lives, anger from those that would have been devastated by their deaths is therapeutic in that it draws their attention to the extent to which others care about them.

We are all entitled to act in ways that may be morally condemned; when we do we are blameworthy for the results of our actions. If caring for others and their lives is important (and that is what I think morality is about) then we must try, in so far as is possible, to refrain from harming innocent others even if this means that at times we cannot do what would satisfy us, without acting immorally. This means that at times we will have to refrain from having sex with those who do not wish to have sex with us, killing our next door neighbour whom we have grown to hate, or telling our students that their work is no good without giving them help to improve it; and at times we will have to avoid suiciding even if to do so would serve our purposes as individuals.

NOTES

1 The idea that one person can act as an extension of another is related to Marshall McLuhan's idea that objects and media can act as extensions of human beings (McLuhan, 1969).

2 The death of Captain Oates is discussed in some detail in Chapter 10.

3 However, I think that moral questions relating to intervention in the serious self harming acts of others have considerable practical importance, because our decisions about right conduct in relation to those that we find suiciding or otherwise self harming may affect the ways in which we respond to them. I turn to such questions in Chapters 11 to 14.

4 My views about these issues are developed elsewhere (Fairbairn, 1991a, 1992b and 1992c).

5 But see Chapter 8, note 2.

3

WHERE DO OUR VIEWS OF SUICIDE COME FROM?

The ways in which we think about self harm and suicide are influenced by a number of factors including the religious and cultural context in which we have been raised. For example, for a committed Roman Catholic, killing oneself would be considered a mortal sin; this, it might be argued, is one reason that verdicts of suicide are rarely delivered in Southern Ireland (Kirwan, 1991).[1] For a traditionally raised Japanese person on the other hand, self killing is required in certain circumstances. Since the sixteenth century, *seppuku*, the ritual self killing of Japan, better known in the West as *hara-kiri*, has been expected of people of the Samurai or warrior class, who have offended or failed in certain ways. It is a means by which the individual can redeem himself to others. There is a striking degree of similarity between seppuku and the renowned death of Socrates by drinking hemlock, in both of which it is at least questionable whether what we have is suicide.[2]

TWO MAJOR INFLUENCES

In this chapter I want to focus attention on two of the most significant influences on our views of self harm. First I will discuss the pervasive influence of medicine. Then I will discuss some of the ways in which the emotive connotations attached to the language that we use to discuss suicide can influence the ways in which we think about it.

Medicine and suicide

In western culture the medical profession occupies a position of considerable importance. Physicians traditionally were, and largely

27

still are, regarded as authority figures by their patients. Medical language is pervasive. Words such as 'disease' and 'cancer' are found in discussions of twentieth century culture; the media carry reports about wars in which people die and are maimed, couched in medical language, referring, for example, to military strikes being carried out with 'surgical precision'. Words like 'treatment' and 'cure' appear both in the reports prepared by those worrying characters who come to deal with the damp in one's house and in the 'diagnostic reports' provided by garage mechanics. Given this, it is hardly surprising that medical language has permeated human services that are closely allied with medicine, such as physiotherapy, occupational therapy and clinical psychology, and also others whose relationship to medicine is less strong, including social work and special education where, for example, teachers of children with learning difficulties talk about the 'diagnostic testing' of children's ability in reading and mathematics.

The pervasive influence of medicine is partly, and perhaps largely, responsible for what is arguably the most common belief about suicide – that anyone who kills or tries to kill himself must be mad, because no one who was sane could want to end his life. Those who have ended or want to end their lives or who seem to want to do so are often assumed to be depressed in the sense of being mentally ill, rather than just miserably unhappy. The idea that suicide always results from psychological disturbance is, I believe, sufficiently well established within the medical community to be considered the orthodox medical view. In the case of genuinely crazy people, psychological disturbance may be responsible for self killing; indeed the species of psychotic behaviour and experience known as schizophrenia is sometimes almost jokingly (though morbidly), and in my opinion tastelessly, referred to as a 'terminal illness', because of the number of people with this diagnosis who go on to kill themselves.

Those who believe in the orthodox medical view of suicide share the conviction that as a result of illness or disease the suicidal self harmer is incapable of rational thought. Often they believe that his illness is compelling him to try to kill himself. As a result they believe that medicine should intervene to treat the illness and prevent his self destruction. Even psychiatry, which we might have expected to have developed a richer understanding of the variety of human acts that may be labelled 'suicide', is dominated by the orthodox medical view and most psychiatrists believe that suicidal behaviour is

always, or almost always, the result of maladaptive attitudes ground-
ed in mental illness, which need therapeutic help. Szasz (1971)
writes, 'It is difficult to find "responsible" medical or psychiatric
authority today that does not regard suicide as a medical, and
specifically as a mental health, problem' (p. 187). Szasz's use of the
word 'responsible' to describe those psychiatric and medical
authorities who believe that people who suicide or attempt to
suicide are fair game for medical paternalism is ironic because he
himself believes that most psychiatric and medical intervention in
suicide is anything but responsible. Nevertheless his judgement that
most doctors, whether in psychiatry or not, believe that suicide
should be regarded as a medical problem, is well founded. For
example, Ringel (1981) writes:

> Anyone who has given serious scientific consideration to the
> problem of suicide knows that death – the state of not-being –
> is for the most part chosen under pathological circumstances
> or under the influence of diseased feelings.
>
> (p. 206)

However, Ringel also seems to take the view that most people who
act suicidally do not intend to be dead but act with the hope that
somehow they will be saved. He believes that, 'The strongest human
driving force is that of self-preservation' (p. 206) and hence that
suicidal action always occurs as the result of distress that causes the
suicider to make mistakes. He writes:

> we must remain aware of the concept of the 'mental crisis'
> during which there is intense psychic conflict and often, as a
> direct result of this, a false assessment of the situation. The
> tragic story of Romeo and Juliet shows how such a misinter-
> pretation can lead to suicide.
>
> (p. 210)

If Ringel was right that most people who suicidally self harm do not
intend to end up dead, it would mean that most people who end up
labelled as suicides would not, to my way of thinking, be suicides,
since it is my view that only those whose acts are aimed unequivocally at achieving their death, are suicides.

Clare (1975) raises the question, 'Is a person who kills himself, by
definition, mentally ill?' (p. 347). He asserts that, 'in practice most
psychiatrists . . . accept that there are cases of self-destruction that
are not a consequence of mental illness' (p. 347). Of course, a

psychiatrist could accept that some cases of self destruction do not result from mental illness while believing that most suicides do and this is what Clare seems to believe.

Though the orthodox medical view of suicide is commonly accepted, there are dissenters from it even within the psychiatric community. For example, Mitchell (1971) considers that the commonly held assumption that everyone who shows a suicidal tendency is for that reason mentally ill, is not necessarily true, because suicidal behaviour 'can be more a measure of distress and despair than of mental disorder' (p. 145). Curran *et al.* (1980) believe that rather than its being the case that everyone who commits suicide or who makes a more or less serious attempt at suicide is suffering from a depressive illness, 'Many people who commit suicide have no true psychiatric illness, but are in chronic pain, lonely, see no hope of improvement, and decide that on balance they might as well be dead' (p. 201). Szasz (1971) does not even believe in the concept of mental illness and thinks that viewing suicide or attempted suicide as indicative of mental illness is 'erroneous because it treats an act as if it were a happening; and evil because it serves to legitimize psychiatric force and fraud by justifying it as medical care and treatment' (p. 186). He contends that the suicidal person is not *ipso facto* disturbed and that even if he is, this does not mean that he is mentally ill. He therefore refutes the claim that since doctors have a duty to treat illness they should frustrate the desire of their patients to kill themselves.

Concluding remarks about medicine and suicide

There is a difference between believing that all who suicide are mad and believing that all who suicidally self harm without intending death are mad. Paradoxically, it might be argued that whereas there are good reasons for believing that all who self harm without intending death must be mad, there is no necessary reason to consider those who wish to die and attempt to bring about their deaths as mad. Whereas no one who was sane could wish to cause himself injury,[3] the argument would go, in certain circumstances life could be so painful or distressing that some people might rationally view death as at best, a release, and at worst, a nothing. In practice however, the orthodox medical view of suicide and its relationship with psychological disturbance is so influential that it leads most people to believe that all of those who suicide, or act in similar ways, must be psychologically disturbed and in need of help.

If those who harm or attempt to harm themselves in suicidal ways were necessarily crazy, it would be the act of a caring person to intervene so as to prevent them harming themselves because, except in situations where some initial harm is necessary for one's long term health (as is the case with surgery), acting in ways that harm him can never be in a person's interests. The orthodox medical idea that suicide always, or nearly always, results from psychological disturbance, would thus lead us to intervene in suicidal self harmings whenever possible.

Emotive and moralistic connotations of the language of suicide

Lebacqz and Englehardt (1980) have little faith in the extent to which our language of suicide allows us to speak clearly about it. They believe that 'definitions of "suicide" are sometimes dependent upon prior judgments about its justifiability' (p. 701). And even in simply describing suicide they believe that 'everyday language may be hazardous to ethical clarity' (p. 672). In relation to the question of how it is appropriate to view certain human acts – those in which one person sacrifices his life for others – they write:

> Some observers classify acts of self-sacrifice as 'suicide'; some do not. While technically the distinction may be said to turn on the 'intent' of the actor, one suspects that those who refuse to classify self-sacrificial actions as suicide do so at least in part because of a prior judgment about the wrongness of suicide; thus actions which seem more ethically acceptable are not classified as 'suicide' because it has already been determined that 'suicide' is wrong.
>
> (p. 701)

Other writers make similar points. For example, discussing the tendency for certain people to refuse to label self destructive acts that arise from altruistic motivations as 'suicides', calling them, perhaps, 'self sacrifice', Martin (1981) writes:

> Possibly the moralists in this tradition find most suicides to be such horrible crimes that the very word 'suicide' gets infested

with negative magic, and rather than admit that certain acts of intentional, voluntary self-killing are acceptable or even praiseworthy suicides, they prefer to deny that those acts are called suicide.

(p. 50)

I think it would always be mistaken to say of a person who sacrifices himself simply for the sake of others, that he was a suicide, because though he may go willingly to his death, death is not the end at which he aims. A soldier who throws himself on a grenade in order to save the lives of his comrades intends only to save them and not to die, though it is inevitable that he will; and a father who rushes into his burning house in order to be able to pass his small children to safety does no more than we would expect any committed parent to do, even if he realises that he is likely to perish as a result. There could even be situations where a person not only accepted his death as a side effect of an action aimed at assisting others, but actually aimed to die as a way of doing so, and yet was not a suicide. Imagine a situation where a spy during wartime killed himself rather than undergoing torture. Such a death would be a suicide if the spy's intention was simply to avoid pain. However, if he killed himself because he knew that he could not hold out under pressure and wished to avoid the possibility that he should blurt out information that would endanger others, it is at least questionable whether his death, though not only accepted but aimed at, should be thought a suicide. My feeling is that it would be inappropriate to think of this spy's death as suicide because his wish was not to be dead, for whatever reason, but to preserve his comrades' lives even at the cost of his own.

So I do not think that the reason that self sacrificial acts are not, in general, labelled suicides has anything to do with prior judgements about the wrongness of suicide. Rather I think it has to do with the question of whether death was aimed at and if so, why it was aimed at. If it was aimed at because the person wished for death, it was a suicide; if not, it probably was not. However, I do think that whether acts that may have been aimed at self destruction are labelled 'suicide' will depend to some extent upon whether the person who is labelling holds the view that suicide is morally wrong.

Beauchamp and Childress (1983) write that since self caused deaths are often inexplicable, 'An emotive meaning of disapproval has . . . . been incorporated into our use of "suicide"' (p. 94). As a result of this, they point out that:

32

we find it hard to view acts of which we approve, or at least do not disapprove, as suicides . . . . Because self-caused deaths under conditions of terminal illness or altruistic actions are commonly understandable, acceptable, and perhaps even laudable, semantic exclusion of them from the realm of the suicidal is tempting and is a *fait accompli* in the English language.

(p. 94)

Beauchamp and Childress claim that where a person who is dying of a 'terminal illness or mortal injury' intentionally allows himself to die, 'we are reluctant to call the act "suicide"' (p. 93) whereas if a patient with a terminal illness takes his or her life by an active means, such as a revolver, we would usually think of their act as a suicide.

What would make people refer to those who achieve their deaths by taking a gun and shooting themselves, as suicides while being reluctant to refer to the act of an individual who achieves his death by allowing it to occur, as suicide? One possible reason could be the tendency to distinguish between actively bringing about a death and simply allowing it to occur. This has been the subject of endless debate. Many people believe that whereas allowing patients to die is sometimes justifiable, killing them never is. I will not enter into a discussion of the literature on the distinction between killing and letting die. I am convinced by the arguments of Harris (1980), among others, that there is in essence no moral distinction between killing a person and allowing him to die; as acts each is just as deadly and must be judged according to the intention of the agent. However, someone who was convinced that killing was somehow worse than letting die might think that the patient who shoots himself is a suicide, because she is already immersed in the idea that suicide is wrong and since killing is wrong, this being a killing and hence to be disapproved of, must have been a suicide. Conversely she might reason that since the person who merely allows himself to die does not do something wrong, because allowing to die is not in itself bad, he could not be a suicide; this would be strengthened by the fact that allowing oneself to die in circumstances where one is terminally ill or mortally wounded and in great pain, is something with which many of us can identify; it makes sense to us.

Beauchamp and Childress do indeed focus on the distinction between acts and omissions, between doing and allowing, killing

33

and letting die, to argue that what makes the difference to our judgement of these two cases is the passive nature of the case where the individual allows himself to die as opposed to the active nature of the death of the person who kills himself. In arguing for this point of view, they write:

if a seriously burned but not mortally wounded patient takes a weapon in hand and intentionally brings about his death, it is a suicide. But if a seriously burned patient is suffering terribly from a terminal wound and refuses to undergo yet another painful tubbing or blood transfusion, we are not likely to regard the death as a suicide.

(1983, p. 94)

The problem with this example is that the passive/active distinction is not the only difference between the two cases. They are also different in that whereas in the second the individual is going to die soon, in the first he is not. In the first the individual shortens a life that looked likely to go on for some time after the worst effects of his injury had been overcome; in the second the individual simply brings rather more quickly to a close a life that was heading towards its end anyway. In coming to a decision about these cases, someone who thought that the first was a suicide whereas the second was not, might thus have focused on the possibility that the second individual's act could be viewed as a kind of self induced euthanasia which the patient embraced in order to avoid a long drawn out, painful and distressing death, whereas the first was intended to avoid a distressing life.

Consider how we would have reacted if the individual who was terminally ill had shot himself dead while the one who was seriously but not mortally wounded, had refused treatment. Wouldn't we, in that case, be inclined to think of both incidents as suicide? Or at least wouldn't we be inclined to leave the decision about whether they were or were not suicide until we could make a reasoned guess at whether either or both wished for death, and intended in acting as they did to arrange that they would die?

Suicide as an act 'committed'

The most common way of speaking about suicide is to talk of its being 'committed'. But to talk of 'committing suicide' is to beg the question of whether suicide is wrong. A number of writers make this point in different ways. For example, Flew (1986) writes, 'If you believe, as I do, that suicide is not always and as such wrong, it is inappropriate to speak of "committing suicide"' (p. 56, footnote 13). It is at least plausible to suggest that this linguistic practice shapes our thinking by associating suicide and the area of human life in which we most often talk of acts being committed, which is crime. Drawing attention to the importance that language may assume in shaping attitudes towards suicide, Barrington (1969) writes:

in itself the tendentious expression 'to commit suicide', is calculated to poison the unsuspecting mind with its false semantic overtones, for apart from the dangerous practice of committing oneself to an opinion, most other things committed are, as suicide once was, criminal offences.

(p. 231)

Making a similar point, Lebacqz and Englehardt (1980) write:

our everyday language may be hazardous to ethical clarity. Common usage employs the phrase 'to commit suicide' – as in 'she committed suicide by jumping off the Golden Gate Bridge.' . . . such usage portrays suicide as a 'crime' to be 'committed' as is, for example, murder.

(p. 672)

Unfortunately the practice of referring to suicide as an act committed is so deeply embedded in our language that it is difficult to find alternative means of speaking that are neither clumsy nor misleading. Some possible replacements for 'suicide' are really contracted definitions and are for that reason longwinded, inelegant and impractical. Consider for example, 'This person killed himself intentionally, aware of what he was doing, and wishing for this result.'

Some writers have offered alternatives which do not work. Lebacqz and Englehardt (1980) agree that common usage 'portrays suicide as a "crime" to be "committed" as is, for example, murder', and write, 'We shall avoid use of the term "commit suicide" by substituting the phrase "kill oneself" in hopes that this term will have a more neutral ring' (p. 673). But this cannot solve the problem because, of course, a person can kill himself without his death being the result of suiciding. A person who arrives home drunk from the pub and pours himself a glass of paraquat mistakenly thinking it to be gin, will kill himself when he drinks it but he will not be a suicide,

35

because he does not intend to arrange his death. Another possible way of getting over the problem of loading the idea of suicide with negative and criminal connotations is simply to avoid referring to suicide as something committed by, for example, saying of a person that 'he performed suicide', 'he enacted suicide' or that 'he did suicide'. However, all of these seem awkward.

I favour the use of the verb 'to suicide'. This cannot in itself remove the idea, embedded by years of use of the expression 'to commit suicide', that suicide is akin to, if not actually, a crime. However, removing the evaluative 'to commit' has the advantage that it leaves open the question of how the particular act of suicide is to be judged. To say of a person that 'he suicided' is simply to describe what he did, which was intentionally to act in such a way as to achieve his death because he wished to be dead; it says nothing about the reasons that he had for doing so, or the effects that his doing so might have had on others; and it does not imply any judgement about his act having been criminal.

The verb 'to suicide' has more in common with verbs such as 'to love' or 'to listen' or 'to think' or 'to appreciate' or 'to agree' or 'to consent' than it does with verbs like 'to compete' or 'to race' or 'to fight', in that what matters is what the suicide intentionally does and not whether he is successful. At the risk of appearing trivial, we might say that suicide is more about 'taking part' in the game of intentional self killing than about 'winning' the game. Whereas 'competing' and 'racing' and 'fighting' and 'trying' have as their focus changes in the external world, 'loving', 'listening', 'thinking', 'consenting' and I think 'suiciding', refer to inward events. Suicide, like listening, thinking, consenting and loving is essentially a matter of things that go on inside the suicide, rather than what he does in the world. Of course in order to suicide a person must act in the world, but what his act means is determined not by what he does but by what he means by what he does and that is an inward rather than an outward thing.

NOTES

1 Making a similar but more general point, Wertheimer (1991) writes: 'In countries where suicide is strongly condemned for religious or cultural reasons there will almost certainly be under-reporting of suicides, the nature of such deaths often remaining closely guarded family secrets' (p. 3).
2 In Chapter 10, among other things, I discuss the question of whether

seppuku is necessarily suicide and reopen the case of Socrates to consider whether he was a suicide.

3   As a result I expect that even those who maintain a liberal view of suicide would be likely to intervene, whether directly or by going for help, in cases of self harm that are obviously aimed at something other than death (I am thinking here of self mutilating behaviours such as cutting, scratching, head banging and so on) while maintaining the belief that it is wrong to interfere in another's attempt to kill himself.

4

OUR IMPOVERISHED LANGUAGE OF SUICIDE AND SELF HARM

> no language – including, as I have made sure from colleagues, Japanese – has a genuinely separate word for suicide. The words denoting it are always qualifications of others, mostly either of 'to die' or 'to kill'. Suicide, that is, is exhibited as a dying or killing, with a twist. Latin *mors voluntaria* stresses the voluntary nature of such dying, English 'suicide', 'self-killing,' the fact that oneself is the object.
>
> (Daube, 1972, p. 390)

The language in which suicide and other varieties of suicidal self harm are discussed is very sparse. In most 'suicide talk', whether among professional or lay people, the whole range of self harmings that can lead to death are subsumed under the umbrella concept 'suicide' and a few variants, along with expressions like 'cry for help'. This is a reflection of a rather limited model of suicidal self harm in which fine distinctions are not made, even in theory, perhaps because they are difficult to make in practice.

The language and concepts that we possess can make a difference to the ways in which we think; they can also influence the ways that we act. In Chapter 3, I offered some observations about ways in which our views of suicidally self harming actions and those who engage in them may be influenced by the emotive and moralistic overtones that typically accompany 'suicide talk'. I have no doubt that this influence is significant. However, in my view the fact that the conceptual apparatus and language that are available are so thin and impoverished, is a much more significant influence on the ways in which we act towards those who have acted suicidally.

In this chapter I want to turn to a more general consideration of the language in which we discuss, and through which we construe, suicide and other self harmings. I will not discuss the history of the language of self harm. Such a discussion is offered by Daube's study

'The Linguistics of Suicide' (Daube, 1972). Among other things, he treats us to a selection of Greek descriptions of the act of suicide. In translation he renders these as: 'to seize death'; 'to grasp death'; 'to break up life'; 'to end life'; 'to be delivered from life'; 'to deliver oneself'; 'to leave the light'; 'to go voluntarily to Hades'; 'to do violence to oneself'; 'to flee living'; 'to carry oneself off'; 'to get through with oneself'; 'to consume oneself'; 'to die voluntarily'; 'to kill oneself'; 'to destroy oneself'; 'to get oneself out of the way' (pp. 399–400). Rather I am concerned to review some of the terms that are currently available for discussing and referring to suicidal acts and to individuals who take suicidally self harming action and to point to some problems with these. Specifically I want to say a little about some of the terms that constitute the current, impoverished model: 'suicide' and its variants 'parasuicide', 'attempted suicide', 'failed suicide' and 'threatened suicide'. In addition I will introduce a new and apparently contradictory term, *non-fatal suicide*, as an alternative to the over-used and degraded term 'attempted suicide' and the less frequently used and hence less degraded term 'failed suicide'. After that, I will say something about the terminological confusion that may arise as the result of the inadequacy of the language that is currently available.

Suicide

Suicide is rather difficult to define which is why I have devoted the whole of Chapter 6 to a discussion of the difficulties in doing so and to the attempt to develop a definition of my own. For the moment it is sufficient to say that most people use 'suicide' to refer to the act of deliberate self killing by a person who knew what he was doing when he acted. In its usual usage suicide thus involves a person not only bringing about his death but bringing it about intentionally.

Parasuicide

'Parasuicide' is a generic term used to refer to acts which resemble suicide in some ways but in which the individual ends up alive. Its definition makes no reference to the outcome intended by the individual – for example, to whether he intends to live or die – and refers instead only to his behaviour. Kreitman (1977) defines it as 'a non-fatal act in which an individual deliberately causes self-injury or ingests a substance in excess of any prescribed or generally recognised therapeutic dosage' (p. 3). Kreitman thinks that this definition will usually be straightforward to operate though he recognises that it will not always be easy to decide that a person was by his definition a parasuicide, because at times it is difficult to tell whether his self harming or poisoning was deliberate.

The fact that the definition of parasuicide does not refer to the reasons that an individual had for acting in the ways that he did, means that it lumps together individuals whose brush with death has come about in different ways. Some acts that end up labelled as parasuicides may thus in fact have been *suicides* that failed; others may have been *suicide gestures* in which the individual feigned suicide successfully; yet others may have been *non-fatal cosmic gambles*.

Though there is an accepted definition for 'parasuicide', the term is rather loosely used at times. Sometimes people use it only in relation to those who deliberately self harm. For example, Lyttle (1991) writes, 'The term parasuicide refers to a deliberate act of self-harm which does not have a fatal outcome' (p. 341). Sometimes, however, 'parasuicide' is used to refer to any case where a person is non-fatally harmed as a result of, or apparently as the result of, an activity that is sometimes used as a means of suicide, and where it is unclear whether he intended to be dead by doing whatever he has done. Thus, for example, some people would refer to anyone who is admitted to casualty as the result of a drug overdose as a parasuicide, even if the individual may have taken the overdose accidentally. It is because of such inconsistencies that I do not think the term 'parasuicide' a useful one.

Attempted suicide

'Attempted suicide' is a weak and often inaccurate term. Taken literally it implies that death was aimed at, though the agent failed to achieve his aim. However, many people whose actions are labelled as 'attempted suicide' had no intention of dying. Like 'parasuicide', 'attempted suicide' is used to refer to a wide variety of situations where people come to harm but do not die. For example, it is used in referring to suicides that have failed, occasions when a person has intentionally self harmed in a way that could have led to death but was unsure whether he wished to die, occasions where an individual has aimed to create the illusion that he intended to die though he actually intended to live, and occasions where a person's brush with death was accidental. There are two varieties of this last category: first cases where, although he acted intentionally to harm himself, the self harming individual did not intend to die, and second cases where there was not even the intention to self harm and the brush with death, though resulting from an intentional act, was the result of a miscalculation. As an example of the first of these, consider the person who, in attempting to inflict superficial wounds on his wrists with a piece of broken glass, accidentally slashes his wrists longitudinally rather than transversely, so that he inflicts major wounds of a kind that he did not intend. As an example of the second, consider the heroin addict who, in a drug induced state, injects himself with a massive overdose; though such an individual acts intentionally in injecting himself, he does not intend to die, or even to harm himself.

In relation to overdosing, Kessel (1965) writes that attempted suicide is neither a diagnosis, nor a description of behaviour but rather 'an interpretation of the motives for the act of self-poisoning – an unnecessary and usually a wrong interpretation' (p. 30). He thus considers that its use is both misleading and clinically inappropriate:

> for four-fifths of the patients the concept of attempting suicide is wide of the mark. They performed their acts in the belief that they were comparatively safe – aware, even in the heat of the moment, that they would survive their overdosage and be able to disclose what they had done in good time to ensure their rescue. What they were attempting was not suicide.
>
> (p. 29)

He continues,

> If the term 'attempted suicide' were just meaningless it could be tolerated, but it is positively wrong and should be discarded. The motives of our patients clearly proclaim this. In the first place the majority of acts were impulsive. Then, too, they were stupid and senseless, and the patients themselves acknowledge this. Not thus does a man drive himself to suicide.
>
> (p. 29)

It is not that Kessel believes that the acts of those in relation to whom he thinks 'attempted suicide' is wrongly applied are meaningless; he thinks that they were focused on some purpose. It is just that 'this purpose was to alter their life situation, not to die' (p. 30).

Another writer who is critical of the term 'attempted suicide' is

41

Lester (1990) who offers a categorisation of acts of 'attempted suicide' (by which he means acts that are usually referred to using this expression), based on a decision about whether 'the harm to the self is foreseen or desired' (p. 1245). He offers five categories. 'Failed suicides' intend to die but fail; 'deliberate self-harmers' wish to harm themselves but not sufficiently to die; 'subintentioned self-harmers' want to achieve some positive consequence and are willing to trade off damage to the self in doing so; 'counterproductive self-harmers' neither foresee nor desire the harmful consequences of, for example, an overdose; finally 'pseudoself-harmers' do not intend to die and only minimally harm themselves by what he calls a 'mild gesture'.

Lester's model is interesting though I think it rests too much on empirical facts and pays too little attention to intention. For example, his exemplar of 'pseudoself-harm' is the situation where a person takes a small number of analgesic tablets, the implication being that a person who takes an overdose that could not kill him could not be a suicide. Of course a person could feign suicide by doing something that he knows would not kill him. However, he could do something that would not kill him believing that it could and intending that it should, and so Lester's exemplar of 'pseudoself-harm' could thus be a genuine attempt at suicide.

As I have already suggested, it is often the case that too little attention is paid to the intention of the individual in acting in a self harming way. Both misconstruing (and hence mislabelling) and mislabelling (and hence misconstruing) a person's self harming can lead to inappropriate and unhelpful treatment on the part of others. For example, if 'attempted suicide' is taken literally, those who are wrongly labelled in this way may be treated as if they really wanted to die and this might lead, for example, to their being 'specialled' on a psychiatric ward (that is, kept under observation at all times) as a precaution against their making another attempt. This in turn might lead to such individuals being put under unhelpful pressure; at worst such pressure might itself lead them towards suicidal acts.

There is another problem about the use of the term 'attempted suicide' that seems to contradict the main thrust of my suggestion that labelling a person in this way might lead to his being treated as if he really wanted to be dead. In certain contexts, including casualty wards and the acute admissions wards of psychiatric hospitals, professionals caring for those labelled as 'attempted suicides' sometimes assume that rather than having genuinely attempted to achieve their deaths, such clients intended nothing more than to attract attention to themselves; this can lead to a lack of sympathy or even a lack of care for such clients. Those who are given this label may thus be treated rather badly by overworked staff in hospitals who may view such individuals as having brought trouble on themselves and object to having to care for them while there are others who also need attention and who they consider to be more worthy of help. The thinking goes something like this: 'Well really he's brought this on himself so why should we give him as much attention as other patients who are here through no fault of their own?'

The phenomenon to which I am referring is recognised by others. For example, discussing the fact that what looks like an attempt at self killing can be effective in getting results where other methods of interpersonal communication have failed, Kessel (1965) takes a benevolent view:

> The girls who resort to it are, all the same, very much distressed; in their despair they do something stupid and senseless, and it works. Should we judge them harshly on that score? Perhaps what we most resent is that, though there was probably a negligible risk to life, they are held by their circle of friends narrowly to have escaped death. They have had their drama; to us it only means work. But we can hardly expect our patients to have borne that in mind.

(p. 23)

There are two extremes in relation to the question of whether those who end up labelled as suicide attempters really were attempting suicide. At one extreme is the view that since a person who really wants to die kills himself, all who do suicidal things but do not die must be hysterical and over-dramatic attention seekers. At the other is the view that everyone who does something that could have been a suicide but survives, either was, or should be treated as if he was, genuinely attempting to kill himself. Both of these extremes may lead to unhelpful treatment for at least some of those who self harm but live. Somewhere between them is the beneficent view that everyone who 'attempts suicide' is making a cry for help. Those who are thought to be making a cry for help by self harming may end up being treated in very different ways. If they adopt this means of communicating their distress once or twice, they may meet with tender loving care and be given a great deal of sympathy and empathic understanding. On the other hand, those who have cried for help too often may be subjected to a more cool, and even aggressive approach.

Since, as I have argued, in current usage 'attempted suicide' tends to be used to cover all self harming acts that could have led to death but end with the protagonist alive, its use does not allow for discrimination between non-fatal self harming acts of different kinds. It is thus often misleading to talk of 'attempted suicide' because only some acts labelled 'attempted suicide' truly are attempts at suicide. This is the reason that I think we would do well to drop it from our vocabulary for discussing suicidal self harm whenever possible; when it is used I think its use should be restricted to occasions when a person has genuinely tried to kill himself and failed.

Failed suicide and non-fatal suicide

Though less common, the term 'failed suicide' tends to be used interchangeably with 'attempted suicide'. In my view it is less degraded and may thus be more easily rehabilitated than 'attempted suicide', perhaps because it is less frequently used and is more often used only in relation to those who intended to die but failed in arranging that they should. In order to achieve its rescue, I want to propose that use of the term 'failed suicide' should be restricted to suicides that have not ended in death, because the intention of the failed suicide is the same as that of the (successful) suicide and different from that of those who self harm but do so without the expectation and hope that they will die as a result. Restricting the use of 'failed suicide' in the way I propose recognises that it is a subset of the set of suicides rather than another, discrete set. Of course this depends upon a radical redefinition of suicide in which those who intend to suicide, and enact that intention, are thought of as suicides whether or not they die. I develop such a definition in Chapters 5 and 6.

Another way of referring to failed suicide would be to use the expression *non-fatal suicide* which in truth I prefer, though I expect it to be more difficult to have accepted by those who believe that suicide is always, and necessarily, fatal. A fatal suicide is one that has resulted in death; a non-fatal suicide is a suicide that has not. Most people would refer to such an event as an attempted suicide but since as I have argued the term 'attempted suicide' has become so loosely and imprecisely used as to make it a handicap to clear thought, this alternative seems worthwhile.[1]

44

Threatened suicide

The term 'threatened suicide' is usually used to refer to the act of a person who says to another or others that he intends to kill himself when he has no intention of doing so. Sometimes, however, suicide threats can be a precursor to suicidal action. Such action may be genuinely suicidal because the individual intends to end up dead. On the other hand, it may amount to a gamble because the individual has not formed a definite intention to die, or it may amount to little more than a gesture at suiciding, because the individual intends to end up alive.

Vera was 73. Though mobile and independent, she thought of herself as a very old woman. She had two sons, one of whom she saw regularly although he had learning difficulties and lived in an institution. Her other son lived a few miles away but did not visit often and so Vera rarely saw her grand-children. She felt very isolated. However, she had regular contact with a social worker, a home help visited two days a week and she had daily meals on wheels.

Vera developed the habit of telephoning Social Services (sometimes more than once in a week) and announcing that she was going to kill herself. For their part Social Services developed the habit of sending in the 'psychological cavalry' whenever this happened. Vera's suicide threats never issued in action.

People who threaten to end their lives most often intend no more than to bully other people into changing their behaviour; they have learned that threatening suicide is an effective way of doing so. Sometimes, as seems to have been the case with Vera, agencies that intend to help are instrumental in shaping habitual suicide threat-ening behaviour. To continue using the jargon of behavioural psychology, we might say that individuals who threaten or gesture suicide are 'positively reinforced' (lay people would say 'rewarded') by the attention they are given by others; as a result they become more likely to act in similar ways again.

However, although threats of suicide are more likely to be about trying to induce change in another person or persons – in the ways they feel or act, for example – than they are to be about announcing the intention of the individual to kill himself, they may sometimes genuinely be a prelude to a suicidal act which is aimed at achieving death. In such a case, announcing to another person that one intends to kill oneself unless she acts in certain ways, would realistically be about giving her the opportunity to save one's life. Consider, for example, the following case.

Geoff telephoned his estranged wife to say that if she did not allow him to return to live at home with his children, he would kill himself. Aware that he had made such threats in the past, his wife told him that until he convinced her that he was a 'changed man' she was unwilling to have him home to live again. The following day Geoff was found hanging from a rope in his garage. Dead.

Geoff's threat was genuine; he said that he would kill himself if his wife did not comply with his wishes, and he did.

Perhaps threatened suicide is best thought of as falling into several categories. In the first a statement of intention such as, 'If x doesn't happen I will . . . ', will be followed, as in Geoff's case, by the threatened action; this might be called a *genuine suicide threat*. By contrast occasions when, though the agent intends to follow up the threat to suicide with action, the action he has in mind falls short of suicide, might be referred to as *threatened suicide gestures*, because although the threat is genuine what is threatened is not suicide but a gesture at suicide. There is another, related but arguably more trivial variety of suicide threat, that is aimed at no more than bringing about a change in others; this might be referred to as a *gestured suicide threat* since there is no intention to follow it up with self harming of any kind; Vera's threats were of this kind. Finally occasions where the individual makes the threat without having formed the intention either to act upon it or not, we might refer to as *impetuous suicide threats*.

Suicide threats that lead to suicide gestures are unlikely to lead to seriously life endangering behaviour and more likely to lead to gestures of a relatively mild kind aimed at creating dramatic effect, as might be the case where a person who has threatened to kill himself flamboyantly takes a handful of mild tranquillisers.

However, just as a genuine suicide threat might, through miscalculation or ignorance, lead to an action that is not genuinely life threatening, so a gestured suicide threat might, by way of miscalculation, lead to a seriously life threatening action. Suicide threats that, like Vera's, do not issue in action of any kind, are unlikely to pose a threat to life. However, some such threats could lead to serious self harm although there was not even the intention to follow up the threat with a gesture. For example, someone standing near the edge of a cliff in a Hollywood movie could threaten to jump though he had no intention of actually doing so, but find that the cliff edge crumbles beneath his feet sending him to his death; and someone in real life could do this too.

The problem with suicide threats is in deciding which are genuine and which are not. There is a hierarchy of danger with genuine threats which are likely to lead to realistic suicide bids at one end, and gestured suicide threats which are unlikely to lead to any kind of self harm, at the other. However, as I have indicated, even those threats that are least dangerous could, by mistake, end in death. The situation is made even more complicated by the fact that a person who habitually threatens with no intention of taking realistically suicidal action may eventually 'up the odds', as it were, and act in a genuinely life threatening way. The most appropriate ways of dealing with threats of different kinds will, of course, be different; but this is not a book about counselling, psychotherapy or even friendship, and so I will not discuss these here.

TERMINOLOGICAL CONFUSION

I have said a little about the terms that are most commonly used in discussing suicide and suicidal self harm. I want now to discuss the terminological confusion that the impoverished nature of our language of self harm can cause, even for those who recognise some of the complexities of the area but are constrained in what they can say by the lack of words and concepts in which to do so. By pointing out inadequacies in the current vocabulary of self harm, I hope to draw attention to the need to think more closely about the range of phenomena that cluster round suicide.

Terminological confusion is common in both lay and professional discussions of the nature of suicidal self harm and in practice settings in which suicidal self harmers are seen by professionals. Consider the kinds of things that are frequently said about those who take what seems to be serious self harming action: 'He seems to have attempted suicide as a cry for help' or 'This suicide was a desperate cry for help from a deeply depressed person.' Such statements are contradictory. Though each uses the word 'suicide', implying the act of intended and wished-for self induced death, in each it is conjoined with the implication that death was not aimed at. In the first an attempt at suicide could hardly constitute a cry for help, since those who intend to die by their own hand do not anticipate being around to receive help. In the second the person's death, if intended, could not have been a plea for help for the same reason; and if it was a plea for help it could not have been suicide. Let me deal briefly with some possible criticisms of my claim that such statements are contradictory.

It might first of all be suggested that whether they are contradictory depends partly upon what is meant by 'a cry for help'; a critic adopting this stance might point out that a person who 'cries for help' need not be doing so in a conscious way, but may simply be acting desperately in response to some dreadful circumstance such as great unhappiness. Such a person, it would be suggested, communicates in his act that he needs help even though he may be unaware of this when he acts.

Secondly, it might be pointed out that though logically contradictory, there is nothing wrong with such statements, given the way that our language works. It just is the case, my critic would claim, that the expression 'attempted suicide' is used to refer to a wide range of self harming acts, some of which are not intended to be fatal. But to argue thus is to ignore the fact that the way we think about self harm will be affected by the expectations to which the labels we use to refer to self harming acts, give rise.

Our familiarity, or lack of familiarity, with the language and culture of a specialist area will make a difference to the extent to which we can successfully understand the matters that arise in that area. When we find ourselves in territory in which the language is unfamiliar, we are apt to make mistakes. It was because of this that a couple of years ago my lack of knowledge of computerese, the language of computer experts, created problems for me in trying to decide what computer to buy. An even worse state of affairs to my mind would have been that I should have had a smattering of understanding of that specialised jargon such that I thought that I understood it like a computer buff when in fact I did not; if that had been the case, I might have purchased a computer that was totally inappropriate for my purposes. And strange though it may seem, computer-illiterate people may not be able to understand the reports about computers being attacked by 'viruses' and 'bugs', that have been common in recent years. It is not just that they cannot understand the illness metaphor that is at work here but that they may not even understand it to be a metaphor, believing that what is being said is that computers are literally being attacked by biological viruses. In a similar way, most people who do not come into regular contact with self harm are unlikely to understand that, for example, the term 'attempted suicide' does not always mean literally that the person tried to kill himself, because they are not part of the culture in which such knowledge is taken for granted. Most people who come into contact with suicidal self harmers will be as ignorant of the idiosyncrasies of the linguistic code used by professionals who work with self harmers and suicides as I was of computerese; and so if it is said of someone they care about that he 'attempted suicide', they are likely to believe that he actually tried to kill himself.

Real and apparent terminological confusion in the literature

But it is not just those who do not come into regular contact with suicidal self harm, or who have not reflected on its nature, for whom our impoverished language can cause confusion in speaking about suicide and related acts. Difficulties can be experienced even by those who have given the matter considerable thought and are aware of at least some of the distinctions that must be made between self harming actions that look similar but may mean different things and hence constitute different acts. Let me illustrate this point by reference to things that other people have written.

Clare

First of all, consider something that Clare (1975) has written: 'No one can ever say with certainty whether the failed suicide really wanted to die or live, the successful one to live or die' (p. 351). One of the biggest difficulties about suicide and related human acts is in telling after a person has killed himself or has taken action that could have killed him but has not, whether in acting as he did, he wanted to live or die. By writing what he has, Clare shows that he is aware of the complexity of the phenomena about which he is talking – that, for example, sometimes those who end up dead did not intend to do so and that sometimes those who end up alive, intended to be dead. However, his adherence to the current conventions for discussing self harm, in which *suicide = a dead person* and *failed suicide = a live person*, leave him seeming to talk as if the question of whether an act was suicide or failed suicide depends on whether the individual whose act is in question ends up alive or dead rather than on the answer to the question of whether he intended to die or to live. By writing in the way that he has Clare has fallen into a trap set by our impoverished language. Other than the fact that he seems to be assuming that in all cases of suicidal self harm death is a success and life a failure, four points are worth noting:

1 His use of the expression 'successful suicide' to refer to any case where a person dies in circumstances that suggest that he may have intended to bring about his own death conflicts with the possibility that death was not what was aimed at and that such a person may really have wanted to live.
2 If a self harmer who ends up dead really wanted to live, he is not a successful suicide or indeed a suicide of any kind; his self killing is, rather, the result of a mistake.
3 Clare's use of the expression 'failed suicide' to refer to any case where the individual ends up alive in circumstances that suggest that he may have intended to end up dead, conflicts with the possibility that he really wanted to live.
4 If a person who ends up alive really wanted to live, he was not a failed suicide. If he really wanted to live, he would not have suicided though he might, for various reasons, including the desire to control others or to attract attention to his predicament, have intentionally acted in such a way that others would think that he had.

A critic might jump to Clare's defence. First, she might point out that a person could both want to live and yet be a 'failed suicide' because he could want to live and yet intend to end his life. This would be the case, for example, where a person had no positive wish to die but decided to suicide because, however much he wanted to live, he could see no prospect of having a life worth living at some point in the future, and therefore decided to kill himself before things got too bad. Or a person with AIDS or some progressively deteriorating condition such as Huntington's Chorea or Alzheimer's Disease, who loved life and was afraid of a gradual decline, might thus kill himself while his life was good. Despite the apparent force of this point, it has to be noted that though, in relation to some imaginable life, the suicider might have wanted to live, in the end it was true that he wanted to die more than to live the life he was living.

Secondly, my critic might argue that a person could be a successful suicide and yet really have wanted to live. In an effort to persuade me of this, she might if she had already got further in this book than you have, remind me about some of the stories from Chapter 5, say that of Alex, claiming that Alex was a successful suicide who really wanted to live. Alex takes an overdose of drugs with the intention of dying and only realises and begins to regret what he is doing as he fades into the unconsciousness before death. But although he brings about his death by actions that were intended to bring it about, Alex dies wishing to live and so he cannot, to my way of thinking, be an example of a suicide who really wants to live.

Glover

Discussing the significance to be attached to a request for assistance in achieving suicide, Glover (1977) writes:

> When unassisted suicide is possible, there is no need to ask for help. A person's unnecessary request for help would be evidence that his suicide 'attempt' was not genuine, but an appeal for support.

(p. 183)

Glover places 'attempt' in scare quotes in order, presumably, to demonstrate his unease about referring to an act that is not intended to end in death, as 'attempted suicide'. Though he thus shows sensitivity to the problems language can cause, I think Glover fails adequately to take account of the possibility that a person might earnestly wish for death and intend to die and yet find that however hard he tries, he cannot take the steps that are necessary to achieve his wish. He might, for example, find that however much he wishes to die, his courage fails him; or he might have difficulty in overcoming a deep-seated religiously rooted aversion to suicide. Such a person might ask a close friend to administer the fatal blow not because his expressed desire to die is disingenuous but because however much he wishes for death, he cannot achieve it alone. A critic might speak out in favour of Glover, arguing that if a person is

51

incapable of taking the steps necessary to end his life, this is a strong indication that really he does not want to die. I think this is a very hard line stance to take and one that does not take account of the possibility that weakness of will might overcome the strongest wish. A critic voicing this view would presumably also wish to say not only that I cannot really want to lose weight because I do not resist eating and drinking food and drink that I know will preserve my overweight state, but also more seriously and more pertinently, that a person trapped in a burning building who has a morbid fear of heights and hence does not jump to safety, really couldn't have wanted to live.

Szasz

Writing about the ethics of suicide, Szasz (1971) has this to say,

> I believe that, generally speaking, the person who commits suicide intends to die; whereas the one who threatens suicide or makes an unsuccessful attempt at it intends to improve his life, not to terminate it.
>
> (p. 186)

I agree that a person who commits suicide intends to die though I think this is always, and by definition, the case, rather than only generally being so. However, things are more complex in the case of suicide threats. Although those who threaten suicide and do not intend to carry it out, generally intend to improve their lives rather than terminating them, those who threaten suicide and do intend to carry it out do intend to suicide, though only if the terms that they have offered to those to whom the threat is made are not fulfilled.

The second half of Szasz's sentence is interesting. Taken at face value its seems contradictory: you cannot both attempt to do something and not attempt to do it, at the same time. An athlete who has accepted a bribe may pretend to be trying to win the race while deliberately losing, but he could not consciously attempt both to win and to lose at the same time. And a person who attempts suicide (which literally means that he is trying to kill himself) cannot, at the same time, be attempting to stay alive. Of course, Szasz believes that the person who is said to be attempting suicide is really doing something else and the apparent problem to which I have pointed is caused by the inadequacy of the language rather than by an inadequacy in his thinking.

Lester

Even those who have noted the problems that the language of suicide can cause, and are attempting to remedy them, can have problems in saying what they want to say. I have already pointed out some of the problems that I have experienced in writing this book, for example. Or consider something that Lester says in his article proposing a classification of acts of attempted suicide, to which I have already referred (Lester, 1990). Though it is clear that he believes that many acts currently labelled 'attempted suicide' do not represent attempts at suicide, he uses this expression in referring to them:

> Some of those who attempt suicide do so because they both foresee and desire the consequences. They wish to harm themselves, risk death, or punish themselves, but (unless they miscalculated) not sufficiently to die. They are not attempting suicide but rather deliberately harming themselves.
>
> (p. 1246)

An aggressive reading of this passage would point out that Lester is contradicting himself here. However, it is obvious that rather than being incoherent he is simply stumbling over the inadequacies of our language. He uses the term 'attempted suicide' to orientate his audience to the point he wishes to make and then points out that people who do things of this kind are not suicide attempters but something else.

It is worthwhile saying something more about this passage because a careful reading of it could raise doubts about whether I am being too kind to Lester. He claims that those he wishes to call 'deliberate self-harmers' do wish to harm themselves and both foresee and desire the consequences; in calling them deliberate self-harmers he wants to deny that they are attempted suicides. But then, why does he put that rider in parentheses? Remember, he writes 'They wish to harm themselves, risk death, or punish themselves, but (unless they miscalculated) not sufficiently to die.' This suggests that they may, after all, have been attempting suicide but miscalculated what they had to do to achieve their deaths. But either a person is a suicide attempter or he is not; either he intends to die or he does not. Since Lester is clearly aware that 'attempted suicide' is a problematic term that is conceptually distinct from his category of 'deliberate self-harm', his seeming to confuse the two is proof of the difficulties that a poverty of terms can cause.

SUICIDE AND CONNOISSEURSHIP

A connoisseur of fine wine, English furniture, art or music is likely to be able to convey his opinion of a glass of Chablis, a Chippendale chair, a painting by Chagall or a Charpentier Chorale more succinctly and more clearly than someone whose acquaintance with these things is more slight. He will be able to do this at least partly because he has available to him a language in terms of which to do so. Any field of study has its own specialised vocabulary in terms of which to discuss its subject matter and those who do not have access to this vocabulary are forever cut off from understanding it in the same way as its initiates can. It is, for example, because I do not understand computerese expressions such as 'megabyte' and 'megahertz', 'RAM', 'CACHE' and 'DOS' that I experienced the difficulty in deciding what computer I should purchase in the example I referred to earlier.

People who are connoisseurs of a particular area of human experience and endeavour can understand and appreciate that area better than those who are not, because they have access to its meanings through their knowledge of its specialised language. But having developed the language in which to convey nuances of meaning, it is likely also that such individuals will be able to taste, look at, touch and listen in different, more precise ways. Language can help us both to express and to experience. For example, since Eskimos have an elaborated vocabulary for discussing snow, they can communicate very accurately about its condition in a relatively simple way. They are connoisseurs of frozen water whose language has developed to allow fine discrimination between different varieties of ice and snow; given the environment in which they have traditionally lived, developing the language in which to make such discriminations was in their interests. On the other hand, we have only a few expressions for snow including words like 'sleet', 'slush' and expressions like 'powdery snow', and are thus limited in what we can say about it; unless, for example, we are skiing or winter climbing enthusiasts, we think about snow in relatively simple ways. In a similar way since discriminating between different varieties of life endangering self harm does not have a high priority for most people, our language for discussing such acts is rather impoverished. As a result we are limited in the ways in which we can speak and think about suicide, and about its relationship to other similar phenomena.

Kreitman (1977) recognises the need for a refurbishment of the conceptual apparatus and terminology with which we approach the problems of suicide and other related phenomena. He writes:

> there are conceptual issues which arise at the very beginning of any study of suicidal behaviour and which must be clarified if any progress is to be made. Even a term like 'suicide' is by no means free of ambiguity; the position is far worse with that form of behaviour which is still widely, loosely and regrettably designated as 'attempted suicide'.
>
> (p. 1)

However, while asserting that a 'clear terminology is a minimum requirement of an adequate theory', Kreitman recognises that 'discussions about terminology are always at risk of degenerating into semantic quibbling' (p. 1). Some people might argue that this book, with its constant reassessment of the language of self harm, and its proliferation of distinctions and new labels for different varieties of self harm, is a degenerate analytic game which puts semantic quibbling before useful thinking about what to do about the problem of suicide in the modern world.

One view might be that the only really useful work to be done in relation to suicide is to work out why people kill themselves, in order that steps may be taken to avoid the conditions that induce them to do so. However, I am not convinced that discovering the causes of suicide would make any difference to the numbers of people who kill themselves. In particular, for example, I doubt whether discovering that, say, unemployment was a major factor in causing suicide rates to rise would lead to significant changes in social or economic policy aimed at reducing redundancy and increasing employment opportunities in this or any country, unless the prevention of self killing suited its government.

Another view might be that quibbling over the language that we use to discuss suicide will not make any difference to the ways in which we deal with it. 'What difference does it make', someone adopting this position might ask, 'how we refer to suicide and other self harming acts?' Such a question would demonstrate that my critic did not understand the nature of my concern with the language of suicide. Of course in a sense it makes no difference whether we refer to suicide as *suicide*, or as, for example, *cotton socks*; the phenomenon is not changed by the label used to refer to it. However, as I have pointed out, the way in which we think about acts of self harm is affected both by the labels used to refer to them and by the expectations to which the use of such labels gives rise.

In any case, what I am concerned to do is only partly a linguistic job; it is only partly about sorting out the labels. More importantly, it is about exploring the wide range of possibilities, both moral and psychological, for meanings and reasons and intentions that might underpin a person's self harming act. No doubt some sophisticated practitioners – psychotherapists, counsellors and so on – will be aware of the range of different acts that suicidal self harming might represent, and be able to utilise this awareness without labelling them in any way. However, for most people, building up a picture of the complexity of this network will be facilitated by the introduction of labels in terms of which to discuss it. By contrast, the way in which intentional self harming actions are at present commonly construed and discussed, limited as it is by the language we have available, fails to take account of the range of meanings that actually or potentially lethal self harmings may have for those who enact them and of the range of different communications that these actions may represent.

NOTE

1   It could be argued that what I have said about suicide has implications for the way in which we conceive of murder and attempted murder. If a failed suicide is just as much a suicide as one who succeeds, the argument might go, wouldn't this mean that a failed murderer is just as much a murderer as one who succeeds? I do not accept this though I do believe that those who attempt to murder and fail are just as culpable, in a moral sense, as those who succeed, given that the reason for the failure lay somewhere other than in the strength of the intention to kill. I discuss the distinction between suicide and murder in Chapter 5.

5

SUICIDE AND INTENTION

In this chapter I want to suggest a new way of thinking about suicide and other forms of suicidal self harm, in which the intentions, wishes and expectations that individuals entertain are centrally important. An examination of intention is helpful in thinking about the moral nature of self destructive acts; it is also essential in determining whether a person was a suicide.

In most talk of suicide, emphasis is placed on the state in which the individual ends up rather than on what he intended when he acted. A person is not normally said to have suicided just because he took action aimed at his death; in addition he has to die. However, the intention of those who suicidally self harm does have an important place in thinking about the nature of their performances. We do not say of all individuals who end up dead as the result of something that they do or omit to do, that they are suicides. For example, we would not normally conclude that a person who died from food poisoning because he unwittingly ate some salmonella chicken was a suicide; nor would we normally say of a person who accidentally drove his car off a steeply curving mountain road that he was a suicide. We talk of suicide only in cases where we are inclined to believe that the individual's action could have been intended to bring about his death.

So the question of whether an act was a suicide depends upon the intention of the individual who is its agent in enacting it. However, in practical decisions, what is generally important is not the actual intention of the person, but rather the intention that others believe he had in acting. Such decisions may be based on rather a cursory consideration of the intentions of self harmers and focus mainly on empirical evidence from the scene of the suicidal act. As a result, assumptions may be made about what a suicidal self harmer intended, without thinking too closely about the range of intentions that could underpin such an act in such circumstances.

A new view of suicide

In thinking about suicide and suicidal self harm I want to focus attention on the inward events that underpin suicidal actions rather than on the consequences of those actions. In contrast to the usual view, where death is necessary for suicide, I want to suggest that all people who wish to die and who intentionally act so as to achieve their deaths, should be referred to as *suicides* whether they live or die. This involves placing emphasis on the importance of the person's intention in acting as he does and on the significance that his act has for him. The model of suicide I am proposing is thus intentional rather than consequential in nature. It places emphasis on the future as planned by the individual who self harms, rather than emphasising the state in which he ends up. It is about what a person *does* rather than about what he achieves, or what happens to him. It is appropriate to emphasise what a person intends by his act because the acts of those who intentionally end their lives and those who attempt to do so but fail, are acts *of the same kind*.

It could be argued that there is a difference in intention between those who kill themselves and those who act in similar ways but don't. Such an argument might begin by pointing out that a person who wishes to die can ensure that he does by adopting a method of suicide that is likely to be successful and then taking steps to ensure that he will not be saved. But this does not take account of the possibility that a person might earnestly wish to die and yet fail to achieve his death. He might, for example, take steps that he has every reason to believe will ensure his death, and yet be unsuccessful.

It is possible to imagine cases where a person acts in order to achieve his death but fails to achieve it in which, to my mind, it would be absurd to deny that he was a suicide, if it is allowed that suicide depends upon what he does rather than on what he achieves. Consider, for example, the man who jumped from the twentieth storey of an office block with the intention of achieving his death, unaware of the fact that a large marquee had been erected earlier in the day, which broke his fall so that rather than crashing to the ground as he had intended, he slid gracefully down to land at the feet of the famous author who was opening the book fair. This is rather a far fetched example but there are other, less fantastic examples of cases where a person might try to die and take precautions designed to ensure that he does, and yet be unsuccessful. For example, a suicide who chooses overdosing as his method of self killing might take careful precautions to avoid discovery, yet be interrupted and saved by another. The first of Sylvia Plath's recorded suicidal acts is perhaps as clear an example of such a situation as we might hope to find. Alvarez (1972) describes the precautions she seems to have taken against being found after taking an overdose:

> She had carefully disguised the theft of the sleeping pills, left a misleading note to cover her tracks, and hidden herself in the darkest, most unused corner of a cellar, rearranging behind her the old firelogs she had disturbed, burying herself away like a skeleton in the nethermost family closet. Then she had swallowed a bottle of fifty sleeping pills. She was found late and by accident, and survived only by a miracle.
>
> (p. 28–9)

So a person might, like Plath, take steps that are as near as possible to foolproof in order to achieve his death, and yet fail because chance is against him.

In Chapter 4, I suggested that a person could do something that would not kill him believing that it could and intending that it should. It is interesting to speculate whether a person could intend to kill himself by performing some action that had no chance of bringing his death. Consider, for example, someone who cuts his wrists so that the blood oozes rather than gushes, spurts or even trickles, or who swallows a bottle of vitamin pills rather than, for example, sleeping pills or tranquillisers. Could he intend by such a seemingly trivial act to end his life? Could he be a suicide? It seems clear that he could, because it is plausible that he could act in any of these ways while entertaining the false belief that he would end up dead as a result. Some people might question the seriousness of such an individual's intention because he has not made sure that his chosen method will actually bring about his death (or even taken steps to ensure that it is very likely to do so). However, the fact that he will not die as a result of his act does not mean that his attempt at self killing is inauthentic.

Kreitman (1977) agrees that a person could really intend to kill himself by doing something that is very unlikely to bring about his death. Discussing how we should think of such individuals, he writes:

59

a patient who has taken a quantity of Vitamin C tablets deliberately and in the expectation of harming himself would not
show any toxic effects. Nevertheless, since patients are not
pharmacists an individual of the kind just cited should not be
excluded from the group.

(p. 3)

A person who did not have the knowledge or skill or tenacity to find
out what would, and what would not, constitute a foolproof way of
ensuring his death, might nevertheless wish to be dead and intend
to bring his death about. Rather than being regarded as a 'cry for
help' or as a gesture at suicide, for example, the acts of those who
intend their deaths by acting in ways that are unlikely to achieve
death should thus be regarded and treated as suicides that have
failed.

So by the account I offer here and elsewhere in this book,
whether a given act is a suicide depends not on whether the individual ends up alive or dead, but on whether in acting, death was
what he wished for and intended. Adhering to this idea has the
result that a person who by a self harming act ends up dead will not
be a suicide unless death was what he intended. It also, as I have
indicated already, has the somewhat unusual consequence that by
my account, a person who wishes and intends to die will be said to
have suicided if he enacts his intention, whether he ends up dead or
alive, provided that he does not rescind this intention. Adopting this
model, a person who intends to die and whose act results in death
may be labelled a *successful suicide*; one whose act does not result
in death, on the other hand, will be an *unsuccessful, failed* or
non-fatal suicide; each, however, will be a suicide.

Some problems with intention

Emphasising intention as I do is fraught with difficulties because
intentions are not on public display. Like wishes, hopes and fears,
they are internal to the intender and not directly accessible to others.
Like the quality of life that he enjoys, like his feelings, we cannot
know another's intentions with certainty. We can guess at them; and
we can gather evidence about them by looking at what he does and
sometimes by asking him what they are. However, others may
deceive us into believing that their intentions are different from how
they really are. Consider the woman who, on asking her husband

his intentions, believes him when he says that he intends to try harder at being a good father and husband on the very day that he is planning to run off with his lover. Things are even more difficult when it is not possible to ask another person about his intentions and one must make a guess at them, because intentions are easy to misread. Consider for example the woman who believes that the rough looking young man with bright pink hair running in her direction means her no good, is terrified when he throws himself headlong at her, and only later realises his courage in moving her out of the path of the runaway bus.

The difficulties in ascertaining what the intentions of self harmers were when they acted mean that it will often, if not always, be impossible to be sure whether a person who dies as the result of self harm was a suicide. So the first problem with emphasising intention is that decisions about the intentions of individuals who bring about their own deaths will always be uncertain, depending as they do on more or less informed guesswork based on whatever knowledge we can glean about the person's lifestyle, beliefs, relationships and any other physical and social evidence which is available.

Another, and perhaps even more significant, problem that is created by my emphasis on intention is that of deciding when the person must have the intention to die if his act is to be considered as suicide, since a person may change his intention even after taking steps that will bring about his death. Initially I thought to say that someone who ends up dead as the result of self harm is not a suicide unless it was his intention, wish and expectation before, throughout and sometimes, depending on the method chosen, in the period following the self harming act, that he would die. I thought that for a person to be a suicide it would have to be the case that in the last seconds before things had gone so far that he could no longer influence events, he must have wanted to die. On reflection, however, I realised that problems arise for this view in cases such as that of a person who, with the wish to die and the intention of bringing about his death, jumped from an aeroplane without a parachute but realised in mid-air that really he wanted to live. The problems arise because in this case, by the time the person (let's call him Chris) changed his mind about what he wished and intended, things had already gone so far that he could not alter the course of events and hence he was going to die whatever he thought about it, whatever hopes, wishes and intentions he now entertained. And so it was his wish up until the point at which he ceased to be able to influence events, that he should die. Yet I want to say that though Chris intended to take his life by acting as he did, and died as the result of a suicide act, when he died he was not a suicide.

Perhaps I can make my case clearer by comparing Chris's story with a scene from the film *Reuben Reuben* (Ellis, 1982), in which the actor Tom Conti plays the part of a poet. In the film Conti's character is depressed because his girlfriend is leaving him. In no mood to live on, Conti arranges things such that he can hang himself. The scene is set.

Conti is standing on a chair with a noose round his neck, ready to kick the chair away and make his voyage into oblivion. But then he reflects a little, for example, about the fact that his girlfriend isn't the only fish in the sea (or woman on the planet); there are other women he could get to know. He changes his mind. Though he intended, when he stood on the chair, to kill himself and wanted to be dead, he now no longer wants death, he is looking forward to the remainder of his life. Then in comes an Old English Sheepdog, the Reuben of the title. Spotting his friend on a chair, he jumps up to greet him, knocking the chair away. Conti (or at least the character he is playing) falls off the chair and dies in the way he had intended to die when he stood on it and put the noose round his neck.

This story seems similar to Chris's; it is clearly a case of self induced death which began with an intention to suicide and ended in death but where death, at the last, was not wished for and intended by the agent. Both men wanted to die and each acted so as to achieve his death. Each changed his mind and each died. I think neither was a suicide because neither, when he died, wished to do so. But perhaps the Conti case is not good enough. Despite the fact that both Chris and the Conti character died after deciding that they wanted to live, a critic would no doubt point out a way in which the two cases are obviously different: whereas Chris had enacted his suicidal act, the Conti character had merely set it up. His death, my critic might argue, was an accident and not a suicide (however suicidal it might look to outsiders); Chris's, on the other hand, is suicide because he had already set out on a suicidal trajectory. It is as if Chris had deliberately put the gun to his head and pulled the trigger, whereas all the Conti character had done was to put it there and think about pulling the trigger until, startled by a loud noise, he had accidentally done so.

Let me take another tilt at the problem by comparing Chris's case with a couple of other cases that are perhaps more similar to it than the Conti case.

Following a serious quarrel with his girlfriend, Alex decided to kill himself and set out to do so by driving too fast down a country lane. He was hospitalised following a major road accident. One day he consumes a large quantity of the pre-scribed painkillers and sleeping pills that he has been putting aside in his bedside cabinet so that having botched the job once he can finally get it over with and be done with his miserable life. He wishes and intends to die and is aware that what he is doing will be construed as suicide. Just as he is lapsing into unconsciousness, however, he thinks 'My God, what have I done?' His life flashes before him. He recalls all the things he hasn't done that he wishes he had done. He changes his mind and tries to get up and make himself sick, to get the poison out of his system. When he finds that he can't, he begins to call out for help.

As a protest to his bosses for taking him off the high speed trains that he loves to drive, Richard lies down on the line just before one of those very trains comes along and only realises as the train is bearing down on him that there are other ways in which he could express his displeasure and that really he doesn't want to die; when he tries to get up he finds that he has caught his foot between the rails. He screams for help.

As in Chris's case, by the time Alex and Richard change their minds about what they wish and intend, things have already gone so far that they cannot, by themselves, change the course of events and hence they will die; and so it was their wish that they should die, up until the point at which they ceased to be able to influence things. There is a difference between their cases and Chris's, however, because whereas Chris had no chance of changing the outcome,

Richard and Alex do have some hope of recovery. Let me tell what happens next in a possible continuation of each of these stories.

Just before Alex finally slips into unconsciousness a doctor passes by and hearing his weak cries for help, goes to him, finds the empty bottle, concludes that Alex has taken an overdose and takes immediate steps to save him; as a result Alex lives.

A passing linesperson, hearing Richard's screams, manages to release him just before the train passes; as a result, Richard is saved.

In these stories, each of the central characters acts intentionally so as to take his life but each changes his mind and each is fortunate both in being within earshot of a potential rescuer and in attracting her attention when there is yet time to save him, and is thus saved. Neither will be thought of as a suicide.

When as in the stories of Alex and Richard, a person has taken action aimed at achieving his death but then, changing his mind, achieves his rescue, albeit via the agency of another, it seems uncontentiously to be the case that he is no longer a suicide. But what if the doctor had been unable to save Alex and the linesperson had been listening to music on her walkman and had thus failed to hear Richard's cries until the train had just about been upon him? In that case both men would have died anyway because although others knew of their change of heart, they could do nothing about it. Here it seems clear since there are these witnesses to the fact that in the end neither man wished to die, most people will not consider their tragic deaths to be suicides. And it seems to me that even if there were no witnesses to testify to their change of mind, the fact that their minds were changed would mean that though they began as suicides, they would end up as something else, just as much as they would had others known about their change of heart. The same is true of Chris and others like him who, although they changed their minds, never had any chance of being rescued after they took their fatal step.

When they wanted to die and acted in a way that they intended and wished to bring about their deaths, Richard and Chris and Alex were suicides; when they want to live, however, they are no longer suicides whether they live or not, provided that they take, or would take, whatever action they could in order to achieve their rescue. Just as a person can be a suicide without dying, because what he intends in acting as he does is to die, so I think that a person can die as the result of a suicidal act aimed at achieving his death and yet not be a suicide, because he does not wish, when he dies, to do so.

How then are we to describe occasions when a person sets out to kill himself, changes his mind *en route* to death, but dies nevertheless?

I was at first inclined to say that in such circumstances the protagonist will have died as the result of accident. However, talking of accidents in this context seems odd because such an individual does not do what he does accidentally, he does it intentionally; and what's more he does it intending to be dead. Chris and Alex and Richard did not accidentally step on the railway line, or take the pills or jump out of the aeroplane; they did these things with the intention of killing themselves. Then I thought that perhaps a better description of what those who die regretting their actions in trying to bring about their deaths do, would be to say that they die as the result of an *irretrievably fatal suicidal act* that was aimed at achieving death but which in the end they regret. Their bad luck in discovering too late that really they wanted to live contributes just as much to their deaths as their having formed and acted upon the intention to kill themselves. Had they been lucky they could, having changed their minds, have been saved.

I do not expect many people to agree with me. Even if they do, this part of my discussion of suicide and self harm will have little practical importance. Unless the protagonist had the opportunity to let someone know about his change of heart, his having changed his mind about his wish to die will make no difference to the decisions others will make about his death. Certainly in the case of those who have histories of serious suicidal self harm, a consideration of life-style, beliefs and relationships, combined with evidence from the scene of the incident, will suggest strongly that the protagonist intended to take his life. As a result, though at the last they wanted to live, such individuals are likely to be thought of as suicides by most people. A critic might suggest that even by my own analysis,

Chris (and Richard and Alex in the versions of their stories in which they die) should be judged suicides because I believe that taking suicidal action with the intention of ending up dead is sufficient for suicide. Some people with very odd views might even argue that the Conti character was a suicide because it was as a result of his own actions – in putting his head in a noose with the intention of killing himself – that he died. However, though I agree that at the point at which he took his intentional suicidal action each was a suicide, I think he ceases to be a suicide when he ceases to wish to die. My critic might continue by making an analogy between suicide and football, inviting me to consider the following case.

A footballer is invited to take a penalty thirty seconds before the end of the cup final. The outcome of the match hangs on this penalty: if he scores his team will win, if he does not, the game will be a draw. He earnestly wishes, as he takes his run, to score; to win the match for his team. But just before his boot connects with the ball, even as the goalkeeper dives in the wrong direction, he reconsiders; he changes his mind and no longer wishes to score. Perhaps he remembers that his wife has a very large amount of money stacked on his team drawing the game; perhaps he looked at his cousin's face as he began his run up and family loyalty got the better of him (his cousin I should explain, is the goalkeeper of the opposing side). Whatever the facts of the matter, he has changed his mind and no longer wishes to score. However, his boot connects and the deed is done. The goal is scored.

More seriously, my critic might also ask me to compare my first four cases with the following case in which a man, unlucky in love, decides to take revenge on his lover.

Peter's lover, Paula, has gone off with another man. Depressed and angry, he has tried to woo her back but Paula is unrepentant. 'I never loved you,' she says. 'Our love was a figment of our joint imagination.' Peter tries to cope with the hurt Paula has caused him but can't.

One afternoon, on a week when her new lover is working

away from home, Peter breaks into Paula's new flat. He laces the gin bottle with a particularly swift acting poison because he knows, as we might expect, that she is in the habit of having a nightcap before going to bed and again as we might expect, he knows that her tipple is gin. That evening, as he is tucked up in bed drinking his cocoa and reading a good book, Peter begins to think about Paula just as she is pouring the poisonous potion into her glass. He tries telephoning to warn her about the gin but she drinks it and expires before he manages even to dial the number.

In relation to these two stories, my critic would ask, 'Wouldn't we call the penalty taker's act that of scoring a goal and wasn't Peter Paula's murderer? And if so, mustn't it also be true that one who successfully and intentionally takes his life is a suicide, whether or not he changes his mind before he dies?' In response to these questions I am inclined to say that obviously the footballer scored a goal and that given what we have been told, Peter clearly murdered Paula. My critic might be delighted, thinking that by this answer I would have shown that I was mistaken in my thinking about Chris, Alex and Richard, and the Tom Conti character. But though she would have boxed cleverly, she would be mistaken. Her understanding of these situations and of my view of them would show no more than that she did not understand the difference between acts of suicide on the one hand and goal scoring and murder on the other. How is the case of suicide distinct from that of penalty goal scoring? And how is it different from murder? Let me deal with each in turn.

Whereas intention is centrally important in deciding whether an act was a suicide, in the matter of goal scoring it is irrelevant. A footballer can score a goal by doing something that he does not intend to do – accidentally kicking the ball into his own team's net. Indeed a player could score a goal by kicking the ball into the back of his own team's net in an abortive attempt to prevent it ending up there. The definition of a goal has nothing to do with the intentions of the goal scorer; it has to do with where the ball ends up, not with who put it there or why he did so. By contrast to the case of goal scoring, we do not normally think of a person's death as a suicide just because his action led to it; what makes his death a suicide is his having intended to end up dead. In other words, whereas it makes a difference in the case of suicide if the suicide changes his mind, it makes no difference to the footballer's act of scoring a goal, whether his intention to do so changes at the last minute (or even, in the case of an own goal, whether his intention was always quite the opposite). The definition of a goal focuses on physical facts. The definition of suicide, on the other hand, focuses on inward facts – on the intentions and wishes of the person who ends up dead, could end up dead or could have ended up dead.

Now to the case of Peter, who successfully arranged his lover's death and grew to regret having done so too late to arrange her reprieve. Peter, I would argue, is more like the goal scorer than he is like a suicide; he is a murderer just because, with the intention to do her harm, he unlawfully and deliberately caused Paula's death, although even as it was happening he wished it was not. Murder is unlawful killing of another from bad intentions,[1] and that is what Peter did. This is the case even though as Paula put the glass to her lips, he was trying to effect her rescue. He is her murderer just as much as if he had put a gun to her head and pulled the trigger or forced the poison down her throat. The fact that Peter regrets what he has done might act as mitigation if he were found guilty and sentenced, but it does not alter the extent or seriousness of his guilt because his deliberate act of killing arose from a wicked intention. He is therefore a murderer; his regret cannot alter that. Regret, on the other hand, does change what Chris, Alex and Richard do. Though they enact suicidal acts, the fact that having done so, they regret what they have done and try to change the outcome or (in Chris's case) would have done had this been possible, means that they are not suicides because they die not wishing to do so.

So when must a person have the intention and wish to die if we are to think of him as a suicide?

As I have said, I was at first inclined to think that a person will be a suicide if he takes suicidal action and wishes, intends and expects to die in the period before, throughout and sometimes following, the self harming act. Following the discussion on the last few pages I now feel able to make another attempt to answer this question.

A person who dies as the result of a self harming aimed at achieving his death is a suicide if, and only if, he entertained the wish and intention to be dead until he ceased to be able to entertain intentions and wishes; it must, in other words, have been his unrescinded wish that he should die.

Conversely, someone who intends to die by his own hand and
takes actions intended to achieve his death, but does not die,
is a suicide at the time that he takes his suicidal step and will
remain so while his intention and wish to die is ongoing and
while he expects to die as a result of that act.

By this account, not one of Chris, Alex or Richard nor any other person who, having set out on a suicidal course wishing to be dead, decides that he no longer wishes to be dead, is a suicide, even if he dies. Conversely those who take actions aimed at achieving their deaths are suicides even if they end up alive, provided that their intention to be dead did not alter during the attempt. In a sense Chris and Alex and Richard each died as the result of an act of suicide, because the act they performed, when they performed it, was a suicide. However, by the time they die it is not; the nature of their acts is, in other words, retrospectively transformed by the changes in intention and desire that occurred in them as they approached death.

My critic might ask why a change of heart should count after the action that brings death in the case of suicide, but not in the case of murder. I think my answer is that since suicide is about what a person means by his action and meanings can alter even after he has acted, in the case of suicide a change of heart and intention changes the act performed. Murder, on the other hand, is about what he achieves. In other words, whereas meanings are reversible while one can yet imagine, facts are not. Though his irreversibly fatal act was a suicide when he enacted it, when a person who wishes to die and sets out intentionally to kill himself changes his mind about what he wishes, the nature of his act changes. Though he started out on a suicidal course, changing his mind changes the nature of his act even in cases where it cannot change the outcome, and so the suicider who changes his mind is no longer a suicide when he dies, because he dies wishing to live. On the other hand, someone like Peter, who intentionally and unlawfully kills another, is a murderer because, with wicked intentions, he wanted another person dead, acted so as to achieve her death, and was successful in doing so.

NOTE

1   Murder is 'The crime of unlawful homicide with malice aforethought; as where death is caused by an unlawful act done with the intention to cause death or bodily harm, or which is commonly known to be likely to cause death or bodily harm' (Saunders, 1970, p. 226).

6

DEFINING SUICIDE

Holland's famous paper about suicide (Holland, 1969) begins by making a distinction between the questions: 'Is arsenic poisonous?' and 'Is suicide all right or not?' Holland thinks that whereas the question about arsenic is susceptible of an answer which, as he says, would be *the* answer to the question, the question about suicide cannot be answered so easily. In the case of arsenic he writes, 'the question what it is, and the question whether it is poisonous, are separable: you can know that arsenic is poisonous without having analysed its nature' (p. 32). In relation to suicide he writes, 'to know or believe that suicide is objectionable is to have analysed its nature or construed its significance in one way rather than another' (p. 32). Though he is primarily concerned with the ethico-religious problems raised by suicide, with the question, that is, of whether it is right or wrong, Holland thus embarks first on an exploration of what suicide is. He writes: 'I do not think it is just one thing and I do not expect to get very far with the question' (p. 32).

While agreeing with his belief that suicide isn't just one thing, I do not share Holland's lack of confidence about the possibility of saying what it is. Much of this book is given over to the attempt to distinguish acts of suicide from other similar acts, in order to be able to say what it is about suicide acts that makes them distinctive. I want now to think a little about some of the problems that arise when one attempts a formal definition of suicide. It is not possible to come up with a rule of thumb that will allow us to tell unequivocally whether any particular human act was a suicide since too much depends on what we cannot tell: what was in the mind of the individual when he took the action that leads, or could have led, to his death, and what was in his mind after he took that action. However, I hope to be able to say enough to allow us to decide in

70

relation to any act that if it was an act of *this* kind, it was a suicide and if it wasn't, it was not.

Suicide is usually defined retrospectively by focusing attention on evidence about the state of the individual after he has done what he does and after he has achieved what he achieves, in suiciding, and not while he is in the process of doing or acting. By contrast the definition of suicide that I hope to establish is prospective, because it lays stress on what the suicide intended by his act; it looks not at what he achieved, but at what he hoped to achieve, in acting.

Suicide as 'self killing' or 'self inflicted death'

By contrast to the way in which 'suicide' is normally used, the expressions 'self killing' and 'self inflicted death' imply only the physical fact that a person has brought about his own death. In spite of this, suicide is sometimes thought of in just these terms, as self killing or as self inflicted death. One problem with defining suicide in this way, is that doing so doesn't take account of the possibility that a person could suicide without successfully arranging his death; of course this is rather contentious, depending as it does on the new way of thinking about suicide that I have proposed. Less contentiously, it does not take account of the possibility that a person may kill himself without suiciding. For example, he could bring about his own death by accidentally driving into a wall or taking an overdose of either prescribed or illegal drugs. Taking account of the possibility of accidental self killing might lead to suicide being defined as 'intentional self killing'. Indeed, 'suicide' as it is usually used implies not only that a person was responsible for bringing about his death, but also that he brought it about intentionally. Those who end up dead but are known (or thought) not to have intended to do so, just are not considered, in the normal way of things, to have suicided, even though their death results from their intentional act.

Definitions of suicide which focus attention on the intention of the individual have a long pedigree. For example, in 1846 a judge ruled that:

> every act of self-destruction is, in common language, described by the word suicide, provided that it be the intentional act of a party knowing the probable consequences of what he is about. This is, I think, the ordinary meaning of the term.
>
> (B. Rolfe, 1846)

71

There are some problems with this definition. One of these is that it is imprecise about the nature of the intentional act that is necessary; there are a range of intentional acts that a person could perform knowing that they were likely to end with him dead, where we would not wish to consider him a suicide. The person who sacrifices his life in saving others is an obvious example. I think, however, that if we allow that what Rolfe means is that the individual must not only have acted intentionally, knowing that he was likely to die as a result, but with the intention of bringing about his death, his definition is quite successful, though it does not attend to the importance, as I see it, of the desire or wish to be dead.

Beauchamp and Childress (1983) come up with a definition which emphasises the fact that death must arise not only from an intentional act, but from one that is aimed at achieving death: 'suicide occurs if and only if one intentionally terminates one's own life – no matter what the conditions or precise nature of the causal route to death' (p. 95). Beauchamp and Childress's definition leaves open the reasons that a person might have for ending his life. It focuses simply on what is done or was done, rather than on the question of why it is, or was, done. It also leaves open the question of what it means to say of a person that he intentionally ended his life.[1] Though it is easy to give examples of intentional acts, it is less easy both to say just what makes them intentional, and to say who is to be counted as being capable of intentional action. There are also difficulties in deciding of a person what his intention was in acting in a particular way and in saying what precisely his intention must be in order that he should count as a suicide. How might we know that a person intended to kill himself? Since a person's intentions are private to him, we can never be sure of what they are; the best we can do is to guess at what he intended. Related to the problem of coming to know or understand another's intentions is the problem of deciding whether in acting, he is rational.

Rationality, understanding and suicide

Sometimes it is argued that for a self killing to amount to suicide it is necessary that the dead person was rational in his intention to bring about his death. If those who hold this view mean that a person cannot suicide if he is non-rational, I agree. A person who is non-rational is for that reason non-autonomous and in my view, although a person who is not autonomous can take his life, his death is not a suicide.

However, the view that a person must be rational before we should count his suicidal self harming as suicide could imply that a person who acts irrationally cannot suicide. In this case I disagree, because I think a person can suicide irrationally. A person can be so irrational that he is non-autonomous; however, he may act irrationally while maintaining his autonomy. Rationality is, after all, a matter of degree; none of us acts fully rationally all of the time. For example, we may react irrationally to a driver who has behaved impolitely towards us when we are hurrying to work, or to the cat or the baby, neither of whom has the faintest idea why the object over which they have been sick is so precious to us, but this does not mean that we are necessarily non-autonomous.

The question of rationality is closely bound up with the question of understanding. Some minimal conception of what death might be like, and awareness of the fact that (religious conviction aside) it is an irreversible state, is necessary before someone could wish and intend to achieve that state and thus be capable of suicide. And so, in deciding upon the nature of his act, I think we should consider the extent to which a person who takes serious self harming action understood and was aware of what he was doing.

Consider a person who does not understand the nature of suicide, who says (whether to himself or to others) that he intends to kill himself but has no notion of what it means to be dead. Perhaps he does not understand that death is irreversible, that he will not be able to change his mind (if he still has one) and come back from wherever he ends up. Such a person could not suicide. He could kill himself but if he could not even envisage what death was like, he could not intend to be dead though he could say that he intended it and he could intend to perform the fateful action. We cannot intend to be something that we cannot comprehend. It is because of his limited ability to comprehend or imagine a state of non-being that though he could kill himself, I do not believe that a young child or a person who had a severe learning difficulty could suicide.

But what, someone might ask, of the eminent astronomer who, after playing with the controls of a disused radio telescope as a child, said to her parents, 'I intend one day to become a radio astronomer.' Wouldn't it be correct to say, they might argue, that this child had become what she intended to become even though, at the time of asserting her intention at the age of 6, she did not know what radio astronomy was but only that she had enjoyed playing with the controls of the disused dish? Though using the notion of intending, she could not have intended (at that time) to be an astronomer. We cannot intend to be what we cannot comprehend, whether that is an astronomer, or dead. And if intending to be dead is necessary for suicide then a person who is incapable (in any sense) of knowing what death is, cannot suicide. It might be argued that since we cannot have the experience of dying and coming to life again, none of us can know what death is like. However, those of us who have the capacity for rational thought and are able to reflect on the nature of life and death, can at least conceive of what death might be like.

So I think that to suicide a person must at least be able to imagine what it might mean to be dead. If he does not have sufficient understanding of life and death to be able to do this, he cannot suicide though he could self kill. Nor can a person suicide if his rationality is for a time so impaired by factors such as psychological distress, intense pain, lack of sleep, the effects of drugs or the range of conditions commonly referred to as 'mental illness' that he is incapable of the necessary level of reflection.

In arguing that a person whose capacity for rational thought is severely impaired cannot suicide, I should reiterate that I am not claiming that whenever a person's rationality is impaired, his ability to reason will be affected so much that if he attempts to kill himself we should think of his action as something other than suicide. To assume, as many people do, that anyone who acts suicidally must have been so irrational as to render him non-autonomous, simply because of the way in which he has acted, seems wrong. To do so makes the assumption that it is never possible rationally to wish to be dead rather than alive, and I do not believe that. Just because a person's rationality is impaired as the result of emotional upset or psychological distress, does not mean that he is incapable of suicide; Ophelia might well have suicided when Hamlet rejected her, however upset at the thought of life in a nunnery. Even a person who is crazy in the sense of having psychotic experience, may at least sometimes be rational enough to suicide, in the sense that he is sufficiently aware both of what he is doing, and of its significance, to want and intend to do it. However, although he may suicide during a rational *window* in his psychosis, a crazy person who acts suicidally while psychotic will not be a suicide whether or not his act proves fatal, because psychotic acts, resulting as they do from inaccurate or false perceptions of the world, are non-autonomous.[2]

Suicide as an 'open textured' concept

Windt (1981) offers a view of suicide which he describes as 'open textured'. He does not believe that it is possible to come up with a set of necessary and sufficient conditions for suicide because he believes that for each characteristic by virtue of which we might be able to call an event a suicide, there will be cases which are not suicides though they display that characteristic, and other cases that are cases of suicide though they do not have that characteristic. However, he believes that: 'characteristics of cases of suicide may be found which are definitional, in the sense that they really are the characteristics by virtue of which an event is a suicide' (pp. 39–40). Further to this he believes that by analysing the concept of suicide it should be possible to 'specify any necessary conditions, indicate criteria and the circumstances under which they are or are not significant, give paradigms, and say something about the general character of the similarities linking the various cases together' (p. 40).

So Windt denies that there is any nuclear set of characteristics which all cases of suicide will share. However, he writes, 'If the concept of suicide is open-textured, then it must involve some criteria' (p. 40) and he attempts to pinpoint such criteria. He adopts Wittgenstein's idea (Wittgenstein, 1974) of family resemblance to describe the way in which different cases of suicide will relate to one another: 'While different criteria may be involved in different cases, we should expect to find similarities among the whole family of cases which justify their assimilation under a single concept' (p. 40).

Windt introduces a number of vivid examples and though I think his analysis is mistaken, a consideration of what he has to say about them will prove instructive and helpful in the attempt to come up with a set of necessary and sufficient conditions in order to be able to say just how suicide should be defined.

Windt's necessary conditions for suicide

Windt stipulates, for the sake of argument, that 'the death either of the person or of the organism' (p. 41) is a necessary condition for suicide. He asserts that the only other necessary condition is that some reflexive description should apply to the death; as examples of such descriptions, he cites cases in which it would be correct to say, respectively, that a person has 'killed himself', 'gotten himself killed' and 'let himself be killed'. Each of these can certainly be found in cases of suicide. Consider, for example, John who achieves his death by shooting himself in the head because he wishes to die and Jason who achieves his by getting Donald to shoot him with the intention of achieving his death. John kills himself and Jason gets himself killed and each is a suicide. Consider also the man in search of a picnic site who has mistakenly wandered onto a firing range before practice begins. If after his cucumber sandwiches he stands up just as a group of soldiers are trying out some automatic weapons, but realising where he is he decides not to duck because he is feeling depressed and wishes to die, he is a suicide. Whereas John killed himself and Jason got himself killed, however, this man lets himself be killed.

But the fact that a person kills himself, gets himself killed or allows himself to be killed is not sufficient for suicide, since all may apply also in cases that are not suicide. If John had shot himself while cleaning his shotgun which he believed to be empty, he would not have been a suicide although he would have killed himself. If Donald had shot Jason not because Jason wanted to die but because he had asked him to do so in order to play a practical joke on Miranda and had believed the gun to be full of blanks, Jason would have gotten himself killed but would not have been a suicide but the victim (though its author) of rather a nasty accident. Finally, if the picnicker hadn't deliberately stood where he was when he realised that bullets were raining down on him but had simply frozen on the spot with fear, he would not have been a suicide though he would still have let himself be killed.

In other words, in order that killing oneself, getting oneself killed or letting oneself be killed should constitute suicide, something more has to be true: the individual must, in addition, have intended by the means in question to arrange his death. Nevertheless, Windt is right in asserting that some such description must be true before suicide will have occurred. However, I do not understand why he talks in terms of 'reflexive description'. A simpler way of describing these situations would be to say that in each case the individual is the instigator or author of his demise whether or not he physically carries it out. If this is what he means then I think he is correct; it is a necessary, but as I have shown not sufficient, condition of suicide that the person who is said to suicide should instigate the act.

What distinguishes suicide from other deaths in which a person has a hand himself?

In defining suicide a number of different features have been given prominence. Windt considers the following:

- that death was caused by the actions or behaviour of the deceased;
- that the deceased wanted, desired, or wished death;
- that the deceased intended, chose, decided, or willed to die;
- that the deceased knew that death would result from his behaviour;
- that the deceased was responsible for his death.

(p. 41)

Windt claims that these are *criteria* for suicide. He believes that though their presence or absence can help us in deciding whether a given act was a suicide, none is sufficient or even necessary to classify an act as suicide. In order to explore his reasons for this, he invites us to consider a person on a hiking trip who uses a slender log to cross a stream, falls in and is drowned. In an attempt to discover some of the criteria that might induce us to decide in a given case that this man was a suicide, Windt examines a range of variations on this story.

First of all he discusses two cases which he considers to be easy. First, the situation where: 'Though he is in high spirits and generally satisfied with his lot, the hiker loses his balance and falls into the stream and drowns despite attempting to swim to safety.' Second, the situation where: 'The hiker is in despair and wants to die, has planned to drown himself at that spot by drowning, deliberately jumps from the log and makes no effort to swim' (p. 42).

According to Windt these are easy cases, and I agree; the first is clearly a simple accident and has nothing at all to do with suicide, while the second seems to be a clear case of suicide. But Windt does not tell us why he believes they are easy. I shall say why I think they are easy presently, but for the moment I want to say something about some other features of Windt's first two scenes that he claims might influence us towards thinking that the hiker in the second was a suicide, while in the first he was not, though they are not

77

in themselves conclusive. In this matter I again concur with his view.

In the case where the hiker does suicide, the non-necessary feature is that he is in despair. Though many who suicide are desperately depressed so that they do not know where to turn, the fact that the hiker was in despair does not necessarily mean that he suicided because, of course, a person can be in despair without intending to suicide, however dangerous the enterprise in which he is engaged. I have often been in despair while trying to work out how to trim this book down to the length agreed with my commissioning editor, without wishing to die and formulating the intention to die as a result.

In the scenario where the hiker does not suicide, the non-necessary features are that he is happy and satisfied with life, the life threatening condition comes about accidentally and he tries to swim to safety. Though these might lead us to suspect that he did not suicide, they are again inconclusive, even when taken together.

First of all, the hiker's being happy does not prove that he was not a suicide; many suicides seem happier in the hours and moments before they died than they had been for a long period before. This is a common experience. One possible reason for this is that the individuals concerned are happier because they have decided once and for all on a way to put themselves out of their misery; another possibility is that having decided to suicide, they are putting on a brave face in an attempt to disguise their real intentions and plans in front of those who might interfere if they knew what was afoot.

Secondly, the fact that his falling in the river is accidental does not mean that his death could not be a suicide. A person could wish to die, intend to die, and by a lucky accident of fate find himself in a situation where death was easily obtained. Consider, for example, the situation if the hiker, wishing to kill himself, was hiking to the top of a very high cliff from which he intended to throw himself but, crossing the stream *en route*, accidentally fell from the log and seizing his chance, successfully refrained from swimming and drowned as a result. Here the life threatening condition would have come about accidentally but the hiker is a suicide nevertheless, because he took advantage of the situation in which he found himself to enact his intention and wish to die.

Finally, the fact that the hiker tries to swim to safety does not mean that he did not intend and wish to die. A man could want to drown, jump into a river with the intention of drowning, but be so shocked by the cold water that he swam to the bank in a reflex way. Or he might discover that he does not have what it takes to allow himself to drown; refraining from staying above the water might prove beyond him and he might find himself unable to stop breathing and attempting to expel water from his lungs. In either case he would be a suicide that saved himself. By my analysis of suicide, provided that he does not lose his will and wish to die, he will remain a suicide even as he swims to the bank; if this is the case, he would probably take up the offer of help in setting up a foolproof method of killing himself, should a handy and helpful suicide liberal[3] offer assistance as he pulls himself out of the water; otherwise he might either go off and immediately try again, or put his suicide on hold for a short time until he has worked out a more practicable way to achieve his death.

Given that none of these features is conclusive in deciding whether the hiker in Windt's first two cases was a suicide, what then makes them easy? The reason I think they are is that whereas the second exhibits features that I consider necessary before we could consider a human act to be suicide, the first does not. More than that, I think these features comprise a set of necessary and sufficient conditions for suicide.

What then are these necessary and sufficient characteristics? They are that in suicide the person's intention and wish to end up dead must underpin an act or omission that is intended to bring his death about. They may be stated like this:

> *For an act to be suicide, the agent must wish to be dead, intend to achieve his death, and whether directly or through the agency of another, he must act so as to achieve it.*

Alternatively we might say:

> *A person who suicides wishes to be dead, intends to die and enacts that intention.*

Next Windt goes on to consider some cases that he considers to be more difficult. First, the situation where: 'the hiker is suffering from depression and wants to die but has not formed any plans for his death; after slipping on the log and falling in accidentally, he deliberately refrains from swimming and drowns.' In this case, Windt claims, the hiker suicides though there is no significant causation on his part. I agree that the hiker does suicide; but Windt is mistaken in thinking that there is no significant causation on his part. Since he

79

does not perform any actions that cause his death, Windt thinks that the hiker does nothing to cause it. But there is significant causation on his part because he does do something: he refrains from swimming and, what's more, by doing so he achieves his death. If any should doubt that refraining from swimming is an active pastime, let her get into deep water and refrain from swimming; then try to avoid spitting out the water when she begins to go under. If any refraining is active this refraining is. This case meets the set of necessary and sufficient conditions I have outlined for suicide, because the hiker aims at bringing about his death by refraining from swimming; the fact that he succeeds in doing so means that his is a successful suicide.

Next Windt considers the possibility that: 'the hiker is neither depressed nor inclined to die but drowns because, falsely believing that he is a better swimmer than he is, he gets into difficulties after diving into the stream to cool off.' In this case, although there is significant causation, the hiker is not a suicide because although his intentional act brought it about, the life threatening condition is not underpinned by the intention and wish to die. Unlike the previous case, this does not match up to the set of necessary and sufficient conditions that I have outlined.

Windt thinks that the distinction between cases that are suicide and those that are not is located in the presence or absence of what he calls 'the desire to die and the decision to do so' (p. 42); Alternatively we might refer to this as the intention and wish to die. I believe that, however expressed, this is a necessary condition for suicide. However, it is not sufficient in itself to delineate all cases of suicide; for an act to be suicide it must have been underpinned by the intention and wish to die, but a person could intend and wish to suicide, be about the business of procuring his death, and yet die as the result of an accident.

Consider, for example, a man who has the desire to die and decides to kill himself by swallowing a massive overdose of drugs. He has accumulated a quantity of sleeping tablets far in excess of the amount needed to kill him and plans to take them on a day when he knows that his wife and family are far away. He intends to die, he desires to die and has decided to do so; he has planned his death to the last detail: he will put on his favourite recording of the St Matthew Passion, wash down the pills with a large glass of decent malt whisky and then, lying on his Victorian *chaise longue* in the conservatory, looking out at the garden he loved, he will dream himself to death. The pills are by the couch; he has his malt to help them on their way. He plugs in his portable CD player and is electrocuted. He intended and wished and planned to kill himself; but despite all that he died as the result of an accident.

In the next version of his story, Windt considers the possibility that the hiker might die as the result of what he refers to as 'a compulsion to suicide', which he fears and has sought aid in combating: 'Eventually the hiker falls prey to his compulsion to commit suicide and as he is crossing the bridge it drives him into the water and he drowns' (p. 42). Windt is in no doubt that this occurrence counts as a case of suicide though the hiker neither wanted nor intended to die and the compulsion operated against his will rather than in accordance with it. He believes that this story shows that 'wanting, willing, intending, or deciding to die are not necessary conditions of suicide' (p. 43).

Surely Windt is mistaken here. Rather than showing that wanting, intending and deciding are not necessary conditions of suicide, I think his analysis of this case demonstrates his unawareness of the question-begging nature of his account. He assumes in the beginning both that intention is not necessary for suicide and that it is possible to have a compulsion to suicide. From there he argues that because his victim did not intend or will or want or decide to die, that intending, willing, wanting and deciding cannot be necessary conditions for suicide. But he has already distinguished cases of suicide from cases that are not suicide on the basis that in those that are suicide, the individual desired (wanted) and decided to die. In any case I think that the notion of compulsive suicide is incomprehensible and that what Windt is referring to as a compulsion to suicide is in reality no more than a compulsion to self kill. A person might decide to suicide as the result of a compulsion to kill himself, for example, because he could not stand the strain of trying to avoid killing himself and decided to get his life over with in order to rid himself of the suffering that avoiding killing himself caused. But that would be different from suiciding because he had a compulsion to do so.

Following his discussion of these variations on his story of the hiker, Windt considers a number of other points that are worthy of note.

First, he addresses the question of whether the knowledge that a given behaviour would result in death might be a necessary condition for suicide. He considers the case where the hiker 'is moody, depressed, and decides to leap from the log and try to swim the stream' (p. 43). When the hiker is unsure whether he will survive or not, Windt thinks that we will count his death as a suicide if that is the outcome. In contrast to this I think this case is an example of cosmic roulette, which I discuss in Chapter 7, because in it the hiker takes a gamble with his life. It is not suicide because it does not arise out of his intention and wish to end his life, though if he thinks it is very unlikely that he will be able to swim across the river, we might consider that he was gambling suicidally with his life. As regards the general question of whether it is necessary for suicide that the individual should know that a given act will bring about his death, I do not believe that such knowledge is a necessary condition. As I have already demonstrated, a person can earnestly intend to die and act so as to achieve his death, believing that his action will kill him, and thus be a suicide, but end up alive because what he does is insufficient to bring about his death.

Next, Windt discusses a feature that he considers is common to all suicides. 'In suicide', he writes,

> we find a peculiar negation of the value of life. Of all persons, we should expect he whose life it is to be most sensitive to the value of a life; but in suicide it is that very person who allows the value of his life to be overridden by other factors.
>
> (p. 45)

Here again I think Windt is mistaken. Though for many people who suicide, death is sought because they do not value their lives, this is by no means true of all who suicide. Some who suicide do so because they *do* value their lives and do not wish to devalue them by living on in a state that they consider is a degradation of what life *can be*, perhaps of what they think it *should be*. For such a person suicide would not result from a 'peculiar negation of the value of life'; rather it would be an assertion of its value. Windt seems, in fact, to acknowledge as much when he writes:

> In some cases a life really may not be worth living further; in others delusion and irrationality may only make it seem so; in still others something of greater worth may be achieved by sacrificing life; and so on.
>
> (p. 45)

At least some suicides might be a celebration of life. In her address to a meeting to honour the memory of Arthur and Cynthia Koestler,

Barbara Smoker, then Chairman of the Executive Committee of the Voluntary Euthanasia Society, clearly thought as much in Koestler's case:

> In the unique pattern of his life, Arthur Koestler manifested the Art of Living – living intensely, whole-heartedly, exuberantly, with intellectual wonder and excitement, and with manifold interests, purposes and satisfactions. When life of an acceptable quality was no longer possible, he manifested the Art of Dying – bringing his life-span to a serene and dignified close, in his own home and at the time of his own choosing. Having partaken fully of the feast of life, he made ready for a brisk departure, with the quiet contentment of a satisfied guest.
>
> (1983, pp. 263–4)

Finally, I want to consider Windt's claim that failing to notice the open textured nature of the concept of suicide may result in mistakes being made in judging what is and what is not suicide. This will happen, he thinks, if we define suicide in terms of some nuclear set of characteristics, because doing so might lead us both to exclude some genuine cases of suicide and to include others which are not suicide.

In arriving at a definition of some phenomenon, it is certain that those who do not agree with the new definition will disagree both about the inclusion of some instances that the definition includes in the category and about the exclusion of some that it excludes. In addition there is, of course, always a danger that some instances of that phenomenon may be excluded when the definition is applied. Or at least there is a danger of this if the boundaries of the definition are hazy or too definite; thus, for example, if I define 'tall men' hazily, as, say, 'men who are tall by comparison with other men', those men who are, say, 6 feet tall will be excluded if they are judged against the members of a North American professional basketball squad. And if I define 'tall men' as 'men who are over 6 feet 10 inches tall', many men who most people would consider tall, say 6 feet 6 inches in height, will be excluded. To avoid similar problems in relation to any phenomenon, we will have to come up with a clear definition that will include all examples of that phenomenon and exclude none, and which will in addition be acceptable to everyone. I think this should be easier to achieve in relation to suicide than in relation to tall men because whereas I think the question 'What is suicide?' is susceptible of an answer, the question

'When is a man tall?' is not. Whereas there are gradations of tallness, there are not gradations of suicide. An act either is, or is not, suicide; on the other hand, the question of whether a man is, or is not, tall will depend upon what he is measured against. The set of necessary and sufficient conditions for suicide I proposed earlier leads towards a definition of the act of suicide that I hope will allow us to answer the question 'What is suicide?' in a way that will include all acts that are suicide and exclude all acts that are not suicide.

Some proposed definitions

Since I use the expression 'suicide' to refer both to acts of suicidal self harm of a particular kind and to those who enact them, I will offer definitions for both acts and persons.

> *Suicide is an act, whether of commission or omission, and whether performed by himself or others, by means of which an individual autonomously intends and wishes to bring about his death because he wants to be dead or wants to die the death he enacts.*

> *A person is a suicide if he initiates an act, whether of commission or omission, and whether performed by himself or others, by means of which he autonomously intends and wishes to bring about his death because he wants to be dead, or wants to die the death he enacts, as long as he entertains that wish and intention.*

I think these definitions cover all cases of suicide. In line with what I have said so far in this book, they focus on the intention and wish with which the individual acts and allow that if he earnestly wishes to achieve his death and takes action intended to achieve it, a person is a suicide whether or not he ends up dead, provided that he does not rescind his wish to die. They allow that death may be brought about either by omission or by commission on the part of either the suicide or some other person. They allow that a person may act in ways that he foresees or even intends should bring about his death, without being a suicide, because he may do this without wishing to die. Finally, they take account of the fact that there is a hazy area surrounding suicide in which there are acts that are performed by those who have not thought out what they are doing sufficiently well for it to be true to say that what they meant was to be done with life. I do not think that cases of this kind are suicides and the definitions I have offered take account of this by allowing that some people who intend to kill themselves may not be suicides because they are, either always or when they act, not autonomous.

Where a person dies as the result of a suicide act he will be a successful suicide; where he does not die, he will be a failed or unsuccessful suicide; where, while he is still able to entertain wishes, he changes his mind about wishing to die he will no longer be a suicide, regardless of whether he lives or dies, though he will still have died as the result of a suicide act.

NOTES

1 The notion of intention is a slippery one into which I shall not delve deeply. I was tempted at first to say something of this kind: 'A person intends to do something if he wants to do it and decides to do it.' But a person could intend to do something that he did not want to do; consider, for example, my intention to do something that I find distasteful but that I know needs to be done, like drinking the awful potion that my doctor has said will settle my stomach upset. I shall assume that when we talk of a person's having intended to end his life, we mean that were he somehow able to witness his state after his act, a person who intended to end up dead would hope afterwards to find that he was dead, whereas a person who did not intend to end up dead would be surprised to find that he was. I have avoided stipulating either that the person who intended to be dead would be pleased to discover that he was, or that the one who did not intend to be dead would be disappointed to find that he was, because it might be that having acted, either might change his mind if he found that death was different from what he expected.

2 Although I do not wish to do so here, I think it might be argued that the apparent 'acts' that a psychotic person performs should not be considered as *acts* but merely as *actions*; this relates to the idea that under certain conditions a person should not be held responsible for his behaviour because he has acted in a state of what is commonly known as 'diminished responsibility' which has resulted from mental instability.

3 A suicide liberal is one who believes that everyone has the right to do away with his life; some suicide liberals would think it right to offer Windt's hiker assistance if he failed to achieve his death. I discuss the distinction between suicide liberals and conservatives in some detail in Chapter 11.

7

EXTENDING THE TAXONOMY OF SUICIDAL SELF HARM

Instances of someone taking poison deliberately to harm himself, but with the intention of surviving, are hard to find. Juliet did so, but Romeo had so little thought that she might not be dead that he killed himself in despair. He knew, as everyone knew, that if you took poison you died. Conversely you did not poison yourself unless you wanted to die. This is not the case today.

(Kessel, 1965, p. 4)

Experts distinguish between the person really determined to make an end of himself and the one who rather hopes he will be saved. Already the ancients realised that a person might go through the motions of suicide while careful to stay alive. As is admitted on all hands, it may at times be extremely difficult to decide which category we have before us.

(Daube, 1972, p. 388)

He committed suicide more than any other man I know but always in the most reasonable manner. If he drowned himself, then the canal was dry: if he jumped down a well, so was that: and when he drank disinfectant there was always an antidote ready, clearly marked to save everybody trouble.

(Laurie Lee, 1959, p. 181)

I have argued that our current conceptual apparatus and language of self harm is limited, and does not allow us to distinguish with sufficient subtlety between suicidal acts of different kinds. In Chapter 6, I discussed some problems in defining suicide and developed definitions of suicide as applied both to persons and to acts. I now want to extend my examination of the natural history of human self destruction by elaborating and extending the vocabulary of suicidal self harm. In doing so, I will be introducing some new expressions, and elaborating and suggesting particular uses for others. I will begin by distinguishing between suicide and two other varieties of human act with which it is sometimes confused: *cosmic roulette* and *suicide gesturing*. After that I will say something about *assisted suicide*.

Cosmic roulette

Suicide should, I think, be distinguished from potentially self destructive self harming actions in which, rather than setting out to take their lives, people take a gamble by intentionally giving up their fate to God or the cosmos. I will refer to a range of such activities by the family name *cosmic roulette*. There is, of course, a sense in which many suicides put their lives into the balance. Except in cases where death will almost certainly follow the suicidal act, as when powerful firearms or particularly swift acting poisons are used, whether a suicide lives or dies is to some extent a matter of luck. However, in suicide the intention is to achieve death and the gamble is a risk created by the means one uses. In cosmic roulette, on the other hand, the gamble is what is aimed at, one of the possible outcomes or pay-offs of which is death.

In cosmic roulette a person intentionally self harms or creates a situation in which self harm might come about, but does not do so wholeheartedly intending either that he should live, or that he should die. As a result of his act, the cosmic gambler may die and bring an end to the troubles that precipitated the gamble; or he may survive, when the pay-off is likely to be lots of attention, sympathy and help. When I first began to think of this species of suicidal behaviour in terms of cosmic roulette, I was thinking of the idea that the cosmic gambler would not calculate the odds of dying or surviving but rather that, acting on a whim, he would behave in a way that could end in either life or death; and some cosmic gambles certainly will be impulsive in character – the agent will act without thinking or with little thought and will hence take little account of the odds of death or survival. Then it occurred to me that gamblers usually have a preference for one outcome or another and I realised that in cosmic gambling this is probably as true as it is in other forms of gambling; but whereas in other forms of gambling the gambler plays for odds controlled by another person, in cosmic roulette he has some influence over the odds because they depend largely on the way in which he acts. In other words I realised that though there may be cosmic gamblers who really do not care what happens to them, and for whom the outcome really does not matter, cosmic

87

gambling is a more richly textured phenomenon than this simple explanation would suggest. I attempt to sketch a little of this richness below.

Some possible sub species of cosmic roulette

A word of caution is called for before launching into a discussion of different varieties of cosmic roulette. The varieties that I outline are the result of my imagining and although my guess is that something like all of them does exist in the real world, they may not. Whether they are real or not my purpose is simply to suggest some dimensions in terms of which suicidal self harmings that seem to have something of a gamble about them may be considered.

Calculated cosmic roulette would be where the agent acts realising that there is a good but not certain chance that he will be saved, or where he does something knowing that there is a good but not certain chance that he will not be saved. For example, a gambling man with a preference for life could greatly increase the likelihood that he will be discovered and saved by taking an overdose at five thirty, knowing that though occasionally she is unavoidably detained, his partner is usually home by six o'clock. On the other hand, one with a preference for death might stack the odds in favour of dying, by taking his overdose at two thirty knowing that though occasionally she comes home much earlier, his wife is rarely home before seven o'clock.

A more *whimsical* form of cosmic roulette might be where the agent acts, aware of the possibility of death but caring little for the consequences. *Impetuous* or *spontaneous* cosmic roulette would be where an individual does something that may result in death without thinking about what the results might be. Though impetuous and whimsical cosmic roulette are similar, they differ in the amount of thought given to the possible outcomes and in the mood in which they are enacted. The whimsical gambler does not care what the consequences will be and says, effectively, 'Do what you will' as he spins the wheel of life and death. The impetuous gambler, on the other hand, acts without considering the consequences and says 'I can't/I won't stay with this situation any longer' as he leaps spontaneously (if metaphorically) into the arms of fate.

Another variety of cosmic roulette is illustrated by a case study cited by Kessel (1965):

A married woman of 27 whose husband was threatening to leave her took 50 aspirins: 'I didn't think they'd kill me. I hoped they wouldn't. I thought of my mother and father. I couldn't let them be hurt. I hoped really it would bring John back. If it didn't I might as well die.'

(p. 19–20)

This woman did not aim unequivocally at death; rather she hoped to change her husband's behaviour. However, she clearly realised the possibility that she might end up in the mortuary; if her act didn't bring her husband back, she claims, *she might as well die*. Perhaps acts of this kind could be referred to as *ambivalent* cosmic roulette, to show that they result from a lack of preference. They are akin to the tossing of a coin by a person who cannot decide between two movies, both of which he really wants to see.

Compulsive cosmic roulette would be cosmic roulette, probably of the impetuous variety, which results from a compulsion that the individual experiences to gamble with his life. Like other compulsive gamblers, an individual who engages in this game of chance might bet on poorer odds each time he plays at the roulette wheel of life and death, until finally he loses everything.

A final and rather extreme form of cosmic roulette might be referred to as *capricious* cosmic roulette; this would be a form of extremely whimsical gamble where a person who does not really wish to die nevertheless challenges both fate and those who care for him. The capricious gambler will probably be one who has had a career in cosmic gambling during which he has gambled on successively higher odds of dying. He may have grown to believe that having survived so often in the past he is invulnerable; or perhaps upping the stakes has been necessary to maintain the satisfaction he gets from playing the game, or to achieve results with others. The capricious gambler is very likely to end up dead when he pushes the stakes too high or makes a mistake in what he thinks he can get away with.

Is fatal cosmic roulette suicide?

To ask this question would be to misunderstand what I mean by 'cosmic roulette' because it emphasises the outcome of a person's action rather than the intention with which it is performed. In suicide the individual intends to be dead, and so success would mean death. In cosmic roulette, on the other hand, it is less clear what success would mean.

At first I thought that it might be useful to conceive of cosmic roulette as occupying a continuum. At one end would be gambles that are so likely to end in death that they would rightly be considered as *suicidal* cosmic gambles because anyone gambling on such odds must have a preference for death; at the limit these would shade into suicide. At the other end would be gambles which are so unlikely to end in death that they would be more like what, in the next section, I refer to as 'suicide gestures'. By this account, the act performed by a person who gambles with his life by taking an overdose of drugs when the odds are high that he will be found and/or small that the action he has taken will kill him, might be thought of as a *gestural* cosmic gamble. On the other hand, if a person takes a gamble with his life and the odds are low that he will be found and/or high that the action will achieve his death, we might think of his act as a *suicidal* cosmic gamble.

However, to think of the continuum in this way would be to place too much emphasis on the empirical facts of the matter and to attend too little to the intention of the protagonist. It fails to take account of the possibility that a person might take action that he thought had very low odds of ending with him dead which actually was very likely to end with him dead, or conversely that he might take action that he thought had a very high probability of ending with him dead which actually had very little chance of doing so. An example of the first might be where a person, wishing to keep the odds of dying low, and expecting to be found fairly soon, took an overdose of some readily obtainable drug such as paracetamol, falsely believing that such a common medicine must be fairly innocuous. An example of the second might be where a person, wishing to make the odds of his dying high rather than low, and falsely believing that taking a large overdose of pills will endanger his life whatever the pills, swallowed large quantities of pills that turn out to be relatively innocuous.

Thus the question 'Is fatal cosmic roulette suicide?' is not to be answered by considering the odds that the agent would end up dead when he gambled, but by considering where on the continuum of odds he thought his act lay. If he thought it lay at the end that was likely to end in death we might think of his gamble as suicidal cosmic roulette or even, in extreme cases perhaps, as suicide; if on the other hand, he thought that it lay at the other end, we would think of it as gestural cosmic roulette, or perhaps in a case where he believed the odds of dying to be extremely low, as a suicide gesture.

Other references to gambling with one's life

Talking of gambling in relation to self harm is not new though those who do so are usually referring to all suicidal acts rather than to a relatively discrete subset of such acts; that is, they tend to believe that all suicidal self harmings are the result of gambles rather than of the wholehearted intention to end one's life. Taylor (1988) cites Stengel:

> Most people who commit acts of self damage with more or less conscious self-destructive intent do not want either to live or to die, but to do both at the same time – usually one more than the other. . . . Most suicidal acts are manifestations of risk-taking behaviour. They are gambles.
>
> (Stengel, 1969, cited in Taylor, pp. 50–1)

Taylor also picks up Stengel's interesting notion (Stengel, 1973, cited in Taylor) that some suicidal acts are akin to the medieval idea of the ordeal: a dangerous test or trial to which individuals were submitted in order to determine whether God wanted them to live or not. Stengel's suggestion is that in modern societies people submit themselves to suicidal ordeals, risking their lives to see whether God thinks they should continue living.

Glover (1977) talks about people gambling with their lives in time of war. Those who volunteer for dangerous missions, he asserts, do not always do so out of altruism, but may do so 'because they do not value their lives much, or even half want to die' (p. 173). Glover seems to think that those who undertake such missions because they don't value their lives won't be doing so because of altruistic feelings. However, I can see no reason why cosmic roulette in such circumstances should not be underpinned by care and regard for one's fellows. Rather than thinking that it doesn't matter whether he lives or dies, the soldier contemplating such a mission might conceivably think that at least by undertaking this dangerous task, he can give his life some meaning. If he lives he will have shown himself to be the kind of man who is willing to risk his life for others and consequently may feel better about himself; perhaps also others will think well of him. If on the other hand he dies, he will have died as the kind of man who is willing to die for others and at least those others will have benefited from his existence. In this case the memories others have of him will be enhanced as a result of his actions, and though that could hardly make him feel better when he was dead, it could make him feel better before he acts (which of us would not like to think that others will think well of us when we die?). Of course, whether he lives or dies, if his reason for acting as he does was primarily the desire to ensure that they should think highly of him, we would hardly consider him to have acted altruistically. Perhaps, however, at least some of the actions that Glover is talking about might be referred to as *altruistic* cosmic roulette.

Cosmic roulette: a final note

I have discussed a wide range of acts that may be thought of as varieties of cosmic gamble, where the individual puts his life in the balance and invites the cosmic croupier to decide whether he lives or dies. I have suggested that in some of these the protagonist's act is probably akin to suicide because the odds are stacked so heavily against his surviving that his act is very likely to end up with him dead and he was aware of this when he acted. In others, where the odds are stacked heavily in favour of survival, cosmic gambles are more similar to suicide gesture, which I discuss in the next section, because in such instances the individual is aware of the low risk he is taking and considers that level of risk worthwhile, given the size of the 'pay-out' he expects if the gamble pays off on the side of life. In yet others the gamble constitutes a metaphorical leap in the dark because the odds are unknown and therefore, from the point of view of the gambler, give a balanced probability of dying or surviving (actual leaps in the dark – for example, from cliff faces or high buildings – would be more like suicides unless the leaper knew that there was a realistic chance that there was a safety net somewhere below).

Gesturing at suicide

Suicide should be distinguished from intentional self harmings that are intended to resemble suicide though they are performed with the intention of ending with the individual alive rather than dead. Such acts, along with situations in which a person pretends to take suicidal self harming action or says that he has done so when he has not, may be referred to as *gestured suicide* or *suicide gestures*.

Sally worked with her husband Ben in a school for mal-adjusted children. One afternoon in the middle of a staff meeting which was being held in their flat, the marital disharmony they were living through spilled into the professional arena when they disagreed violently. Sally burst into tears and ran to the bathroom, slamming the door loudly behind her. When Ben broke open the door a few minutes later he found Sally sitting on the floor; she had swallowed a large quantity of tranquillisers.

It seems unlikely that Sally had any real intention of ending her life and more likely that her actions were intended to achieve some effect in others. The fact that Ben broke the door down fairly quickly suggests that he had reason to believe that she may have done something unwise; indeed on a number of previous occasions and in similar circumstances, she had acted in similarly dramatic ways.

Whereas in suicide the person wishes, intends and expects to be dead after his suicidal act, the person who gestures at suicide wishes, intends and expects to be alive afterwards. Suicide gestures may be thought of as a performance; like an actor in a one man play, the individual who gestures suicide stages, directs and performs in an *enactment* of his death. In the theatrical performances that we call plays, actors intend, by their performance, to move and produce emotional reactions in the audience; in a suicide gesture, the actor – the suicide gesturer – also intends, by his performance, to move and produce emotional reactions in others.

My use of the theatrical analogy is not unique. For example, Kessel (1965) also uses it, in arguing that far from having attempted something at which they have failed, so called 'suicide attempters' are actually often successful in what they attempt. He writes:

Moreover what they are attempting they commonly achieved. To that end the simulation of death, consciously or not, the hint of suicide, heightened its effectiveness. But the act was not attempted suicide. Doctors do not have to be deceived by their simulation; the drama was enacted for their own circle only.

(p. 29)

Whereas, in addition to achieving his death, the suicide often intends to achieve some other purpose or purposes, the suicide gesturer always has some other purpose which his feigned enactment of deliberate self killing is aimed at bringing about. Some suicide gestures are intended to draw attention to the agent's despair or need for help; others are intended to punish another person or persons, or to induce in them some emotion such as guilt, anxiety or fear.

Elsie had recently left hospital after several months as a psychiatric in-patient. She was attending an out-patient clinic and receiving social work support in the community, from Miss MacMinn. Elsie's husband, David, had received treatment for depression in the past but had not attended an out-patient clinic for a considerable time. He seemed to be anxious to support Elsie and was usually present when Miss MacMinn called.

One day while Miss MacMinn was visiting, David, who had clearly been unaware that her visit was planned, burst into the living room; a quarrel ensued between him and his wife at the height of which he became very agitated and rushed into the kitchen saying 'Well, that's it then.' When Miss MacMinn and Elsie went into the kitchen David was swallowing large quantities of sleeping pills. When David refused to go straight to casualty with her and began leaving the room, Miss MacMinn followed, saying that as soon as the pills began to take their effect, she would phone for an ambulance and have him taken into hospital. And she did.

David's action may have been an impulsive cosmic gamble; it is possible that he took the pills not caring what should happen to him. It is also possible that he simply intended to die and what's more, to die at the first available opportunity. But consider some things he said to Miss MacMinn two days later. First of all he said, 'You had no right to bring me into hospital. I've got the right to kill myself. You shouldn't have interfered.' When Miss MacMinn explained that though she agreed in a way, she had no intention of ruining her career by allowing a client to die, whatever that client's rights as she saw them, David went on, 'You people are all the same. You don't care. You should've stopped me taking them pills.'

These remarks suggest that David expected Miss MacMinn to stop him taking the pills. Their contradictory nature suggests that in them David is not concerned to communicate with Miss MacMinn in a straightforward way, but rather psychologically to beat her in whatever ways he can. Despite the fact that the number of pills he had taken was enough to kill him, it seems likely that his dramatic action was an aggressive suicide gesture performed as an attempt psychologically to beat those who witnessed it, rather than an attempt to kill himself.

A more generous reading of David's remarks might suggest the question of whether he was simply ambivalent about whether he wished to die or live. I reject this. If he had been ambivalent about his wishes we might have expected him to be angry at Miss MacMinn for preventing him from dying, if on waking up he realised that really he would have preferred to have been dead. On the other hand, if on waking he had suddenly realised how very much he liked life despite its difficulties, he might reasonably have felt angry at Miss MacMinn for allowing him to risk his life by taking the overdose. However, he could not rationally accuse her of both things.

Success and failure in suicide gestures

In thinking about whether a suicide gesture was wholly successful or not, two dimensions are important. Physically speaking, success for the suicide gesturer involves exactly the opposite of success for the suicide; whereas for the suicide success in a physical sense means death, for the suicide gesturer it means remaining alive. Personally and socially speaking, on the other hand, success in suicide gesturing will be the same as success in suiciding and depend on the extent to which a gesturer achieves the changes in his life, and in others, at which he was aiming. So the wholly successful gesture will end with the agent alive and well and with the changes to others that the gesturer hoped by his gesture to bring about, having been achieved.

Failure in suicide gesturing could mean several things. On a personal and social level, failure for the suicide gesturer would be identical to failure for the suicide and involve failing to achieve the changes in others that he wanted to bring about. Physically speaking, on the other hand, things are again opposite for the suicide and the suicide gesturer: for the suicide, death represents success though not a success he will experience; for the suicide gesturer, on the other hand, death represents failure, though not a failure he would experience. Losing his life, the unsuccessful suicide gesturer pays a greater price in attempting to achieve his purpose than he intended to pay.

Things are, however, more complicated than the account above might suggest, because it could be argued that there is a failure which is worse than death for the suicide gesturer: ending up horribly disabled and hence in a worse state than before. Consider, for example, what happened to Elizabeth.

Elizabeth wanted her husband, Eric, to change his job which involved long absences from home. One evening she climbed on a high stool by the open window and said that if he did not promise to find another job, she would jump. Then she slipped, falling heavily onto the concrete patio, fracturing her skull. As a result of the accident she was paraplegic. After that Eric gave up work and stayed at home to care for his wife.

Although Elizabeth managed to bring about some of the changes in her life that she wished for, she ended up greatly incapacitated. Though she managed to arrange that Eric stayed at home with her, this did not happen because her gesture was successful, but because it failed. Objectively speaking, her life became worse rather than better. She could not walk and was doubly incontinent; and although Eric left his job and no longer stayed away for weeks on end, their income was drastically reduced and, materially at least, Elizabeth was thus much worse off. Psychologically she was also worse off because Eric resented having been forced to leave his job and as a result the marriage suffered.

Usually we think of death as being the ultimate misfortune that can befall a person because death deprives us of the possibility of benefiting from anything in this world. However, many people would feel that ending up horribly incapacitated as Elizabeth did is a fate worse than death, especially since she had to live with the knowledge that she was responsible for her incapacity.

Some people might want to say that the events in Elizabeth's life that I have described would be better thought of as a *gestured suicide threat* because Elizabeth did not intend to jump from the window but merely and accidentally slipped. However, although she did not intend to harm herself, in setting up the act that she was threatening to perform she had already embarked on an apparently suicidal path; and that seems to make her a gesturer rather than a threatener.

Chapman (1970) uses the term *miscalculated risk* to refer to cases where acts of the kind that I am calling gestured suicide go wrong and result in death. He cites the case of Frances who had suffered years of apparent physical illness which allowed her to exert power over her family. Finally she was persuaded to see a psychiatrist and after resisting treatment for a while, she appeared to be making progress. However, at the same time, she began to use aspects of her alleged psychiatric condition – depressive episodes and dramatic agitation – to control her family again. Chapman writes:

> Now her most potent weapons were suicidal threats and gestures which stampeded her relatives into being whatever she wanted and made her home a nightmare. Repeated psychiatric hospitalisations for suicidal gestures, most of which were harmless, gave only a brief relief to her family. Psychiatric treatment ground into a stalemate.
>
> (p. 165)

It was then that Frances took her fatal miscalculated risk. After telephoning her husband to tell him what she was going to do and why, she took a cocktail of pills. She thought that a moderate dosage of anti-depressants as opposed to sedatives would cause neither death nor unpleasant symptoms. Unfortunately she was mistaken. Though the amount she had taken of neither drug would have killed her on its own, the mixture of anti-depressants Frances took produced a grave reaction when taken together. Chapman explains what happened:

> By the time her husband arrived Frances was in a semi-stupor, trembling and gasping for air. She had tried to call a doctor or an ambulance, but the receiver had slipped out of her hand, and it hung dangling at the end of its cord. She managed to tell her husband what she had done and begged him to rush her to the hospital. Before the ambulance arrived she had a convulsion. In the ambulance on the way to the hospital she had two more convulsions. After the second convulsion she vomited her breakfast and in her condition of semi-stupor she inspirated large clots of half-digested food into her bronchial

tubes and lungs. Her lung passages became obstructed, and she became purple as she gasped for air, her eyes bulging, in terror through the mist of her semi-stupor. By the time she arrived at hospital she was dead.

(p. 166)

Some other views of the phenomenon of gestured suicide

Though the expressions 'suicide gesture' and 'gestured suicide' are not as common as expressions such as 'parasuicide' and 'attempted suicide', the phenomenon to which they refer is common enough. For example, Clare's comment (Clare, 1975) to which I referred in Chapter 4, to the effect that we cannot know for sure whether a successful suicide intended to die or to live or whether an unsuccessful suicide intended to live or to die, shows that he knows that at least some of what commonly passes as suicide, or attempted suicide, does not result from an attempt to self kill. Proposing that the term 'attempted suicide' should be replaced by other terms such as 'deliberate self poisoning' and 'deliberate self-injury', Kessel (1965) also recognises that some of what looks like suicide is not aimed at death:

If he has taken only a small quantity of drugs then he was not really attempting suicide, so the argument time and again runs, he was just making a suicidal gesture which need not be taken seriously.

(p. 29)

Kessel, as I have already said, was writing in the context of a study of self poisoning; suicidal gestures are particularly easy to stage via a non-fatal overdose. Again in relation to gestures that take the form of overdoses with drugs, Curran et al. (1980) write:

In the last few years there has been an enormous increase in the number of 'suicidal gestures' by taking overdoses of drugs, often trivial. In many cases there is no suicidal intent at all, and they are perhaps better called 'self poisonings'.

(p. 203)

Using drugs it is easy to give others the impression that one has tried to kill oneself while ensuring that the amount one takes will cause no real harm.[1] One can achieve this by leaving an empty bottle or bottles lying around or by brandishing them in front of the intended

98

victims of one's gesture when one has flushed the contents down the toilet instead of into one's body. By comparison, other methods of suicide are harder to use as gestures because they are harder to regulate. So, for example, shooting oneself in the head, leaping from high places or attaching a hosepipe from the exhaust to the passenger compartment of one's car in a locked garage, tend to be fatal.

Chapman (1970) writes:

> In some instances suicide is an accident by a person who uses threats of suicide and suicidal gestures as whips to manipulate his family. In some of these the empty nature of the suicidal gesture is obvious.
>
> (p. 164)

He describes a number of scenarios which he considers typical; in one, a young woman, following a row with her husband, calls him into the dining room where he finds her standing with a tin opener at her throat. He also discusses a number of other manoeuvres that can be employed as suicide gestures; these include calling one's spouse into the bedroom for a final reconciliation after swallowing eight aspirin tablets; brandishing an empty pistol while protesting that one intends to end it all; making a few light nicks on one's wrists with a razor; or rushing out of the house ostensibly headed for the motorway.

Discussing the nature of suicidal acts that are not intended to be fatal, Mitchell (1971) writes:

> Some clinicians use the phrase 'suicidal gesture', implying that the act is primarily an attempt to draw attention to oneself and that although the setting may be dramatic, the actual injury sustained will be minimal.
>
> (p. 139)

Mitchell believes that suicide gestures occur most often among young people – with a peak around age 20. This claim is based on the higher incidence of non-fatal suicidal acts among the young. He gives no evidence for his further assertion that suicide gestures occur most frequently among women. However, this would be supported to some extent by the higher incidence among women of non-fatal suicidal acts, since it seems unlikely that women are simply less efficient at killing themselves than men.

Purposefulness and gestures at suicide

Discussing his reasons for considering that the term 'attempted suicide' does not describe what the majority of people who gain this label in hospitals have done, Kessel (1965) writes that their acts 'demonstrated some purposefulness; but this purpose was to alter their life situation, not to die' (p. 29). I agree. The purpose suicide gesturers have is not about ending their lives. Rather their acts are aimed at changing their lives by bringing pressure to bear on others; they are manipulative maneouvres intended to change the ways others behave by, for example, inducing in them feelings of guilt, remorse and perhaps fear.

Sometimes the changes that are brought about in others will be more than the gesturer bargained for. Discussing the adverse reactions that those who gesture suicide may meet with from professionals with whom they come in contact, Mitchell (1971) writes:

> This is very disturbing behaviour, and cynically one can say that this is exactly what it is meant to be – maximally disturbing to others so that they will be moved to do something. A young person behaving in such a way is usually angry, and anger is often the feeling mobilised in those around her. Angry work-mates demand that something should be done. If the police are called in they demand that a doctor do something about it. If a general practitioner is called he can be angry too, and his anger is revealed in notes hurriedly scribbled to the casualty officer, 'This foolish young woman has taken an overdose', or 'This manipulating young psychopath has done it again', or 'I'm sorry to bother you but Miss Smith has made another of her hysterical gestures.' Violence or potential violence is frightening to most of us. We are not sure how to deal with it. We also feel angry because we can see the fraudulent component in the patient's behaviour. 'This girl is pretending to be disturbed. She's cheating in some way.' Cheats annoy us.
>
> (pp. 140–1)

Mitchell characterises the reasons for suicidal gestures and their intended and likely effects. He writes that suicide gesturers 'resort to a show of intending to harm themselves as a way of drawing attention to their situation, perhaps as a protest, perhaps in an appeal for something to be done' (pp. 140–1). The argument would go that by actually (but in a minor way) harming themselves or by

100

pretending to do so, such individuals are simply trying to attract attention to their sorry plight. Many people believe that suicidal behaviour always represents a 'cry for help'. I think that in at least a large number of cases, this is mistaken. It is not that I do not believe that such actions indicate that the individual needs help, only that in acting he is unlikely to have thought something along the lines of 'I think I'll cut my wrists/take some pills/jump in the canal/put my head in the oven, because then people will perhaps believe that I am so distressed that I need help.'

Though no doubt some suicide gestures are about asking for help, I believe that gesturing suicide is more likely to be about controlling others. Other writers seem to agree with this point of view. For example, though he refers not to 'gestured suicide' but to 'unsuccessful suicide' it seems clear that Szasz (1971) would support this view when he writes that 'unsuccessful suicide is generally an expression of an individual's desire for more control over others' (p. 186). And acknowledging not the validity but the efficacy of such actions in bringing about effects in others, Kessel (1965) writes, 'Admission to the ward, having poisoned oneself, can be for instance a powerful weapon in bringing back errant boyfriends' (p. 23). Even in those cases where it is true to say that the protagonist is making a plea for help by acting in a self harming way, it is clear that what is going on is largely about control. The suicide gesturer does not ask for help but demands it; those from whom help is demanded do not, if they are decent people, have any choice about helping a person who self harms and then presents himself to them, or who has self harmed in a place that means that they have come upon him by chance. They must help or be *care-less* and insensitive. So whether or not they act to help the suicide gesturer, he has an effect on them; if he does not change their behaviour or feelings, he changes their character.

Postscript to cosmic roulette and gestured suicide

As acts, gestures at suicide and cosmic roulette are distinct from suicide, though each may be performed via actions and sequences of actions that look identical from the point of view of an outside observer. They are different because of their internal grammar, that is because of the intentions with which they are enacted and the meanings they have for those who perform them. However, it is important to note that a person could change from a habitual suicide

101

gesturer or cosmic gambler into a suicide. Consider for example Debbie, whose death as the result of fire was discussed in Chapter 1. Debbie's suicide gesturing behaviours and other self harmings had included scratching herself on the legs, cutting her wrists badly enough to cause real damage but not death, setting fire to herself in a way that was probably a gesture at suicide and taking small and large overdoses of various prescribed drugs. The fact that in the end she died after setting fire to herself in a shopping precinct, might mean that for years Debbie had simply been inefficient in her attempts at suicide. Or it could simply be that on this last occasion she was unsuccessful in her gesture. If Debbie wanted to die, she was lucky that no one managed to smother the flames that killed her. If she did not want to die, she had a stroke of bad luck.

Assisted suicide

The term 'assisted suicide' is usually used to refer to occasions when one person physically assists another in delivering a death blow to himself, or actually delivers it on his behalf. However, not all assisted suicides involve the assister so directly and a whole range of activities could be construed as assisted suicide. These may be conceived of as lying on a continuum from situations in which the assister's role is minimal and in which she plays no part in either setting up or triggering the events that are intended to bring death, to situations in which she delivers the death blow or arranges for its delivery.

Supplying general information

First of all, the assister may share information of a general kind about ways of achieving death, which the suicider then uses in ending his life.

Supplying detailed information

Again information is shared but this is now of a detailed kind, referring, for example, to the calibre of bullet that will be best, and where best to aim the gun that will fire it, or to the length of time a cut of a given size and seriousness will take to produce blood loss significant enough to bring death. Most commonly, perhaps, such an assister will give information about the names and quantities of drugs that may be used and the best way in which to take them. This sharing of information may be deliberate as in the case of associations such as the Hemlock Society in the USA and Exit in the UK, whose members believe that everyone should have the right to die at the time of their choosing and have set about making such information available in order that their members may truly have the choice of whether to live or die. On the other hand detailed information about how to kill oneself may unwittingly be given to a person who intends to kill himself by another who is unaware that the person to whom she passes on the information intends to end his life. For example, a physician may share information about the effects of different drugs that are commonly used in suiciding with a philosopher who claims to be writing a book about suicide; if he goes on to kill himself using her advice to help him not to bungle the affair, she will truly have assisted him in doing so; of course she will be an unwitting assistant, if not an unwilling one.

The book *Final Exit* by Derek Humphry of the Hemlock Society (Humphry, 1991) contains explicit instructions about how best to kill oneself using various drugs and including recommended dosages and instructions for taking them. Humphry's instructions about the best way to go about arranging one's death via an overdose are very detailed:

1 An hour beforehand have an extremely light meal – perhaps tea and a piece of toast – so that the stomach is nearly vacant but not so empty that you would feel nauseous and weak.

2 At the same time take a travel sickness pill such as Dramamine which will ward off nausea later.

3 Take about ten of your chosen tablets or capsules with as large a drink of spirits or wine as you are comfortable with. Vodka is extremely effective. If you cannot drink alcohol, use your favourite soda drink.

4 Have the additional powdered tablets already mixed into a pudding and swallow that as fast as is possible.

5 Throughout, keep plenty of alcoholic drink or soda at your side to wash this all down. It will also help to dilute the bitter taste.

(p. 112)

These instructions, by Humphry's testimony, seem to constitute as near to foolproof means as it is possible to adopt to ensure one's death, though there is still about a 10 per cent chance of failure. It is because the drugs alone are not totally certain that Humphry suggests the employment of what he calls the 'plastic bag technique' after taking the drugs; this refinement to his method of self destruction involves putting one's head in a plastic bag and closing it off with an elastic band round the neck. Humphry himself is obviously satisfied that with this addition death is 100 per cent certain since he tells us that this is what he would do if he ever needed to take his life because of terminal suffering.

Humphry's book is unambiguous and clearly aimed at assisting those who intend suicide to make as dignified and easy an exit as possible, while making things as untraumatic as possible for those who have to clean up afterwards. In spite of this, however, and in spite of the fact that aiding and abetting another in the act of suicide is a crime, it is unlikely that someone like Humphry would be found guilty of assisting another in suicide because of the difficulties in proving that a given piece of advice was significant in shaping the person's act.

Brazier (1987) discusses the case of *A.G.* v. *Able* in which the Voluntary Euthanasia Society was accused of committing an offence in selling a booklet to its members in which various ways in which suicide could be achieved were set out in some detail. The Society claimed that though its members did not advocate suicide, until legislation was brought in legalising voluntary euthanasia, it could see no alternative to supplying such information in order to allow its members to bring about 'their own deliverance'. Although evidence suggested that in the eighteen months following the booklet's first distribution there were fifteen cases of suicide which were directly linked to the booklet and another nineteen in which it was found that the deceased had had some contact with, or was a member of, the Society, the Society was not found guilty of any offence. In order for an offence to have been committed it would have to have been the case that the booklet had been supplied to someone who, at the time, was known to have been contemplating suicide. More than that, it would have had to have been true that the Society's intention in supplying the booklet was the facilitation of that particular person's suicide by means of its contents, and further, that the booklet had actually assisted and encouraged the person to kill, or attempt to kill, himself.

Supplying the means

Here, the assister supplies the means – the gun, the drugs, the razor blade, the petrol, the poison, the rope – with which the individual can achieve his death. More strangely, in this category, it might be argued that the driver of a train, car or other vehicle that kills a suicide may be conceived of as an unwilling or even unknowing assistant in the death of one she kills, because she supplies the vehicle (and the speed) that does the killing.

As with the giving of detailed information, those who supply the means whereby suicide may be achieved may do so wittingly, although in many instances this form of assistance will be unwitting. So, for example, whereas someone might supply a friend with a gun knowing that he intends to shoot himself in the head, it is much more likely that those who provide the heroin that an addict uses to overdose will do so without the knowledge that this is what he is going to use it for; and it is unlikely that the people who supplied Paula, whose case I discuss in Chapter 1, with the means (the petrol can, the petrol, the lighter) by which she could achieve her self immolation were aware that this was her intention.

There may be cases where although an assister who supplies the means either could have, or perhaps should have, been aware of what the suicider was doing, she will claim to be unaware, or perhaps really will be unaware, however improbable that may seem to outside observers. Kessel (1965) reports an experiment in which a very distressed looking girl was sent:

> sobbing into six chemist's shops within a mile of each other in Edinburgh. In each she said: 'May I buy 200 aspirins, please?' There could have been no economic motive for purchasing such a quantity, for the largest bottle contained only 100 tablets. Nowhere was she refused, whether she was served by an assistant or by the manager. Only once was any concern expressed: 'Two hundred? Are you all right? You ought to go and have a cup of tea,' though she received several curious glances and was watched through the window as she left more than one shop.
>
> (p. 25)

The people who supplied this young woman with the means to kill herself assisted in her possible suicide. Had she been suicidal and killed herself afterwards, they would have been partly responsible for her demise. Of course they could not have known, but they might have guessed what she was about. Though, despite the curious glances that Kessel refers to, and the fact that she was watched through the window as she left the shop, it is possible that those who supplied the aspirins did not stop to consider why she wanted them, it is also possible (and in my opinion more likely) that they guessed that she might be going to harm herself, but deceived themselves about the extent of the danger.

Supplying the specific means

Here again the assister supplies the means with which the suicide may achieve death but this time more specifically what the individual needs. This species of assistance could vary between supplying a person with the necessary drugs in appropriate quantity, to much more complex arrangements. Though an individual might supply drugs unwittingly, without suspecting that the person in question had suicide in mind, she could also do so purposefully, with the intention of giving the individual help in procuring his death. Consider, for example, a situation in which a prescriber provides sufficient of some painkilling medication to allow a person to kill himself, knowing that this is a possibility; it is likely that in the terminal care of patients who are suffering dreadfully with pain, perhaps particularly in the case of patients dying at home, at least some doctors and nurses might supply sufficient morphine or some other pain relief to give patients the opportunity, should they so decide, to end their pain by ending their lives. Doing this has some similarity to what happened in a well known case in the USA, that of Barney Clark.

On 2 December 1980, Clark made medical history by being the first human being to receive an artificial heart. Although his artificial heart allowed him to live, he faced a life permanently attached to some rather cumbersome machinery. His doctors, believing that only he could be the judge of whether the life he would have permanently attached to a machine would be worth living, provided a key by which Clark could switch off his life support should he wish to do so. Rachels (1986) believes that giving Clark the key was obviously 'a way of saying that cutting the connection would be all right' (p. 86). He is arguing that the significance of this arrangement is not that it gave Clark the opportunity of arranging that he should die (he could have done that anyway simply by cutting or disconnecting the tubes) but rather that it was an acknowledgement on the part of those caring for him that in his case, suicide would have been permissible.

Rachels' line of reasoning is interesting. However, it is not necessarily true that had he turned the key, Clark would have been a suicide. He was given the possibility of actively ending himself instead of being constrained, should he have wished to do so, to refuse treatment in order to bring his death about. In spite of this whether turning the key would have been suicide or not would depend on his reasons for doing so. If he had turned the key because he wanted to be dead, he would have been a suicide; if on the other hand he had done so because no matter the inevitable consequence, he did not want to endure *this treatment* any longer, he would not have been.

Supplying the specific means and the means of delivery

Rather than simply supplying even the specific means by which a person might achieve his death, a suicide assister could provide both the means and the means of delivering it, without actually doing the delivery herself. The much discussed death in the USA of Mrs Janet Adkins, using Dr Jack Kevorkian's suicide machine or *mercitron*, is an example of assistance in suicide at its most sophisticated, though by all accounts Kevorkian's machine itself sounds quite primitive. Humphry (1991) describes Kevorkian's killing machine, and the way in which Adkins used it to kill herself, in these terms:

> Dr. Kevorkian constructed a small frame of aluminium scrap from which he suspended three inverted bottles. One contained a saline solution, the second sodium pentothal, and the third a solution of potassium chloride and succinylcholine. A small electric motor from a toy car powered the intravenous lines.

The steps to death were as follows:

1 Mrs Adkins was hooked up intravenously to the harmless saline solution.
2 Her heart was monitored by cardiograph electrodes on her arms and legs.
3 When Mrs Adkins was ready to die, she pushed a button

that caused a valve to shut off the saline solution and open the adjoining line of pentothal (thiopental). This drug put her to sleep within about 30 seconds.

4 A timing device connected to the line between the second and third containers triggered after one minute. The potassium chloride and the succinylcholine (a muscle relaxant) began to flow into the arm of the now unconscious woman. Death occurred within six minutes.

(pp. 134–5)

Janet Adkins was 54 years old and suffering with Alzheimer's Disease. She was happily married and the mother of three sons. She had been a member of the Hemlock Society before she was diagnosed with Alzheimer's. She was physically and intellectually active, and horrified when the disease began to affect her faculties. Before making contact with Dr Kevorkian, she had asked two doctors in Portland, Oregon, to help her die. She and her family had discussed the matter fully with the help of a family therapist.

Mrs Adkins and Dr Kevorkian met in Michigan because it was not a crime to assist in suicide there and taped a forty minute conversation recording her competence and wish to die. Two days later, on 4 June 1990, Kevorkian inserted a needle into Adkins' arm as she lay in the back of his Volkswagen van and instructed her about which button to push for a lethal injection. Following Kevorkian's instructions, Adkins successfully brought about her death. Though Kevorkian was charged with murder he was acquitted by the judge after listening to the tape.

This case is an example of assisted suicide but it is different from the other varieties I have described. Kevorkian did more than simply give advice to Adkins about how she might kill herself; and he did more than simply supply the means. Though he did not deliver the death blow himself, his assistance went beyond simply providing the drugs that would bring Adkins' death about but stopped short of delivering them to her body.

Supplying the death blow

Finally, there will be cases where a suicide assister actually supplies the death blow. Some people would want to refer to such an act as murder, others as euthanasia; the truth of the matter, however it is decided by others if they ever come to hear of it, will depend upon what was in the minds and hearts of two people: the person who dies and the one who does the killing, as the means of death is delivered.

Where the assister actually helps the suicider to achieve death by laying hands on him to help secure a noose or a plastic bag round his neck, pointing a gun at him and firing, or injecting a poison into his body (or pouring it down his throat), a case could be made for thinking of the assistant as an extension of the person who intends to die, in bringing about his suicide. In such a case the assistant's actions represent, for her, the act of assisting another to accomplish his death while to the suiciding person they might represent the act of suiciding itself.

The morality of assisting another to suicide

Some forms of assisted suicide, as I have described them, are acts for which a person may be prosecuted in relation to the crime of 'aiding and abetting suicide'. I have already pointed out in Chapter 1, that the only way in which sense may be made of the fact that 'aiding and abetting suicide' is illegal in a country where there is no legal prohibition on suicide, is to guess that there is a fear that those who apparently 'aid and abet' others in suiciding do so for corrupt reasons, so that whereas from the point of view of the person who dies the other aids him in suiciding, from the point of view of the one who does the aiding what happens is, at best, incitement to suicide and, at worst, murder.

The crime of aiding and abetting suicide, for which the Suicide Act, 1961 provides, may be engaged in for a variety of reasons. A young man may assist his mother to die because she can no longer bear the anguish caused by the multiple sclerosis that has gradually eaten away at her life to the point at which she no longer wishes to live. On the other hand, he may help her to die in order that he can inherit her fortune; in this case helping his mother to die might involve first of all persuading her that she wishes to die. In such a case, though from his mother's point of view his act would be the merciful one of assisting her to come to a peaceful end, from his point of view (barring the power of self deceit), it would be murder.

Brazier (1987) discusses a similar, this time real-life, case. In *R. v. McShane* a daughter was found guilty of trying to persuade her 89 year old mother, who lived in a nursing home, to kill herself, in order that she could inherit her mother's estate. The police had hidden a camera in the nursing home where her mother lived and thus obtained film of the daughter handing her mother drugs concealed in a packet of sweets and pinning a note to her dress saying 'Don't bungle it'. This case seems clearly to be one where the daughter was corrupt in her intention.

By contrast, consider April who, having nursed her husband for several years, finally administered a large overdose of morphine when he asked her to do so. They had agreed some time before that if the time came when he could no longer go on with life, she would help him to die and after they had said their final goodbyes and she had given him the fatal dose, she cuddled up with him expecting that in the morning he would be dead. In this case even those who believe suicide and euthanasia to be morally wrong and always the result of a mistaken judgement, will surely recognise the presence of a virtuous (and even, given the possibility of discovery and hence prosecution, heroic) intention on April's part, even if they think in the end that her act was immoral as well as illegal.

The reasons one person might have for assisting another in suicide will thus vary from the morally corrupt to the morally virtuous.

NOTE

1 Although this is true it is also paradoxically the case that the easy availability of one of the most common non-prescription drugs – paracetamol – combined with public ignorance about its potency, means that there is at least one route to overdose via which it is easy for a person to kill himself while making a gesture at doing so; and because of the way in which the drug works, it is even possible for a person who has taken a relatively small overdose one evening to wake up the following day believing that he is well when he has already done the damage that will kill him.

8

LIVING DANGEROUSLY, HEROISM AND EUTHANASIA

In Chapter 7, I distinguished suicide from gestured suicide and cosmic roulette. I now wish to distinguish it from a range of other human activities in which, although the risk or even the probability of death is accepted and perhaps willingly embraced, death is usually not aimed at and intended. In relation to each activity, I will also point out some scenarios in which an individual may act so as to achieve his death.

Engaging in dangerous pursuits

Most trivially, suicide is to be distinguished from a wide range of high risk activities including the smoking of tobacco, the use of pleasure inducing drugs such as alcohol and other so-called 'hard' drugs, driving fast cars recklessly, climbing mountains and hang gliding. Though the individuals in question may be aware of the possibility that what they are doing will lead to death and accept the risk that this is so, in general they do not intend to die. However, in such cases if death comes it will be true to say that it came as a result of the intentional actions of those who die. This is why it is not uncommon for others to say of a person who smokes or drinks to excess, who takes hard drugs, drives too fast or engages in dangerous sports, that what he is doing is 'suicidal', in an attempt to persuade him to change his lifestyle to make it less dangerous. Engaging in hazardous pursuits is clearly life threatening. Nevertheless, to say of someone who engages in such pursuits that what he is doing is suicidal, is most often to use the notion of suicide metaphorically.

However, at least some of these activities could be followed with the intention of dying and the expectation that death may thus be

111

achieved. A person might use them suicidally in two clearly distinguishable ways.

1 He could choose to engage in dangerous pursuits because he wishes to die and anticipates that, by increasing the chances of death, he will eventually die as a result of what he does.
2 He could aim more directly at achieving his death by undertaking a particular course of life threatening behaviour which he expected, in the short term, to result in his death, intending that it should do so.

A person who chooses one of these courses of action in an effort to arrange his death might do so because though he wants to die he finds himself unable to kill himself in a more direct fashion. Each time he tries to do so he might find himself smitten with guilt because he has been brought up to believe that suicide is wrong. Or it might be that his courage simply fails him, that he can neither find it in him to come so close to the mess that is involved in some methods of suicide (those that involve the spilling of blood), nor to take the risk inherent in others (especially, perhaps, the ingesting of drugs and other poisons) that rather than ending up dead, he may end up alive though horribly handicapped. Such a person might find it easier to engage in a pursuit that he believes to have a very high risk of death, imagining it to be inevitable that he will eventually be a victim of fate and of the dangerous lifestyle he has adopted. Let me give some particular examples.

First, a person might develop the habit of driving too fast in the hope and expectation that he will eventually meet with death; if he drove his fast car on the wrong side of the motorway at rush hour, he could be virtually certain of arranging his death. Another way of thinking of someone who acted like this (whatever he himself thought he was doing) would be to think of him as an irrational cosmic gambler: a gambler because there is clearly some chance that though he might kill others, he himself will survive; irrational because in the scenario where he survived the chances that he would be terribly injured are very high indeed.

Second, a person could intend to die, however slowly, by abusing drugs or alcohol; for example, he might intend to die of alcohol poisoning, by regularly drinking to excess, knowing that if he does it is very likely that he will precipitate his death. However, even if such an individual had announced his intention to bring about his death, this would not in itself mean that when he died he should be considered a suicide. It could be that though he set out on his self destructive alcoholic or hard drugs lifestyle with the intention of ending up dead, as he settled into that lifestyle, he lost this urge.[1] Thus I would be wary of deciding that such a person was a suicide, unless there was other evidence to suggest the presence of an ongoing suicidal intention underpinning his actions. On the other hand, a person could intend to die and inject himself with a massive overdose of heroin intending that it should finish him off once and for all. Or he could drink an excessive quantity of alcohol over a very short period with the intention of immediately precipitating his death. However, this would be unusual since, though alcohol is commonly used in association with some other method, alcohol poisoning is relatively difficult to achieve.

Finally, a keen mountain climber might decide to pursue his interest in climbing at the expense of other safer ones, in order to put himself at grave risk as often as possible. A person could even decide to become a mountaineer because he believed this was one way of eventually ensuring his death. Of course, someone who decided to be a mountaineer in the hope that it would eventually kill him could find that the solace of the mountains, the close contact with fear and the threat of death inherent in the game, cured him of his wish to die. A more clear cut example of suicidal action in this context would be where a rock climber climbed beyond his capability, solo and without protection, in poor conditions, with the intention of putting himself in a situation where death was likely.

In relation to mountaineering, and other high risk sports such as hang gliding, there seems to be a slippery distinction between the motives and intentions underpinning the behaviour of individuals who otherwise might seem to be acting in just the same way. In such sports the excitement produced by the danger that is involved is very often at least part of what is aimed at. For example, rock climbers and mountaineers functioning at the highest levels often speak about enjoying living 'close to the edge' (of life as well as of precipices), presumably because doing so gives added spice to their lives by inducing a heightened awareness of the fact that death is always lurking near by.

There is an element of a gamble here that raises the question of whether such sportsmen may be thought of as engaging in cosmic roulette. For this to be the case, it would have to be true that the individual deliberately set out on a particular risky course of action, or pursued a risky lifestyle, with the intention of tempting fate. For some this is probably true; a climber might, for example, seek out danger as a way of inviting God to decide whether he should live or not; if he did his act would constitute cosmic roulette rather than suicide, though if the chances of survival were slim, it might be a *suicidal* cosmic gamble.

However, a person who climbs in order to keep the adrenalin flowing, wishes to stay alive and does what he does simply to make his living as pleasurable as possible. He is not, by any stretch of the imagination, a cosmic gambler because he favours life and his brushes with death are about helping him to experience life as fully as possible. We might say that the risk to life and limb is the cost he pays for his pleasure; this would be like the person who engages in illicit sexual affairs because the risk of discovery (or even, in the case of some very odd characters, of contracting some dread disease) enhances the excitement he experiences. On the other hand, a climber may push himself to the limit because unless he obtains the high that he gets from dicing with death, he feels that life is not worth living. Such a climber, it could be argued, is a cosmic gambler, because for him whether he ends up dead or alive is in a sense immaterial; if alive he will be living on the knife edge that gives his life purpose; if he dies, he will have died doing what he wanted and in any case he will not be around to regret his demise.

In each of these examples an individual who pursues a risky life course with the intention of ending up dead will be a suicide. However, where such a person does not intend to die but merely accepts the risk of death as a foreseen but not intended consequence of the activity, he will not in any sense be suicidal. All that lots of climbers really want to do is simply to get to the top of the mountain; many heavy drinkers really want no more, for example, than to enjoy the taste of decent malt whisky as often as possible; many drug addicts either simply want to enjoy the sensations their use of drugs induces in them or to avoid experiencing those that it helps them to avoid; and mad, self centred and uncaring though it is, many apparently suicidal drivers simply enjoy driving fast.

Heroic actions as the result of which the protagonist expects to be dead yet does not intend to die

Suicide is to be distinguished from heroic actions where the agent recognises that he may or even will end up dead, but does not intend this result. Most heroic deaths are not suicides even where the person knew that he was certain to die; they are not suicides because the person did not intend to die but merely to save those he set out to save. Even in the case of the soldier who throws himself on a grenade to save the lives of his friends, the intention is not to die but to save the lives of others; the act is the act of saving others rather than the act of ending his life. Things would be different if there was a choice of two methods by which he could save his friends, one of which would end with him dead and the other with him alive, and he chose in favour of death. Provided that he knew and understood the alternatives, this would plainly be suicide because the only reason he could have for taking this option would be that he intended not only to save his friends, but to achieve his death.

A person could suicide by actions that bring about his death as he saves or attempts to save others in a heroic fashion. Consider, for example, a father who rushes into a burning building in a bid to rescue his little children. As I pointed out in Chapter 3, most parents who did this would be doing no more than we would expect any committed parent to do; they would act, in other words, with no thought for themselves; their aim would simply be to rescue their children, and death if it came would be accepted rather than gladly embraced. However, a parent in such a situation could act with the intention not only of saving his little ones, but of ending his life. For example, realising that his child was going to die, and feeling guilty about having left her in the building alone, he might rush into the building in a vain attempt to save her life because he would not be able to live with himself if she died, and so chose to end his life.

Intentional omissions as the result of which death might be expected yet the protagonist neither wishes nor intends to die

In Chapter 2, I discussed the possibility that a person might suicide by omitting to take some action that is necessary to preserve his life or by arranging that others should omit to take such action. Suicide as the result of such omissions is to be distinguished from deaths that come about as a result of intentional omissions where the intention was not to end up dead. Consider, for example, the following situations.

115

Jehovah's Witness

Consider first a Jehovah's Witness who refused to receive a blood transfusion. Rather than resulting from the intention to arrange his death, this would usually result from the intention to obey the perceived will of God. However, a Witness could suicide by refusing blood. To do so he would have to refuse blood with the intention of ending his unhappiness by ending his life, rather than for religious reasons. Of course this would involve a departure from the usual beliefs and practices of Jehovah's Witnesses. However, someone who professed to be a Witness and hence to believe in the rightness of the traditional stance against transfusions, might actually believe that this was a silly rule. In most circumstances such a person might have consented willingly to a transfusion, preferring to sin rather than to die. In the event, however, he might refuse the necessary transfusion because it fitted in neatly with his plan to kill himself; it would also fit in neatly with his wish to appear a faithful Witness in the eyes of other Witnesses, if not in the eyes of God.

Anorexia nervosa

Secondly, consider an individual suffering from the so called 'slimmer's disease', anorexia nervosa, who has begun refusing all sustenance and is at risk of dying as a result of malnutrition. Such a person is unlikely to be refraining from eating as a means of suicide. Many of those diagnosed anorexic have a greatly distorted body image such that though they are nothing of the kind, and in spite of evidence to the contrary, they believe that they are grotesquely overweight. Others are intent on using the question of their weight, and how it relates to their health, to manipulate those around them. But in general, although by their behaviour they may damage their health, they do not wish to die. However, an anorexic person might refuse food because he wished to die; if he died as a result, his refusal of food would amount to suicide provided that it resulted from a rational and ongoing wish to die rather than because lack of nourishment had impaired his judgement.

There is some similarity between the case of an anorexic who claims at a certain point that he is giving up food altogether because he wants to die, and that of a person who goes on hunger strike to make a political point. After going without food for a time, each might lose touch with reality. Whatever their public declarations, such people may never have intended to die and might simply miscalculate the extent to which they can go without food while remaining rational. In refusing food the anorexic may have intended no more than to further manipulate those around him; and at the start of his hunger strike the hunger striker may have expected that the authorities would cede whatever point he was trying to persuade them to cede, before he died. Each of these acts would amount to gestured suicide rather than suicide, even if in each the protagonist died and even though they may be construed as suicide by some people. In the case of a hunger striker it is especially likely to be the case that his death is viewed as suicide by those who shared his political point of view, because as suicide it would have more point, politically speaking. But there is a distinction in meaning and in fact, if not in end result, between an individual who starves to death although his hunger strike was a gesture aimed at inducing a change in policy, and one who starves to death because he had decided at the beginning that he would die a martyr's death to help his cause.

Refusal of treatment

I talked in Chapter 2 about the possibility that a person might suicide by refusing medical treatment. Such actions are to be distinguished from those of an individual who refused to undergo painful though life saving treatment, not because he wished to die but because he did not wish to undergo *this treatment* for whatever benefit. Consider, for example, a cancer patient who refused treatment even if it was likely to prolong his life for a considerable time and with a good quality. He might be prepared to pay a lower price should a treatment that was personally less costly become available before he died, and hope fervently that such a treatment should become available; by contrast one who wanted to die would not accept such a treatment even if it was available.

Where death, though aimed at, results from the intentional acts of others

Suicide is normally distinguished from deaths which, though intended and wished for by the dead person, result not from his own intentional actions but from those of others. In other words it is usually distinguished from what might normally be referred to as

117

voluntary and requested euthanasia. Before addressing the distinction between suicide and euthanasia, however, I want to say a little about euthanasia itself.

Euthanasia and suicide

In use 'euthanasia' has moved far from its derivation from the Greek as a 'painless, happy death' or 'good death' or 'easy, happy, painless death' (Dyck, 1980; Kamisar, 1980; Louisell, 1980). Such views have some attraction and they have influenced the definition I shall give below. However, I have avoided drawing directly on the terms traditionally used in defining euthanasia because many people who are committed to helping others to die good, painless, happy deaths believe euthanasia always to be morally wrong. They believe this because they hold as a primary value the idea that life is sacred and therefore believe that we should neither kill nor deliberately refrain from treatment in order to achieve death, however peaceful. Though euthanasia can be performed by other means, it is usually thought of in connection with medicine; indeed some definitions of euthanasia refer to it as a species of medical treatment. For example, the Linacre Centre's *Report on Euthanasia* (1982) defines euthanasia in these terms: 'there is euthanasia when the death of a human being is brought about on purpose as part of the medical care being given him' (p. 2).

I shall not enter deeply into a discussion of the various uses to which the word 'euthanasia' has been put. However, I should like to say something briefly about the distinction that is usually made between 'voluntary', 'involuntary' and 'non-voluntary' euthanasia.

Whereas I believe that voluntary and requested euthanasia is sometimes not only morally right but morally required (Fairbairn, 1991a; Fairbairn, 1992c), so called involuntary euthanasia I consider always to be wrong; indeed I consider it to be wrongly named as euthanasia – killing a person cannot be about assisting him to die a good death, if that death is forced on him.[2]

The notion of non-voluntary euthanasia also makes little sense, especially when applied to those who because they are comatose or in what has become known as a *persistent vegetative state*,[3] are often referred to as being 'as good as dead', because they are beyond human experience. Such individuals may be referred to by a variety of terms including 'ventilated cadaver' and 'the living dead'; the implication of such terms is that though biologically alive, they have ceased to display any of the attributes of personal life; in Rachels' terms (Rachels, 1986) though they are still biologically alive, they are not living a life.

A person who is dead cannot receive medical care and one who is 'as good as dead' may receive medical care but cannot benefit from it. If those who are comatose or persistently vegetative cannot experience, because they are as good as dead, they cannot benefit from having their biological life terminated, whether this is done as part of their medical treatment or simply because someone has decided it would be in their interests to die; nor can those who are already brain dead; the only benefits that can result from such deaths must be reaped by others.

I do not intend to pay detailed attention to the disjunction that is common between views of the moral rightness of killing or 'allowing to die', in the case of adults and in the case of the small people that we usually refer to as babies. Whereas it is common to believe that killing babies, or allowing them to die, is OK, most people do not believe that it is OK to kill big people or allow them to die, even when they have not only expressed a preference for death but have taken some pains to communicate their wishes to others. It is, however, interesting to speculate on the reasons that people might have for thinking it is OK to arrange the deaths of babies who are unable to express an opinion about the value of their lives and how much they would like to live them, while maintaining the view that big people should not be killed even when, as a result of disease, their lives have ceased for them to be worth living and they have requested death. [4]

Whatever decision we come to about the reasons for this disjunction in moral thinking in relation to the lives and deaths of big and small people, it is clear that the killing (or 'infanticide' as it is usually called) of little children cannot, by the definition of euthanasia that I offer below, be euthanasia. It is killing, plain and simple; and though killing may sometimes be justified even in relation to small people, I do not think we should make it more palatable by referring to it as euthanasia, which is associated for many people with the idea of the merciful ending of suffering. Interestingly, of course, many if not all of those who defend the right of parents to decide that their disabled neonate should be killed or allowed to die begin their arguments with references to the suffering the child may face in the future, but fall back, when pressed, to a position where what is centrally important is the effect the child will have on the lives of the parents and siblings.

119

I would like finally to comment briefly on the distinction that is often made between active and passive euthanasia. Usually this distinction is used in referring to the practice of actively killing and (merely) allowing to die, respectively. The reason this distinction is made relates, I think, to the desire to protect the psychological sensitivities of those who want to arrange the deaths of others but do not wish actually to kill (killing seems to be such a bad thing to do, doesn't it?). Somehow engaging in passive euthanasia seems to be thought, or to feel, different from killing because it doesn't involve actually doing anything. However, I think it is legitimate to think of situations in which a person is allowed to die as active euthanasia because though they involve doing nothing, they involve doing it deliberately and actively. Allowing a person to die involves not treating him in life preserving ways and/or not feeding or even watering him, until he dies. No one puts poison or bullets into the person's body; no one puts a needle in his arm or covers his face with a pillow. Nevertheless, however beneficent the reasons might be in some cases, his death is arranged by actively refraining from doing to him what he needed to have done were he to live and which, were it not for the desire to arrange his death, would have been done.

So how are suicide and euthanasia different?

Euthanasia must always be intended to benefit the individual who dies and should never be carried out in order to benefit another. It must always be directed by him, whether at the present time or by an advance directive of some kind; it cannot be imposed upon a person because in the opinion of others, it would be better for him to die; nor can it be carried out in relation to those who are unable to give an opinion about whether in the circumstances, they would like to die and have not previously made plain their wishes should such circumstances arise. Killing a person cannot be about helping him to die a good death if he does not wish to die; nor can it be about helping him to die a good death if has not expressed an opinion about whether he would like to die. In my opinion, killing a person who has not expressed a wish to die is plain killing, however beneficent the intentions of those who do the job.

I would like to propose the following definition of euthanasia:

*There is euthanasia when the death of a person who is dying
is arranged in order that he may die a death that he wishes to
die or has previously expressed a wish to die, in preference to
a death that he wishes or has previously expressed a wish to
avoid.*

This definition limits euthanasia to those cases that are usually
referred to as 'voluntary euthanasia'. In saying something about the
overlap between suicide and euthanasia, I want to limit attention
even further by focusing on requested euthanasia, because this is
the only way in which the term 'euthanasia' is used that overlaps
with the central feature of suicide – that the protagonist should wish
for death and intend to give up life. So in comparing suicide and
euthanasia, it is (voluntary and) requested euthanasia to which I am
referring.

In both suicide and euthanasia, a person wishes and intends to
be dead and takes steps to arrange that his death is achieved. The
distinction that is usually made between them resides partly in the
way in which acts labelled in these two ways are regarded both
socially and legally, partly in the means by which death is achieved,
that is, who delivers the fatal stroke, and partly in the physical and
mental state of the person who dies or wishes to die.

Euthanasia is not legally permissible. On the other hand, since
the Suicide Act of 1961 it has not been a criminal offence to commit,
or attempt to commit, suicide. As I pointed out in Chapters 1 and 7,
however, the Act makes it illegal to assist (or 'aid and abet') another
in suiciding.

Whereas 'suicide' is usually used to refer to a person dying as the
result of his own intentional action, 'euthanasia' is usually used in
referring to deaths that come about as the result of another's actions.
This fails to take account of the possibility that a person could wish
for euthanasia conceived as a peaceful death, and be able to achieve
it without assistance, because he had access to the necessary means
and had the necessary skill to administer this means of release.
Some years ago on the BBC1 Wales programme *Family Matters* a
nurse living with AIDS announced his intention, when the time was
right for him, of hastening his death because he had no desire to go
on living when life ceased, for him, to be worthwhile. He referred to
this intended death as 'euthanasia' rather than suicide. He wished
for and intended to arrange that he should die the gentle and

peaceful death that he assumed euthanasia would be. He wanted to die at the time he chose, rather than leaving things to chance and risking the possibility of a horribly slow death over which he would have little control. His only regret was that because of the legal restrictions about euthanasia, he would have to die his peaceful death alone, without his friends and family, rather than in their company as he felt was proper.

The distinction usually made between suicide and euthanasia also fails to take account of the possibility that a person could wish to suicide and yet be unable to take his life. In such a case he could, as I have already argued, use another person as an extension of himself in order to administer the means of death. Again in such cases, suicide and voluntary euthanasia seem to overlap. However, since to my mind there must be some medical reason for euthanasia, most acts of suicide cannot validly be considered as euthanasia because in most there is no valid reason for considering the act in question to be a medical act. In my opinion suicide and euthanasia do not overlap, unless the individual who kills himself or gets others to arrange that he dies is in such a state that other than arranging his death, nothing more could have been done either by himself or anyone else to make life bearable for him, and his life was fore-seeably short. Situations in which one person administered a death dealing device to another when that other's reason for wishing to be dead was purely (or dominantly) the result of psychological distress, should not, to my mind, be classed as euthanasia.

Other than the issue of who is the agent that deals the death blow, perhaps the most obvious and frequent difference between acts usually considered to be suicide and euthanasia relates to the state of health of those who die or wish to die in each case; indeed this, I think, is the central difference between the two. Whereas suicide is most commonly associated in the public imagination with individuals who are, physically speaking, relatively healthy but who have decided that death is preferable to living the life they seem destined to live, euthanasia is most often associated with individuals who, for reasons of illness, are nearing a natural death and who wish to die well rather than miserably. Of course there are overlaps. For example, someone who is pretty certain that he is imminently going to die from an awful disease may choose to die and be able and fit enough to obtain the means to perform a suicidal act. The young nurse I have already referred to was an example of this. A case that shares some similarity is that of Janet Adkins which I discussed in Chapter 7; one difference here is that although Adkins had received intimations of the way in which Alzheimer's Disease would affect her, and presumably had received accounts of the later and more severe effects, she was still relatively healthy when she hired Jack Kevorkian to assist her in dying.

And where do I think the difference between requested euthanasia and suicide chiefly lies? Well I think it is located in the intention that a person has in acting so as to achieve his death and in the meaning that his death holds for him as he enacts it.

In an act of euthanasia, steps are taken to allow a person who is dying to die a death that he wishes to die, in preference to a death that he wishes to avoid.

In an act of suicide a person arranges his death to avoid a life that he does not wish to live, or in order to die a death that he wishes to die.

NOTES

1 By this I mean not that as a result of alcohol or drug induced amnesia he forgot the urge, but rather that he began to rather enjoy his sorry life and, however bizarre it might seem, to want to live it to the full.

2 An argument could be made for the view that at least in some circumstances killing a person who does not wish to be killed could be seen as helping him to die a good death – say if he is killed in his sleep. Why, the argument would go, should a person's autonomy matter more than, say, the pain and anguish that he is suffering as the result of his condition? Though autonomy is considered an especially good thing, it would be argued, there is no reason why this should be so and if we put stress on a person's experience of distress and pain rather than on his experience of being in control of his life, we might, in a paternalistic way, believe that interfering to 'put him out of his agony', even if he did not wish to be relieved of it, was to do him a great service of a kind that would justify thinking of our act as one of euthanasia. I find it disturbing that I cannot come up with a rejoinder to this argument which could have distasteful repercussions.

3 There are problems with the diagnostic category 'persistent vegetative state' which stem from the fact that it is very loosely used. Though it would be contentious to do so and perhaps offensive to many of those for whom the term 'PVS' is a meaningful one, it might be argued that one reason for its popularity in relation to those who are severely brain damaged as the result of accidents is that its use might make it more likely that legal authority might be gained to allow such individuals to die, as occurred in the case of Tony Bland who was said to be PVS following his injury during the tragic accident at the Hillsborough

football ground in 1989 during which many people were crushed to death.

Mr Bland died on 3 March 1993 following the withdrawal of feeding on 22 February 1993. The legal decision that allowed his death to be performed involved, among other things, the decision that in his case, feeding amounted to medical treatment (Dyer, 1993). In December 1993, the inquest into his death produced the curious decision that Mr Bland had died as the result of an accident. Even though failing to feed someone in the state that he was in might be justified, it might be argued that it would never be right to do this in relation to many of those who are labelled PVS because they appear to be leading lives, however qualitatively different from the lives they led before their accidents.

4   Some of these issues I have addressed, though in different terms, elsewhere (Fairbairn, 1991a, 1992b).

9

VARIETIES OF SUICIDE

Jude stood bending over the kettle, with his watch in his hand, timing the eggs so that his back was turned to the little inner chamber where the children lay. A shriek from Sue suddenly caused him to start round. He saw that the door of the room, or rather closet – which had seemed to go heavily upon its hinges as she pushed it back – was open, and that Sue had sunk to the floor just within it. Hastening forward to pick her up he turned his eyes to the little bed spread on the boards; no children were there. He looked in bewilderment round the room. At the back of the door were fixed two hooks for hanging garments, and from these the forms of the two youngest children were suspended, by a piece of box-cord round each of their necks, while from a nail a few yards off the body of little Jude was hanging in a similar manner. An overturned chair was near the elder boy, and his glazed eyes were slanted into the room; but those of the girl and the baby were closed . . . . a piece of paper was found upon the floor, on which was written, in the boy's hand, with the bit of lead pencil that he carried: 'Done because we are too menny.'

(Thomas Hardy, *Jude the Obscure*, 1957, pp. 346–7)

The romantic suicide, for example, says: 'They'll be sorry,' and imagines a sad, sentimental funeral which may or may not come to pass. The angry suicide says: 'I'll fix them,' and may be equally misguided, since they may be glad to have him out of the way. 'I'll show them' may fail by not getting his name in the papers much beyond the obituary file. On the other hand, the futility or frustration suicide, who tries to kill himself unobtrusively with the fantasy that nobody will really notice or care, may make the front-page headlines due to some unforeseen complication.

(Berne, 1979, pp. 196–7)

Probably the most famous classification of suicide is that by the sociologist Durkheim who believed that in order to understand what people did, we had to look at the way in which they interacted with their social as well as their physical environment. In his study of suicide (Durkheim, 1897) he attempts to show that variations in suicide rates result from differences in the form of social life in different places and classifies suicide according to the extent to which the individual was integrated with, or separated from, society. His sociological model sets out four categories of suicide. *Egoistic suicide* is carried out by an individual who is under-integrated within society. Since such a person is relatively speaking detached from society, Durkheim thinks he is more vulnerable to suicide because at times of stress he has less to hold on to than those who share common beliefs with their fellows. In contrast an individual who is over-integrated into society would be said by Durkheim to carry out *altruistic suicide*. Such a person, he thinks, is too weak to resist the demands of society that he must suicide. His third type of suicide, *anomic suicide*, he believes is performed by individuals who are under-regulated by the norms and values of society, while its converse, *fatalistic suicide*, results from over-regulation of the individual.

I have referred to Durkheim's classification because it is probably the most cited discussion of suicide. My approach to the classification of acts of suicide is different because it involves looking at the intentions of the individual in acting so as to achieve his death and at his reasons for doing so, rather than trying to make sense of his act as a reflection of the way in which the society of which he is a part is functioning. The classification I shall offer is based on the different reasons a person might have for killing or attempting to kill himself.

No hope suicide

Perhaps the most common reason for suicide, at least in western societies, is an extremely unhappy or unfulfilling life with little likelihood of change so that the suicider decides that he would be better off dead than living the life he seems destined to live. Such suicide might be called *no hope suicide* because the reason that the suicide has for ending his life is that he believes there is no hope of changing it for the better. Strictly speaking, of course, the decision that no life would be better than the life that one is leading does not make sense. Living no life could not be better than any life, however bad, because when we are dead we are not around to experience anything.

Some people who kill themselves because they have no hope of achieving a better life may do so rationally because their lives are not amenable to change in directions in which they would wish them to change; others, because they are irrational, will misjudge the possibilities that exist. If such a person was so irrational that we considered him no longer to be capable of autonomous action, he could not suicide.

Existential suicide

A second reason for suicide, related to the first, would be given by a person perhaps in some ways satisfied with his life, who nevertheless has so much anxiety about the future that he decides that being dead seems preferable to living the present until the future comes along. An example would be an individual who is so fearful of the possibility of a nuclear war that he would rather be dead than wait for what seems to him to be inevitable. Another related reason would be given by an individual, deeply reflective and realising his mortality, who decides that since life cannot go on forever and hence that he has no chance of completing what he takes to be his life's work, it must be futile and voluntarily ends it. Camus (1975) seems to concur with the view such an individual entertains about the world:

> In a sense, and as in melodrama, killing yourself amounts to confessing . . . that life is too much for you or that you do not understand it . . . confessing that 'it is not worth the trouble'. Living, naturally, is never easy. You continue making the gestures commanded by existence for many reasons, the first of which is habit. Dying voluntarily implies that you have recognised, even instinctively, the ridiculous nature of that habit, the absence of any profound reason for living, the insane character of that daily agitation and the uselessness of suffering.
>
> (p. 13)

For Camus, then, to kill oneself means simply recognising that life isn't worth the trouble. This form of suicide could perhaps be called *existential suicide*.

127

Dutiful suicide

In some cultures there is (or has been in the past) a duty for some people to kill themselves in certain circumstances, and self killings in accordance with such duties may by some people be thought of as *dutiful suicides*. One example might be *suttee*, the traditional self immolation of Hindu wives; another might be seppuku in Japan, though in Chapter 10, I argue against generally considering seppuku to be suicide.

Altruistic suicide

Yet another reason for suicide might be given by an individual who decides that he would rather be dead than be a burden to his family and friends. *Altruistic suicide*, as I would call it, is perhaps most often associated with individuals who by reason of illness, disability or old age are dependent on others. Those who believe that Captain Oates (Scott, 1935) suicided might wish to argue that his death was a suicide of this kind.

Mitchell (1971) uses the term *philanthropic suicide* in referring to a range of suicidal self harmings. There is some similarity between the examples of philanthropic suicide that he cites and what I am calling altruistic suicide:

the Buddhist monk who sets fire to himself as a declaration of his faith; the old man who kills his wife dying painfully of cancer and then kills himself to be with her; the soldier who willingly gives up his place in the rescue plane so that a wounded companion may go back to safety in his place; Captain Oates in the Antarctic; the man who takes out an insurance policy and then kills himself hoping his family will benefit financially from his death.

(p. 145)

The upsurge of interest in recent years in the possibility of individuals selling organs for profit raises the interesting, though ghastly, possibility that a person, wishing perhaps to arrange that his family were well educated and cared for, might kill himself in order to fulfil the terms of a highly profitable arrangement by which he sold off his organs to the highest bidder prior to his demise. There might even spring up a new breed of medics known as *vivimorticians* who would offer a service to those who wished to raise money for their families by selling their bodies as a source of spare parts for transplant surgery. They would offer specialist skills both in the redistribution of bodily parts and in turning altruistic patients into corpses; with skill they could arrange that patients only gradually approached death by selling off less essential parts to begin with so that death was not necessary in the early stages.

Though the scenario I describe is ghoulish and awful, it does have historical precedents which are discussed by Alvarez (1972). For example, he writes about the fact that at one time in Imperial Rome:

> people would offer themselves for execution to amuse the public for five minae (about £120.00), the money to be paid to their heirs . . . . the market was so competitive that the candidates would offer to be beaten to death rather than beheaded, since that was slower, more painful and so more spectacular.
>
> (p. 57)

Alvarez also discusses a case in the late eighteenth century in which a man advertised that in order to raise money for his poverty stricken family, he was willing to commit suicide publicly in Covent Garden if enough people were willing to pay one pound each. Of this case he writes, 'Nowadays, someone making a similar offer would qualify only for the nearest psychiatric ward, or as a suitable case for treatment in the Theatre of the Absurd' (p. 57).

Revenge suicide

Some people who kill themselves do so as a way of getting at others, or having a negative effect on them. We might refer to suicides of this kind as *revenge suicides*. Perhaps the most frequent purpose that suiciders have in acting – other than ending up dead – is to hurt and punish others who they believe have offended against them in some way.

Douglas (1970) cites the following vivid example of a case in which a suiciding man seems clearly to have the intention, by his suicide, of having revenge on others:

> A young clerk twenty two years old killed himself because his bride of four months was not in love with him but with his elder brother and wanted a divorce so she could marry the brother. The letters he left showed plainly the suicide's desire

129

to bring unpleasant notoriety upon his brother and his wife, and to attract attention to himself. In them he described his shattered romance and advised reporters to see a friend to whom he had forwarded diaries for further details. The first sentence in a special message to his wife read: 'I used to love you; but I die hating you and my brother too.' . . . another note read, 'to whom it may interest: The cause of it all: I loved and trusted my wife and trusted my brother. Now I hate my wife and despise my brother and sentence myself to die for having been fool enough to ever have loved anyone as contemptible as my wife has proven to be.' . . . The day before his death, there was a scene and when assured that the two were really deeply in love with each other, the clerk retorted: 'All right, I can do you more harm dead than alive.'

(pp. 311–12)

This young man wanted to create guilt in his wife and in his brother both of whom had been unfaithful to him and paid the ultimate price in the hope that he could ruin their lives in the way that he perceived them to have ruined his. However, though he may have wanted to be dead because life for him was so miserable, it seems clear that harming his wife and his brother was uppermost in his mind not only at the time of his self destructive act, but for some time before. It is thus at least conceivable that causing harm was his aim and that death was simply a route to inflicting it. Something similar is true of the following story.

John and Lucy had been married for three weeks. They had always had quarrels and lots of people thought they made a mistake in becoming married. Then one morning they had a major row before leaving for work. Later that morning John parked his car outside Lucy's workplace, connected a hose to the exhaust, ran it into the passenger compartment, then turned the engine on. He died of asphyxiation caused by exhaust fumes.

Did John kill himself? Yes he did. But it is perhaps less clear whether his killing constituted the act of suicide. It is difficult to say just what was going on in his mind as he took the fatal steps. Nevertheless it

130

seemed likely to everyone who knew him that John had done what he had done to spite Lucy: to make her feel guilty about the things she had said to him in the morning, to pay her back for all the unkind things she'd said during the course of their stormy relationship and brief marriage; indeed the note he pinned to his clothes said as much.

By his actions John intended to cause pain, hurt and guilt for another person and he was clearly willing to pay the price to achieve this. But it is less clear that he wanted to be dead. The strength of the sentiments he expressed in his note suggested that what was uppermost in his mind when he died was his desire for revenge. He had clearly worked out that he could inflict the maximum amount of pain on his wife by killing himself, and set out to do so. However, if he had been able to achieve this amount of pain for Lucy by some means that fell short of death, he would probably have done so. He intended to die but did not wish to do so. This is the reason that it is at least plausible to view John's death, and others like it, as self killings that do not amount to suicide.

Political or ideological suicide

Sometimes suicide is enacted with the intention of making a political point. Deaths of this kind might be termed *political* or *ideological suicide*. Consider, first of all, the Buddhist monks who set fire to themselves as a protest about the war in Vietnam in the 1960s and 1970s. They set out to make a political point by showing that what they believed in was so important that they were willing to die for it. Death in itself is not what they wanted. However, they did intend to die because by dying they could achieve their ultimate objective. Thus they were genuine suicides.[1] Whether such suicides are successful or not depends in this case not only on whether they die, but also on whether they attain some other end. Though death is intended, it could for them be a failure unless accompanied by the other results they intend to bring about, because if they die without achieving these, their death is pointless and their opportunity to achieve what they wish to achieve has gone.

Suicidal deaths of a political kind are different from other deaths that occur as a result of actions which are intended, among other things, to make a political point. I am thinking now of situations where an individual accepts that though it is very likely, or even certain, that he will die in the process of carrying out a mission, death is not necessarily aimed at. Terrorists who drive lorry loads of explosives at buildings know that their chances of surviving are slim. Some will be suicides because they acted having resolved to die because by dying they could make a greater point. However, for others the intention will not have been to die, but only to deliver the explosives. For these death would have been an inevitable, though undesired, result of the execution of their task, the price they had to pay for success. They will not have suicided. The fact that when they are dead, the deaths of those who did not wish, in undertaking such fatal missions, to die may also be paraded as 'suicides' to make such political points, does not make their deaths into suicides.

The kamikaze pilots of the latter part of World War Two are a well known example of dying for a cause where it is equivocal whether the intention was to die or merely to carry out a mission that involved self sacrifice. Though some of the kamikaze pilots may have wished for death, it is arguable that perhaps many of them undertook the task of flying their plane loads of explosives at enemy targets simply with the honourable aim of serving their country, willing to sacrifice their lives, but not aiming to be dead.

Haring (1972) seems to take this view. He writes:

> The Japanese pilots who assured the success of their attacks on ships and other military targets by plunging themselves and their aircraft onto their objectives could not but lose their lives. Their direct intention, however, was not self-destruction but a noble military gesture that demanded self-sacrifice.
>
> (p. 72)

The act of the self immolator is that of giving up his life for a cause and giving it up, what's more, in the most dramatic way possible. The aim of those who deliver lorry loads of explosives or who fly on kamikaze missions, on the other hand, may simply be to deliver the explosives; in that case death is not aimed at but accepted. And so, while the kamikaze pilot and the lorry driving terrorist may be suicides, the self immolator who intends to die undoubtedly is. Whereas the kamikaze pilot and the terrorist might entertain the hope of a miraculous escape, this is not possible for the person who burns himself to death, because death is what he aims at – it is a necessary part of his plan.

Judicial suicide

The term *judicial suicide* might be used to describe situations in which an individual takes his life believing that there is some legalistic reason why he should die. This might be true of an individual who, believing that he had offended against others or against God, took his life because he believed that this was the only suitable punishment. There may be more than one variety of judicial suicide, distinguished from one another by the extent to which the individual's reasons for believing that he deserves to die make sense. Consider, first of all, a person who had committed awful crimes against children, who decided that prison was too good for him and as a result resolved to kill himself. Though we might question his judgement in deciding on suicide, there is a sense in which such an individual's suicidal decision rests upon rational argument and so we might refer to his suicide as a *rational judicial suicide.* On the other hand a mother, blaming herself for her baby's cot death when it is unlikely that anything she could have done would have saved him, might suicide in the belief that she was a bad mother who deserved punishment; in this case the fact that her suicidal decision does not make sense because there is no evidence to suggest that she could have prevented it by acting differently, suggests the possibility that hers could be referred to as an *irrational judicial suicide.*

Other-driven suicide

Only the person whose life is concerned can suicide though, as I have said in Chapter 2, a person may suicide through the acts or omissions of another and one person may certainly be pushed into, or as we say 'driven to', suicide by another or others. Daube (1972) discusses the use, in Germany, of the expression *jemanden selbstmorden*, 'to suicide somebody', to refer to occasions when one person has been driven to suicide by another or others. I would like to refer to this variety of suicide as *other-driven suicide.*

Interestingly there could be cases where a person was both driven to suicide by another and drove the other to suicide. Shakespeare's Juliet drinks a potion designed to give the impression that she is dead, then falls asleep in the monument at Capel. Out of his mind with grief when he hears the news of her apparent death, Romeo goes straight to the apothecary, buys the means of his own destruction and travels directly to Capel; drinking the poison by Juliet's side, he dies. Waking from her sleep Juliet finds her lover dead beside her. Distraught beyond measure, she kisses him in the hope that sufficient poison will remain on his lips to enable her to join him but to no avail. Finally she stabs herself with his dagger. By setting up the circumstances in which he would think she was dead, Juliet drove Romeo to suicide which in turn drove her to suicide. So each was driven to suicide by the other and each drove the other to suicide.

I should draw attention to a particular sub species of other-driven suicide, in which the individual is not driven to kill himself, but ordered to do so. I am not thinking here of deaths such as that of Socrates, who drank hemlock at the decree of an Athenian court; as I suggest in Chapter 10, whether Socrates is a suicide is a matter that we cannot decide without knowing what was going on for him as he drank. Rather I am thinking of the death of the composer Peter Illyich Tchaikovsky. Attention has recently been paid to the possibility that Tchaikovsky died as the result of a suicide into which he was pushed by a so called *court of honour* convened by former school chums who believed that he had acted in a way that would bring disgrace upon the school and its former students (BBC, 1993). Of course, even if things happened like this, Tchaikovsky need not have been a suicide. It could be that though he killed himself, he did so because otherwise he would have been killed. Rather than a suicide this would have made him the instrument of his own murder by these others. However, given what we know about his lifestyle and temperament, it does seem plausible that unlike the philosopher, the composer may have wished for death when faced with the accusations of his old school friends.

Multiple suicide and mass suicide

Some cases of suicide involve more than one person suiciding at the same time. Such suicides could result from the whole range of reasons that people can have for ending their lives. One very famous recent case of joint suicide, or suicide by pact, was that of Cynthia Koestler and her husband, the writer Arthur Koestler. Koestler was already dying; his wife's reason for ending her life was that she did not want to live without him.

Some multiple suicides do not come in ones or twos, but in much larger numbers. Where large numbers of people suicide together, we usually refer to it as *mass suicide*. Such communal self destruction has occurred throughout history. One historical example is that of the thousand or so Jews in the desert fortress of Masada who in AD 72 killed themselves rather than submit to Roman rule. Though suicide is seen as murder and therefore condemned by Jewish law, this event is often held up as an example of courage in the face of an enemy. Another more recent example was the mass suicide on the island of Saipan towards the end of World War Two. A documentary on British television (*Suicide Island*, Channel 4, February 1994) reported that in 1944, following a massive invasion of the island by American troops, the civilian population and eventually some troops from the Imperial army, went into hiding. Some weeks later many hundreds leaped to their deaths from high cliffs above the sea.

Alvarez (1972) offers a fascinating, though appalling, account of mass suicide during the Spanish conquest of the New World which he writes amounted to 'deliberate genocide in which the native inhabitants themselves cooperated' (p. 50). He writes that:

> Their treatment at the hands of the Spaniards was so cruel that the Indians killed themselves by the thousands rather than endure it. Of forty natives from the Gulf of Mexico who were brought to work in a mine of the Emperor Charles V, thirty-nine strangled themselves to death. A whole cargo of slaves contrived to strangle themselves in the hold of a Spanish galleon, although the headroom was so limited by the heavy ballast of stones that they were forced to hang themselves in a squatting or kneeling position.
>
> (p. 50)

Notoriously, in recent times, mass suicides have often been linked to guru-like figures in cult movements. One example of this was the so called Jonestown massacre of 1978 in Guyana in which hundreds of followers of the Reverend Jim Jones killed themselves and their children. Most of the 913 people who died, died of poisoning by cyanide which had been put into a soft drink; whereas the adults drank the potion that killed them, the children had it squirted down their throats (Humphry, 1991).

Where a number of individuals act together or at the same time in order to achieve their deaths, there could be problems with deciding whether each individual was really a suicide, or whether, for example, he was simply carried along by his companion or companions into acting in a way that he would not individually have chosen to act. If he was, then though he self killed, it is at least debatable whether such a person should be regarded as a suicide.

Looking in; looking out

The classification of varieties of suicide that I have outlined is not intended as a coherent system in the way that Durkheim's classification was. However, the varieties I have presented are all amenable to further discussion in terms of whether the individual in each case acts for reasons that are personally or socially motivated, in other words according to whether in acting he was self regarding or rather looking out into the world.

The no hope suicide most likely acts from personal motivation – he wishes to get rid of the world for him, in order to be rid of despair and bad feelings. The revenge suicide and the other-driven suicide each look in both directions; as a result of the feelings he has, the revenge suicide wants to punish others; as a result of the actions of others, the other-driven suicide is either compelled or driven to kill himself. The political or ideological suicide also looks in both directions. Since in acting he wants to change the world for others, he may be construed as looking outwardly; however, his act is likely also to be underpinned by the belief that he cannot live with society as it is but hopes that he can change it and for this reason he may also be construed as looking inwardly at his belief system and acting for personal reasons. In judicial suicide the individual again looks in both directions at once and acts for both personal and social reasons; he believes he ought to die because what he has done does not match up to what he believes society could legitimately have expected of him. No hope suicide and existential suicide might be thought self regarding to the point of selfishness, though the reason for an existential suicide's despair might be his close relationship to, and feeling of responsibility for, the rest of humanity. On the other hand, the dutiful suicide acts primarily because of his relationship to others; like an English gentleman, he 'does the right thing'. The altruistic suicide probably acts for both social and personal reasons because he wants to do what is best for others and possibly could not live with himself if he did not. The difference, in my classification, between the altruistic suicide and the dutiful suicide is that the dutiful suicide acts in accordance with society's expectations whereas the altruistic suicide acts out of personal feelings towards some particular others; a person could, of course, be an altruistic suicide in circumstances where dutiful suicide would otherwise be demanded.

Finally I should note an apparent difficulty with the brief overview of varieties of suicide that I have offered. Some and perhaps many acts that will fall into these categories would not be suicides by the definitions that I offer in this book, though they will be considered as suicides by many people. The objection might therefore be raised that I am suggesting a categorisation of suicide that does not match up to my own definition. Naturally I consider that whether a self killing is thought of as a suicide should depend on whether it matches up with my criteria; indeed in relation to some of the categories I have offered, I have pointed out occasions when a person's self harming act that might seem to be a suicide should not be considered as such because it does not satisfy my criteria. However, my classification of acts of suicide could be combined with my taxonomy of suicidal self harm so that, for example, an act that to my way of thinking should count as a suicide gesture or a cosmic gamble might be thought of as a revenge suicide gesture or an existential or no hope cosmic gamble.

NOTE

1   It might be suggested that if it is possible to think of the acts of people such as John and the young clerk, who kill themselves to wreak revenge on others, as falling short of suicide though they intentionally self kill, this must be true also in the case of ideological self killers and others who kill themselves in an attempt to bring about something else. I do not agree although it is difficult to say why. One possible, though unsatisfactory, explanation would be that self killings by those who are seeking revenge are likely to be undertaken in a state of considerable emotional turmoil, whereas ideological self killers are more likely to be calculated and cool in their actions. Another is that, whereas ideological self killers can be thought of as wishing to die the dramatic deaths they die, in order to make the point they wish to make, those who kill themselves to harm others are more likely to be thinking only of punishing those others rather than of dying a particular death themselves.

10

DIGGING UP THE PAST
Explorations in the philosophical archaeology of suicide

In Chapters 1 to 9, I have mainly addressed conceptual questions about the nature of suicide, comparing it with a variety of more and less related human phenomena. In doing so I have been attempting to sketch out a richer conceptual framework in terms of which we might talk about suicide and other suicidal self harmings. In Chapters 11 to 14, I want to turn to moral questions that suicide raises for those who unwittingly and unwillingly become involved with what, for the suicide, is the most personal of acts and for the suicider who does not intend by his act to end his life, is perhaps the most public of acts. Before doing that I want, in this chapter, to reopen some famous cases in which death was brought about by the actions of the person who died.

In the title of the chapter I have referred to *philosophical archaeology* rather than, for example, *pathological archaeology* or *archaeological pathology*, because though for a short time after their deaths it would be possible to dig up the bodies of those who may have suicided, the bodies of those that I want to discuss are long gone. And even if we could dig them up this would do little for us when it comes to answering the question of whether the inhabitants of those bodies died as the result of suicide. Only an intimate knowledge of the intentions that underpinned the fatal actions of those who may or may not have suicided can tell us whether they were suicides or not, and access to the intentions of dead people is even more difficult to gain than access to the intentions of those who are still alive. My intention is to attempt, however sketchily, to examine some of the circumstances, both physical and psychological, of these deaths, in order to see what can realistically be said about the intentions that led to them.

Some people might think it rather gory to be digging up corpses from past suicides (or possible suicides). Still, I think it will be interesting to reopen these now famous cases. I will begin with the case of Titus Oates, who died during Captain Scott's last expedition to the Antarctic; then I will reopen the inquiry into the death of Socrates, the Greek philosopher whose penalty for corrupting the young of Athens was that he should drink the hemlock that killed him. Before convening the inquiry into Socrates' case I will discuss the ritual form of self killing which in Japan is known as seppuku and in the west is more commonly known by its literal name of hara-kiri or belly slitting, with which I shall compare it. In both Socrates' case and in cases of seppuku, it is possible to ask whether the death of the individual, though self induced, constitutes suicide given its social context. Finally, I shall return to ancient Greece and consider the case of Aegeus of Athens who leapt from a high place because he believed that his son, who was alive, was dead.

Did Captain Oates suicide?

Captain Scott's last expedition to the South Pole is so famous that it has become part not only of history but of folk lore and the cultural literacy not only of most highly educated but of many relatively uneducated people. One particular event which occurred as the expedition drew to its close, much cited and much discussed, has so caught the public imagination that it has given rise both to comic sketches and to philosophical discussion. The members of the team were all weakening rapidly and, so the story goes, one of the team members, Titus Oates, believing that he was a burden, asked his companions to leave him to die in his sleeping bag. They refused and Scott records what happened next:

> He slept through the night before last, hoping not to wake; but he woke in the morning – yesterday. It was blowing a blizzard. He said, 'I am just going outside and may be some time'. He went out into the blizzard and we have not seen him since . . . . We knew that poor Oates was walking to his death.
>
> (Scott, 1935, p. 462)

Many questions may be asked about the death of Captain Oates and much has been written about it. Was he a suicide? Did he kill himself? Or at any rate did he let the storm kill him? Did he intend to sacrifice his life for his friends, and if so was this a good thing to do?

Discussing what we should say about Oates' death, Holland

139

(1969) writes: 'What Oates decreed was that his hard-pressed companions should be relieved of an encumbrance: of this there can be little doubt' (p. 79). Holland denies that Oates' death was a suicide because he 'remained cheerful right to the end' (pp. 79–80). He maintains that the 'sentiment that he was entitled to quit, or that anyway he was going to quit, never entered into it' (p. 80). The question may be raised how Holland came by such intimate details of Oates' last sentiments and feelings; being able to obtain this degree of knowledge (if it is knowledge) about the internal workings of another's mind is a useful skill, especially when they have been dead for many years and did not overtly share them with others before they died. Perhaps Holland's view of Oates' death is guesswork based on more general knowledge of his character; but perhaps it has its roots in the tendency to avoid labelling acts of which one approves as 'suicide', which I discussed in Chapter 3.

Part of Holland's reason for denying that Oates was a suicide is that he did not die by his own hand. He writes 'Had Oates taken out a revolver and shot himself I would have agreed he was a suicide' (p. 80). It is difficult to make sense of this, since as I have shown in Chapter 2, one can suicide just as easily by omission or by putting oneself in the way of harm, as one may by causing harm to oneself directly. In any case, if, as Holland claims, it had not occurred to Oates that he 'was entitled to quit, or that anyway he was going to quit', the scenario where Oates took the revolver and shot himself would not have arisen. Or at any rate it would not have arisen unless Oates had wanted to die for reasons that had nothing to do with the belief that he was entitled to quit or his intention to quit anyway. He might, for example, have intended to sacrifice his life in order to make sure that his friends had more chance of survival than he believed they would were he alive. In other words it is conceivable that Oates both wanted to die (for altruistic reasons) and did not believe that he was entitled to quit. Rather than being what I have referred to as an *existential suicide* or *no hope suicide*, which is what I think Holland wishes to reject, though he does not use these terms, he may have been what I have referred to as an *altruistic suicide*.

Holland thinks that it makes sense to say of Oates both that 'the blizzard killed him' and that 'he killed himself by going out into the blizzard'. Midway between these two he thinks there is another description: 'He let the blizzard kill him.' While it is a truism to say that the blizzard killed Oates, it is simply untrue to say of Oates that he killed himself by going into the blizzard. On the other hand, it seems to be a reasonable description of the facts to say that he let the blizzard kill him, though it was not that having found himself by chance in a blizzard, he allowed it to do its worst; he intentionally walked out into it and the implication in Scott's account is that in doing so, he expected to die. As I have already pointed out, a person can suicide by arranging that he is in a situation where some external force can kill him. If it was a suicide Oates' letting the blizzard kill him was a suicide of this kind because, presumably, had he wanted to, he could have saved himself or at least given himself some hope of escape, by returning to the relative warmth and shelter of the tent.

So Holland wants to avoid the conclusion that Oates suicided and opts to do so by showing that the best description of his death is that the blizzard killed him. He cites two reasons for thinking this. First, that what Oates did himself – walking into the blizzard – is somewhat remote from the event of his death. Secondly, there was the time factor – his death did not follow immediately after what Oates did, but when the blizzard was good and ready and had had time to take its toll. Let me consider these reasons in turn.

In relation to the first I think Holland is simply mistaken; far from being remote from his death, Oates' walking into the storm brought it about. There is a direct causal connection between his walking into the blizzard and his death, nothing remote about it. In any case, why should his death being somewhat remote from his action in walking into the blizzard have anything to do with whether he suicided? The second of Holland's reasons also seems to have nothing at all to do with whether Oates was a suicide. A man can arrange that he dies or is killed sometime in the future – some minutes, hours, days, weeks, months or even years later and still be a suicide. Frey (1981) discusses such a case:

> Suppose Sir Percy decides to commit suicide but simply cannot face cutting his wrists or shooting himself in the temple; instead, he plants hundreds of pounds of gelignite under his house and attaches the fuses to his telephone, so that, if his telephone rings, his house explodes; and then he sits down to wait.
>
> (p. 38)

This seems clearly to be suicide, given that Sir Percy's telephone rings fairly frequently. If it didn't he could always make his death much more certain by utilising the telephone alarm service offered

141

by British Telecom; then, barring mistakes on the part of the operator, he could be sure not only of dying, but of when he would die.

Sir Percy could also arrange his death at some non-specific and perhaps rather remote future time, by omission. For example, he could arrange that the brakes on his Bentley were not repaired even after he had been warned by a mechanic that unless he had his brakes seen to, he was heading for disaster. If he did this with the intention and expectation that he would eventually have a fatal accident, Percy would be taking suicidal action. Whether and when we would say that he was a suicide, is more difficult to say. However, if as a result of driving with defective brakes, he was involved in a fatal accident within hours or even days, and he had not changed his mind about his intention to cause it, he would clearly have suicided.

Oates did not kill himself, the storm did that for him. But the fact that a person does not kill himself hardly constitutes a reason for saying that he was not a suicide. Most instances of suicide may be restated in terms that deny that the individual directly killed himself. For example, though it seems odd, it could be argued that the man who dies hanging from the end of a rope does not kill himself, but that the rope, combined with gravity, does it for him, or that the person who jumps in front of a moving car does not kill himself but that the car does. It could even be argued that the man who fires a gun at his head does not kill himself, that the bullet does it for him. Harris (1980) makes a similar point. Discussing Duff's claim that if Captain Oates had shot himself instead of walking out of the tent into the storm, this would make a difference to what he did because in that case he would have done something other than disassociating himself from Scott and the others, he writes:

> Had Oates lacked the strength to remove himself from the group physically but possessed a revolver, he might have equally effectively disassociated himself by putting the barrel in his mouth, pulling the trigger and thinking 'Whether I die or not is up to God.'
>
> (p. 54)

Clearly it is possible (though in my opinion only barely so) that a person who puts a gun in his mouth might think something of the kind; in that case by his actions he would participate in cosmic roulette by gambling at the table of life and death over which God the cosmic croupier presides. But the odds seem pretty stacked against life in this case and so most people, I guess, would be willing to take such an act as the act of one who wishes, intends and expects to be dead, whatever he says as he pulls the trigger. It is, I suppose, just possible that someone might really believe that there is the possibility, when he pulls the trigger, of some kind of miraculous change in the causal nature of the universe, or that some cosmic intervener (such as God) might arrange things such that the bullet does not enter his head or at any rate that it does not cause much damage as it passes through; but it seems unlikely.

In conclusion, then, what can we say about Oates and his famous demise? It would be plausible to say that he arranged things such that there was a good but not certain chance that the blizzard might kill him. Like the scenario discussed above, in which Oates puts the gun in his mouth and thinks 'Whether I die or not is up to God', this would make his act in leaving the tent a cosmic gamble, though given the low odds of his being saved, we would probably consider it to be a suicidal one.

However, I think the most accurate description of Oates' actions would be to say that he arranged, by going into the storm, that the storm *would* kill him. If he acted with the intention of ending up dead because, say, he could no longer stand the misery and pain of being stranded or the uncertainty about whether or not he would survive, and therefore decided that he would rather be dead, he would clearly have been a suicide. If, on the other hand, his primary motivation in walking into the storm was, as Holland insists, to ensure that 'his hard-pressed companions should be relieved of an encumbrance' (p. 79), then he was an altruist who gave up his life for his friends; in that case his act was the act of relieving them of dead weight in order that they might have some hope of survival, and his death was the price he paid for helping them. Whether he would then have been a suicide would depend on what precisely he intended. If he intended to arrange his death because that was the only way that he thought he could rid his comrades of the burden that he had become, many people would say that he was a suicide, albeit an altruistic one. My own inclination, in line with what I said about the spy who kills himself to avoid the possibility that he should give away secrets that would endanger others, is to think that in this scenario, Oates would not have been a suicide but simply someone who cared so much for his friends that he was willing to pay with his life to give them the extra chance of survival that he thought they would have without him.

143

In order to be able unequivocally to say whether Oates was a suicide, or rather an altruistic martyr, we would need to know what was in his mind as he left the tent. Since we cannot gain access to this information about Oates' biography, we cannot say unequivocally whether he was a suicide or not and neither can Holland or anyone else.

Socrates, seppuku and suicide

Seppuku is usually thought of, at least in the western world, as a special and rather ritualised form of suicide. In Japan it seems to have been thought of as something more than suicide. Campbell and Collinson (1988, n. 2, p. 19) cite T. Harada, who writes: 'It was not mere suicide. It was an institution, legal and ceremonial . . . by which warriors could expiate their friends or prove their sincerity'. In contrast to this, given the view of suicide that I outline in this book, and given the social context in which it takes place, it is at least questionable whether thinking of seppuku as a variety of suicide is justified. Given the social context in which it takes place, the seppuku's death may not be suicide; this is not to say that some who seppuku might not be suicides, but simply that the act of seppuku in itself need not be suicide.

There may be occasions when seppuku will unequivocally be suicide. This might be the case if, say, an individual had been contemplating taking his life when, by accident, he acted in a way which demanded seppuku. If he then killed himself by enacting seppuku, not simply because in such circumstances it was his duty to do so, but because it fitted well with his own plans to die anyway, he would be a suicide. In this case, his act of seppuku would also be an act of suicide. Indeed, bizarre though it might seem, he could even act in a way that meant seppuku would be required of him, to make it easier for him to suicide, because, for example, though he could bring himself to engage in the ritual act of seppuku, simply killing himself in cold blood, as it were, was beyond him.

So I think it is possible that seppuku is best thought of as being distinct from suicide, as being simply the intentional act of one who aims to do what he ought to do, which is to enact the ritual required of him by custom, tradition and honour. Conceived in this way what is of primary importance in seppuku is not the achievement of death but the enactment of a ritual act of atonement. Suicide, on the other hand, involves not only that the protagonist should arrange his death but that in doing so he should wish and intend to be dead.

When it first began about 1,000 years ago seppuku involved disembowelling oneself beginning with two incisions to the abdomen:

> At first he stabbed a short sword into the left abdomen, moved to the right, and then pulled it out. Again he stabbed it into the epigastrium, and cut down vertically. Finally he gouged the throat by it. This act was a show of bravery because instant death was not expected.
>
> (Tatai, 1970, cited in Iga and Tatai, 1975, p. 258)

About 400 years ago, hara-kiri began to be an honourable form of death for the Samurai. A short sword was thrust into the left abdomen, cut to the right, cut up and then pulled out, after which the seppuku would be beheaded by one of his friends using a long sword (Tatai, cited in Iga and Tatai, 1975). Nowadays, a person may seppuku without inflicting any wounds, by simply reaching out to a ceremonial weapon as the signal to his aide who will then cut off his head (Soya, 1992).

It does not seem to be beyond thought that an intending seppuku might stretch out his hand to his ceremonial weapon, giving the signal to his aide to behead him, without wishing to be dead but merely wishing to do what must be done; that is, the sequence of actions which culminated in his stretching out his hand might, for him, represent an act of seppuku but not, at the same time, an act of suicide. On the other hand, in the case of an intending seppuku who wished for and wanted to arrange his death, the action of stretching out his hand, knowing that it would signal to his aide that his head should be cut off, could at the same time constitute not only the act of seppuku but also the act of suicide.

Imagine that the ritual of seppuku was further attenuated so that it involved nothing more than reaching out to a ceremonial dagger after which the seppuku's aide whirled a ceremonial sword round his head three times, then shook the seppuku's hand. In this case, seppuku could not be suicide because the individual engaging in it would be aware that by doing so he could not arrange his death. And yet he would have done seppuku. Those of whom seppuku is required and for whom tradition matters would perform the pre-scribed ritual even if seppuku changed in the kind of way that I have postulated and so did not involve ending their lives. Of course, a critic might suggest that whereas in the old-fashioned lethal variety of seppuku what one did was to suicide physically, in this new form he would suicide symbolically. But this simply begs the question of whether seppuku is suicide, or in the attenuated case, symbolic suicide.

The fact that seppuku has traditionally been a ritual form of self killing in prescribed circumstances, that now need not even involve the individual in spilling his own blood, suggests that a reading of the culture of seppuku as being about something other than suicide – about, for example, something more like etiquette and 'doing what's right' – is at least of some interest. Indeed it seems clear that the principal focus in seppuku is on doing what one is required to do rather than on ending one's life, though at the present time, doing seppuku involves arranging one's death (Soya, 1992). Whereas, because of the resemblance they bear to the actions involved in some forms of suicide, the western observer takes the seppuku's actions to constitute suicide, for the seppuku, they represent the act of honourable atonement or of making things right. A critic might contend that the fact that a person who does seppuku is doing his duty makes no difference to what he does. She would argue, by analogy, that just as an examiner who does his duty in relation to a poor PhD thesis *fails it*, so a Samurai who does his duty in circumstances that demand seppuku *suicides* because he intentionally kills himself (or arranges by reaching out for the ceremonial dagger that someone else does it for him) and therefore he suicides because intentionally killing oneself (or arranging that one is killed) is what suicide is. But this makes the assumption that all intentional self killing is suicide which I would contest.

So I am claiming that though seppuku could be suicide, it need not be. Things are more complicated than this, however, because it could also be that what looks like seppuku is in fact something else; for example, it may be suicide which, while embracing the traditional rituals of seppuku, does not carry the meaning and intention of atonement, which characterises seppuku.

The brilliant Japanese novelist Yukio Mishima was also a charismatic supporter of traditional Japanese values. His celebrated death is often cited as an example of seppuku and perhaps it was. But perhaps not. After performing ritual disembowelling, Mishima was beheaded by his friend Issho Morita, who afterwards killed himself.

We cannot be certain of Mishima's reasons for dying in the way that he did at the time that he did. It may be that he believed seppuku was what he must do because of some failing on his part. However, rather than the reasons for his act being related to a purely traditional motive for suicide, they seem often to be analysed in terms of aspects of his life experiences. For example, Iga and Tatai talk in terms of his narcissistic temperament, feudalistic philosophy of life, limited life experiences, nihilistic attitude towards life and death,[1] and his homosexuality. Indeed they postulate that his suicide was not a straightforward case of seppuku, and point out that some critics 'regarded his suicide as iyoshi, or love pact suicide, stemming from his homosexuality (with Issho Morita)' (p. 262).

So was Mishima's death seppuku? I cannot say. However, in the absence of the kind of reason that would traditionally lead a person to seppuku, some people might question whether it was, in spite of the fact that in its ceremony and ritual it had the appearance of seppuku. It is at least feasible, they would argue, that his ritualised suicide was a theatrical performance cast in the mould of seppuku in order to give it more point in terms of his aspirations for Japan and for his followers.

Let me turn now to the celebrated death of Socrates which has been much discussed by philosophers. Socrates' death is recorded by Plato in the Phaedo (Tredennick, 1959). He had been accused, among other things, of introducing unusual religious practices and of corrupting young people. At his trial he defended himself but was found guilty and sentenced to death. In the month leading up to his execution by means of a self administered cup of hemlock, Socrates did not accept the possibility for escape arranged by friends because it would have gone against his sense of duty to avoid the punishment decreed by Athens. Then on the appointed day, he drank the hemlock before the hour stipulated for his death.

Holland (1969) believes that Socrates did not suicide because he was doing what had been decided upon by others. He writes:

> Socrates took the cup of hemlock and drank it, and thereby might be said strictly to have died by his own hand. Yet even this cannot make a man a suicide, given the fact that his death was not decreed by him.
>
> (Holland, 1969, p. 74)

He anticipates, but is unimpressed by, the objection that if Socrates knowingly and deliberately drank the poison, it follows that he killed himself and was therefore a suicide. He writes that drinking hemlock 'does not, in the context of an Athenian judicial execution, amount to slaughtering oneself' (p. 75).[2] The point Holland is making is similar to the general point I have made in relation to seppuku: that if a person acts so as to bring about his death simply because he is required by social convention or, in this case, by judicial decision to do so, he is not a suicide. To be a suicide it would have to have been the case that by acting as he did Socrates intended not only to do that which he ought to do or had to do, but that he wanted to be dead and intended to bring about his death. Thus we cannot decide that either a seppuku or Socrates were suicides unless we know what they intended by their individual actions.

Holland thinks that it is clear that Socrates was not a suicide because in the circumstances in which he drank the hemlock, his act 'is no more an act of suicide than the condemned man's walk to the scaffold in our society' (p. 75). He is denying that Socrates was a suicide because he did no more than a condemned man has to do. Of course, we could take him literally as Campbell and Collinson (1988) do and point out that whereas Socrates actually brought about his death by drinking the poison, all the condemned man does in walking to the scaffold is to bring death nearer, 'for when he has completed his walk to the scaffold he has not begun to die' (p. 11). They offer an alternative, and rather closer, analogy 'with a condemned man who actually presses the switch to operate the device that kills him, so that he is his own executioner' (p. 11). Rather than weakening it, this further story serves to strengthen Holland's point because we would no more refer to the one condemned man's pressing the switch as suicide than we would refer to the other's walk to the scaffold as suicide. Even though he brings about his death voluntarily we would not say that the condemned man was a suicide because he pressed the switch; as Campbell and Collinson claim, there is available an accurate and explicit description for what he does: 'self execution'. They point out further that in a judicial system where condemned criminals were given the choice of pressing the switch themselves or of having it pressed by an executioner, if we saw the headline proclaiming 'Condemned man commits suicide' in the newspapers we would think immediately that he had killed himself in his cell. A better headline to intimate that he had pressed the switch himself would be: 'Condemned man opts for self execution' (p. 11).

Holland anticipates the possible suggestion that Socrates might have been a man who wished to suicide and for whom the sentence of self inflicted death from hemlock poisoning 'came in handy'

(p. 75). He deals with this objection by invoking an account of views Socrates had expressed. He asserts that Socrates

> did not wish to die before it was time for him to die. He did not wish to run away from anything. And it certainly cannot be said of him that he wished to die because he found no sense in living. On the contrary the sense he found in living was what on the one hand made him reject suicide and on the other hand enabled him to look on death, whenever it should come, as something to be welcomed rather than feared.
>
> (p. 75)

In contrast to Holland, Frey (1981) argues that Socrates did commit suicide. His argument begins with a day (or a death) in the life of Sir Percy. One day while cleaning his gun, Percy accidentally shoots himself dead. 'Did Sir Percy commit suicide?' Frey asks. The answer, he claims, is that he did not because though killing oneself may be part of what it is to suicide, 'it is not the whole' (p. 36). Sir Percy did not intend to kill himself and therefore he is not a suicide. On the other hand, Frey believes that Socrates did intend to kill himself:

> If suicide, then, is killing oneself intentionally, then Socrates . . . certainly did commit suicide. For he drank the hemlock knowingly, not unknowingly or in ignorance of what it was or what its effect on him would be, and intentionally, not accidentally, or mistakenly.
>
> (p. 36)

Frey is arguing that since Socrates intended to drink the hemlock and knew what the results of doing so would be, he must have wanted to be dead. This just isn't true. A person can do something knowing what its result will be without wanting that result. For example, he could eat too much, drink too much, or smoke too much, or engage in too many unprotected promiscuous sexual encounters knowing that the result is likely to be heart or liver disease, lung cancer or the likelihood that he will contract some dreadful sexually transmitted disease, respectively, without wanting any of these results to come about; and a soldier, as I have argued elsewhere, could fall on a grenade that lands in the shell hole that he is occupying with some mates, to protect the lives of his fellows, knowing that he will end up dead as a result, without wanting to be dead.

But Frey goes further, drawing attention to a number of objections

149

to his view, each of which he considers to be unsuccessful. One of these objections concerns the possibility that it might be argued that as a good citizen, concerned with the law, all Socrates wanted to do was 'not to die, but to uphold the laws of Athens' (p. 36). If this was the case, it would then be wrong to claim that he suicided because, like the seppuku who does not wish to die but only to do what is required of him, all Socrates would have done would have been to have done what was required, which was to kill himself by taking the hemlock.

Though it is true that Socrates drank the hemlock voluntarily rather than having it forced down his throat and though he drank it before the appointed time, Campbell and Collinson (1988) argue that it might be more correct to describe him as 'acting as a virtuous and honourable Athenian citizen' (p. 10). Socrates' overriding desire and intention was to be a good and dutiful citizen; and so, since the law required that he should bring about his death by drinking the hemlock, his doing so, we might say, represented for him the act of one who was doing what a good citizen in his circumstances should, and nothing else. According to Campbell and Collinson then, drinking the hemlock was Socrates' way of fulfilling his duty as an honourable citizen; the fact that he knew it would bring about his death was incidental to what he intended. Of course it could have been that he wanted to die because that was what was required and he was an honourable citizen who wanted what Athens did. This is what Frey thinks. He writes that it could be argued 'that Socrates wanted to die, sentenced as he was by the city to do so, in order to uphold – and be seen upholding – these very laws' (p. 36).

If Socrates wished to be dead because he believed it to be his duty as a good citizen to be dead then he suicided and we could refer to his suicide using the classification that I offered in Chapter 9, as a *dutiful* suicide. If the seppuku wishes to be dead because he believes that it is his duty as a Samurai to die, then he is also a suicide of a dutiful kind. However, since we cannot tell what is in his mind as he takes the dagger in hand or gives the signal to his aide to do his duty, we cannot tell in relation to one who performs the rituals of seppuku whether for him, the act of seppuku and the act of suicide are one and the same. And since we cannot tell what was in his mind as he reached out to take the hemlock and put the cup to his lips, we cannot say whether Socrates suicided or not and all the discussions and guesses of philosophers and others are in vain. All we can do is to say that if by acting in the way that he did, Socrates or the seppuku intended to take his life because he wished for whatever reason to be dead, then he was a suicide and if he did not, he was not.

Aegeus of Athens

According to legend, Aegeus, King of Athens, leaped into the sea because he believed that his son, Theseus, was dead. Theseus had said that when he returned from fighting the Minotaur he would change his black sail for a white one to let his father know that he had been victorious. If he had failed in his mission, on the other hand, his ship would appear on the horizon with its original black sail and Aegeus would know that his son was dead. The story goes that when Theseus' ship appeared under its original black sail, Aegeus leaped to his death.

Suicide is usually defined as the act of a person who intends and wishes by his own autonomous act to end his life. At first sight it thus seems natural to say that Aegeus suicided since he jumped to his death intending, expecting and wishing to be dead. However, there is a sense in which it is possible to argue that despite all this, Aegeus did not suicide and more generally that self killing under false information should not be viewed as suicide.

There are two separate arguments in favour of these conclusions, each of which begins with the observation that though his ship returned under its original black sail, Theseus was in fact alive and had just forgotten to change the sails over.

The first argument focuses on the belief that since autonomy depends partly on a person's state of information, a person cannot act autonomously if he is badly informed. If this is correct, and I believe that it is, then if suicide is defined as resulting from the autonomous intention of an individual to end his life, then though he killed himself, Aegeus was not a suicide.

The second, more complex and perhaps less plausible, argument focuses not on Aegeus' state of information, though it refers to it, but on his intentions. He intended to kill himself if Theseus was dead and he believed that he was; that is why he jumped. But Theseus was not dead. And so although he intended to take his life, his act in leaping was not what he thought it was. Since Theseus was alive, the reason that Aegeus had for killing himself could not have been that Theseus was dead. Aegeus was unwise to act on impulse, without ensuring that Theseus really was dead. However, since he intended only to take his life if his son was dead and his son was alive, it can be argued that his self killing was not a suicide.

Some people might wish to argue that what Aegeus did was to suicide under a misapprehension of fact, that though his leap was based on false information, he nevertheless did what he did with the intention of dying and that this makes him a suicide. They might point out that a murderer who kills the wrong person by mistake nevertheless commits murder and argue, by analogy, that a suicider who suicides by mistake is still a suicide. But this begs the question of whether Aegeus was a suicide and fails to notice the difference between the two concepts, murder and suicide. The question of whether a murder has been committed depends upon the facts of the matter – is there a corpse that has been turned into a corpse by another person's intentional and malicious action? On the contrary, whether suicide has been enacted depends on the intention and the wish of the individual in question and Aegeus wished to kill himself and intended to kill himself if and only if Theseus was dead. Though his act was intentional the result was not what he wished for, or even what he intended. Whereas he intended that if his son was dead, he (Aegeus) should die; the result of his act was that his son was alive and he (Aegeus) was dead.

If this is not convincing, consider the situation where Theseus wishes to benefit from his father's death. Returning from slaying the Minotaur and knowing his father's temperament, Theseus deliberately refrains from changing the black sail for the white one, in order to induce his father to jump. In this case, wouldn't we be inclined to say that Aegeus is murdered by his son, though his son does not lay a hand on him?

The following case is similar to that of Aegeus.

Mr Pailin has heard that his daughter was aboard a ship which has sunk, with considerable loss of life, in Plymouth Dock. Like Aegeus he has resolved to take his life if his daughter, who means everything to him, is dead. But rather than leaping from a high place as Aegeus did, Mr Pailin's chosen method is poison. In front of him he has placed two cups of wine, one laced with poison, the other unadulterated; the one to end his life, the other to celebrate his daughter's survival. A short time later the police, mistaking his daughter's identity, come to the door and report that they believe that she has been drowned in the incident. Drinking the poisoned cup, Mr Pailin expires.

What would we say in this case? Aren't we inclined to say that Mr P died accidentally because really he should have been drinking the good wine rather than the poisoned wine? Isn't it because we think this that, had we known that his daughter was alive and that the police had simply made a mistake in identifying the body they took to be hers, we would have stopped him – because we knew that killing himself in these circumstances was not his intention? Consider the situation if, after hearing the news about his daughter's ship, Mr P had telephoned his estranged wife asking that she should contact him if she heard any news of their daughter, and telling her about his intention to kill himself if their daughter is dead. Imagine that some time later his wife came round to report that (unfortunately) the police had been to see her to report their daughter dead and in spite of her pleading and begging him not to take the poison, Mr P drank the cup and expired. Imagine that his estranged but terrible wife immediately telephoned her lover, laughing at their stroke of luck that the incident with the boat occurred because as a result of that incident they will not now have to enact their plan to murder him; he has done the deed himself. Incidentally, as you may have guessed, though Mr P's daughter intended to be on that ship she was delayed and never even boarded it; as a result at the very moment that her father was polishing off the poisoned cup in his distress at her demise, she was celebrating her good fortune at the delay that caused her to miss the boat. As in the scenario where Theseus contrives things such that his father would jump to his death, wouldn't we be inclined, in this case, to think of Mr P's death as the result of murder on the part of his estranged wife, rather than a suicide on his part?

Mr Pailin's case is different from that of Aegeus because we can construe him as having drunk the wrong glass of wine by mistake. Imagine the situation where the police came to tell Mr P that although his daughter was on the ship when it went down, she had survived. If on hearing this news Mr P was so relieved and excited that he picked up the wrong glass we would have thought him the victim of a horrid mistake. Now in the case where he believes that his daughter is dead, whether because he has been told it by the police or by his scheming wife, he also picks up the wrong glass, isn't he then also the victim of a horrid mistake? Since I do not think a person can suicide by mistake, it follows that Mr P's death by deliberately drinking poison because he believed his daughter to be dead, could not be a suicide.

Aegeus and Mr P and others like them, who kill themselves intentionally because they are in possession of wrong information, should not be considered suicides. Just as Mill's bridge crosser would not have chosen to cross the bridge had he known it to be dangerous,[3] so Mr P and Aegeus and others like them would not have chosen to jump, or drink the poisoned wine or act in other ways that bring about their deaths, if they had known the truth of their situation. And so, although they self kill, they are not suicides because death in the circumstances that actually prevailed when they jumped and drank was not what they either wanted or intended to achieve.

Closing remarks

In reopening some celebrated cases of self killing that might have been suicide, I have tried to reinforce some aspects of my view of suicide. Of course I have been selective in choosing those that I have chosen, and there are many others that I could have raised including those of the deaths of the many rock stars and other well known figures of the twentieth century. For example, I could have said more about the death of the writer Arthur Koestler, who I discuss above (pp. 82–3). Or I could have spent some time re-thinking the death of the poet Sylvia Plath, who survived one very serious attempt only to die ten years later in an act that some people, including the novelist Al Alvarez, believe did not amount to suicide. I myself believe that the evidence is overwhelmingly in favour of the conclusion that Plath was successful in ending her life, rather than unsuccessful in either crying for help or in acting in such a way that others believed she had been attempting to arrange her death, while managing to stay alive (Alvarez, 1972).

So there is much philosophical archaeology to be done among the lives of people who have died at their own hands and I have merely gestured at reopening a few famous cases. I have chosen to discuss the cases I have discussed not only because they are among the most famous and analysed in human experience but because of the interest that they hold for me and because they seem to me to raise questions that are worth asking and to direct us to ways of thinking about suicide in general that are worth pursuing.

NOTES

1   For example, they cite him as writing 'If our biological life is limited, I would like to live forever' (Iga and Tatai, 1975, p. 270).
2   I take Holland's use of the expression 'slaughtering oneself' to mean 'suiciding'. He could not mean, literally, that taking hemlock in this context does not involve killing oneself though in other contexts it would, because 'to slaughter' means 'to kill'.
3   Mill introduces us to his bridge crosser in the context of a discussion of an exception to his *Liberty Principle* (see p. 156 below).

11

THE LIBERAL AND CONSERVATIVE POSITIONS ON SUICIDE

> failure to intervene (in suicide) indicates a lack of concern about others and a diminished sense of moral responsibility in a community.
>
> (Beauchamp and Childress, 1983, p. 100)

> concern for the welfare of others has to be part of respect for persons which must give ultimate priority to respect for their wishes.
>
> (Harris, 1985, p. 204)

> If either a public officer or anyone else saw a person attempting to cross a bridge which had been ascertained to be unsafe, and there was no time to warn him of the danger, they might seize him and turn him back, without any real infringement of his liberty; for liberty consists in doing what one desires and he does not desire to fall into the river.
>
> (Mill, 1859, p. 151)

Those who witness or come across a suicide, or what looks like a suicide, will be affected by it. Aside from the feelings, both physical and emotional, that they experience, they may suffer intellectual and moral turmoil as they attempt to wrestle with the dilemma of deciding how they should react, what they should do. Most will act immediately to do what they can to 'help' the suicider. However, those who have given some thought to the question of whether it is possible that death is something that a person could rationally want and set out to achieve, and/or to the possibility that death might realistically be in a person's best interests, might pause, however briefly, before intervening, especially if the person they come across is well known to them. As a result they may decide that intervention in the person's act may not be helpful and decide to do nothing. However, I think this will be unusual, especially among those who have also thought about the range of aims that a person may have in mind when he behaves in apparently suicidal ways, and hence the number of acts that his suicidal actions may constitute.

The dilemmas that coming across suicide or apparent suicide can cause are doubly difficult for those who are convinced, as I am, that refraining from action in this as in any other situation is in itself a positive act. It is doubly difficult for them because they will know that having become aware of the suicidal incident, they cannot fail to have an effect on the outcome, whether they act to prevent it proceeding or act to allow it to continue.

In this chapter I want to discuss what I refer to as the *liberal* and *conservative* positions on suicide and the ways in which occupying extreme versions of these positions or a range of positions between them, might affect the beliefs that a person entertains about the propriety of intervention in suicidal acts.

The liberal position

Many people, believing that one of the most important values for humankind is autonomy, believe that everyone has the right[1] to do what he wants with his body and hence, for example, that a person may choose to accept or reject medical treatment and should not have treatment forced on him that he does not wish to undergo. In the case of a woman this belief may underpin both the view that she is entitled to decide whether or not to carry a baby to term or to have it aborted, and also the view (at least in affluent countries) that she should have the right to choose the place and manner of the birth of her child should she choose to carry it to term. Paradoxically, although few people would believe that (other than minor mutilation such as the piercing of ears) a person should have the right to have her body mutilated, many would express the view that everyone has the right to decide whether he lives or dies and hence the right to suicide. This might be called the *liberal position* on suicide. Those who occupy an extreme version of this position believe that an individual who has embarked upon a self destructive course has the right to be left to die by any who come upon him. Consequently they believe that no one should intervene in the suicidal acts of others. By contrast, those who occupy a less extreme liberal position might believe that it would often be legitimate to intervene in a suicider's act in order to ascertain whether he was acting autonomously or not. This view is likely to be very common, since most liberals probably believe not in the right to take one's life, but in the right to do so autonomously.

The conservative position

A conservative on suicide believes that whenever possible we should intervene in the self destructive acts of others. There are, I think, two varieties of suicide conservative:

1 Those who believe that since killing himself is not something that a rational person could wish to achieve, an individual who is acting suicidally must be psychologically disturbed, and hence that intervention to save his life would always be in his best interests.
2 Those who believe that suicide is simply wrong, and that anyone who is found trying to kill himself should be prevented from doing so because where possible what is sinful should be prevented.

A person could be doubly conservative by adhering to both of these beliefs.

A continuum of views

There are many suicide conservatives, but I think it is unlikely that there are many genuine suicide liberals, though there are people who claim to hold such a view. Those who claim to hold liberal views are, I think, likely to have given little thought to the nature of suicide. By contrast, I think that someone who has thought about the nature of suicide and about the range of acts that suicidal self harm can represent will probably believe that in most circumstances where, by chance, one person comes across another who appears to have acted suicidally, they are entitled (perhaps even morally obliged) to take action to prevent the apparent suicide dying. I think this will be true of those who are unashamedly conservative both on the question of whether suicide is in itself OK and on the question of whether death can rationally be chosen. More surprisingly perhaps, I think it will be true of those who believe both that there is nothing wrong with suicide in itself and that it is a perfectly reasonable thing, in some circumstances, to prefer death to life.

In an earlier version of this chapter I claimed that a good test of whether a person's claim to hold a liberal view of suicide was authentic would be to place a person who claimed to hold such a view in front of a dearly loved friend who had cut his wrists or taken a massive overdose when she could see no earthly reason for him to wish to be dead. John Harris (Harris, 1991) wondered whether this was a genuine test and asked whether I proposed to apply it and if so how I proposed to do so. He suggested that if I did not intend to apply my test, I should not refer to it as a test. But although this is not a test that we could apply straightforwardly to everyone who claims to be extremely liberal on suicide, because we could hardly arrange for them all to be faced with the apparent suicides of dearly loved friends, we could apply it retrospectively to those claiming liberal views or who claim to have held such views in the past, who have been faced with the possible death of a loved one who has acted suicidally.

Asking those who claimed to hold liberal views about how they responded to such traumatic experiences, about whether, for example, their views changed as a result, would give some indication about the strength of those views. This information could then be extrapolated to others who claim to hold such views, at least in a general way. More effectively, and perhaps more usefully, we could apply the test in relation to hypothetical situations. One possible way of doing this would be to adapt an approach that I have used in working on controversial moral issues with students and with practitioners in the caring professions (Fairbairn and Mead, 1990, 1993a and 1993b). For example, during a teaching sequence in which I consider the moral issues raised by abortion, I distribute a number of short vignettes from the lives of women or couples who have decided either in favour of an abortion or against having one and ask students to imagine themselves into the life of one of the characters in the vignette they have been given. I ask them to imagine the feelings and thoughts that this person would be having, and then to write more of the story from that person's point of view. I have found that asking my students to inhabit the stories lived by people in traumatic situations helps them to come to a fuller understanding of those situations.

Those who claim to hold liberal views about suicide could be invited imaginatively to inhabit the life stories of individuals faced with a suiciding friend in circumstances that make it difficult to believe that the friend has good reason to wish to die. They could then be asked whether they would intervene or simply allow this person to die. This would give some indication of the authenticity of their liberal views.

Faced with a suicidal self harming, I believe that most of those who claim to be liberal on suicide will act in ways that do not match up to their professed beliefs. Of course, they might act differently from how their avowed beliefs would suggest that they should act not because their beliefs had changed, but because they were not emotionally or constitutionally strong enough to implement them. Some people who really wish to suicide might not do so because they find that when it comes to actually enacting their death, they are incapable of doing so; in a similar way, some suicide liberals might find that they are incapable, even for reasons that they consider to be morally reprehensible, of allowing another person to die. Such individuals might thus maintain an extremely liberal belief about how it is appropriate to act in relation to suicidal self harmers, while acting in a particular case to save the person's life.

Though I have offered a characterisation of two extreme positions, in reality there is a continuum of views about whether individuals are entitled to take their lives and should be freely allowed to do so; most people will occupy positions between the two extremes. They might even occupy different positions on the continuum depending on the circumstances. For example, a person might feel generally conservative, believing that it is most often better to prevent a suicider dying than to refrain from intervention, because the odds are stacked against a person's potentially fatal self harming having been intended to bring death. And yet she might believe that sometimes it would be right to allow a person to die; for example, she might think this in the case of an individual who had decided to kill himself because he was dying and in irremediable pain.

Liberal or conservative?

It is difficult to predict who will be conservative or liberal on suicide, but religious beliefs apart, I think the more contact a person has had or may have with suicide and self harm, the less likely it is that she will tend towards a liberal position. Those who have had close contact with suicide and suicidal self harm or who are likely to have it in the future, are unlikely to view suicide romantically and more likely to view it as an assault on those who are left behind. As a result, they are I think much less likely to be willing to allow another person to die if they find him acting suicidally, than those who have not had such contact. By contrast, those who have not had close contact with suicide (and who do not especially expect to have it in the future) are unlikely to have thought through the practicalities of actually allowing another human person to die. If they share what I think is the commonplace belief that the ability and freedom to be in control of one's life is one of the most important values for human persons, they may believe in a general way that human beings are entitled to decide what to do with their lives. And they are more likely to find it easy to look at the phenomenon in rather a romantic way, viewing it (through rose coloured spectacles) primarily as an expression of autonomy, than they would if they had had close contact with human self destruction. Some people might object to my use of the expression 'romantic' to describe a possible view of suicide. However, I think it describes the kind of attitude I am using it to refer to rather well: an attitude as the result of which, like the person engaged in new love, people do not examine too closely the complexity of the situation they are considering, because they are seduced by some particular aspect of it.

Moving from the liberal to the conservative end of the continuum

I used to think of myself as a suicide liberal because I believe that taking personal responsibility for one's life is a very important feature of what it is to function fully as a human person. I thought that suicide was simply a matter of personal choice, that a person had a right to do away with his life if he wished to do so, because our lives are our own and we are entitled to do with them what we will. I therefore believed that someone who came across a suiciding individual should stand back and allow him to get on with it, that to interfere in another's suicide would be wrong.

Then, as a psychiatric social worker, I was asked to go out in the middle of the night to identify the body of a client who had jumped in front of a car. I had to deal with the aftermath of this death and of that of another client who poured a gallon of petrol over himself and set light to it. On numerous occasions distressed clients threatened to kill themselves unless I went to visit them immediately. I was involved with clients who had suicided unsuccessfully, and with others who had gestured suicide successfully. On one occasion a client swallowed large numbers of pills in my presence and on another I discovered a client lying in a pool of blood, because following a large overdose which had damaged her stomach, she had vomited up its contents. As I stood by Gloria's bedside the thought ran through my mind that since her life really was dreadful and I could see no realistic hope for improvement in the circumstances that repeatedly caused her to lose hope of change for the better, perhaps I should leave quietly and allow her suicide to proceed as I had no doubt she intended it to proceed, till it ended with her dead. But then I thought about how much I would miss her in all her madness, of how much poorer I thought the world would be without her. This didn't persuade me that I was right. But then I thought about how I would feel after she was dead; I thought about the worry I would have that my action (or lack of it) might be misconstrued by my managers and/or the media so that I might be thought of as a social worker who did not care enough to save my client. After all, they would not see the act of leaving a client to die as one born out of compassion; that was not their style. So I moved quickly and telephoned for an ambulance and had Gloria taken to hospital where she remained unconscious for many days before waking up, fortunately none the worse for her long sleep.[2]

As a result of these and other experiences my attitudes changed; I became less liberal, more conservative. They changed not simply because I was emotionally wounded by these experiences, though this was certainly true, but because they caused me to reconsider the basis of my beliefs, to take stock of what I judge to be important and to reflect upon the fact that suicide can be harmful to people other than the person who kills himself. In many circumstances, others will be the only ones who will be harmed by suicide because death may well be in the interests of the person who dies; sometimes, indeed, suicide may be intended to harm others. The change in my views also came about partly as the result of reflection upon the range of acts that self harm can represent. Since, as I have already discussed, a sequence of self harming actions may represent more than one act, it is difficult to be certain when a person who has taken such action really did want to die. Realising not only that this was the case but also that most apparent suicide attempts are nothing of the kind,[3] I came to believe that it will most often be best to intervene in order to prevent apparent suicides dying.

NOTES

1   I do not intend to enter into a discussion of 'rights'. What is most often meant when people claim that a person has the right to suicide is something like, ' He should be able to kill himself without interference.'

2   Lest anyone should think my brief flirtation with the idea of just allowing Gloria to die scandalous I should offer the further information that the time that elapsed from entering her home by kicking the door down to calling for an ambulance, was very short – perhaps two minutes. Perhaps I should add that the visit, which was prompted by a hunch that something bad was going on, was an impromptu one which occurred while I was on the way to a restaurant with my wife to celebrate our wedding anniversary. Our celebratory dinner did not happen that night.

3   I do not intend to offer statistical information to support my remarks; those who doubt what I claim can easily reassure themselves that there really are far fewer suicides than there are acts that resemble suicides but are not intended to end in death.

12

AUTONOMY, PATERNALISM AND INTERVENTION IN SUICIDAL ACTS

The two concepts autonomy and paternalism are frequently linked to one another because action that is taken by one person that denies another the possibility of exercising autonomy over his life is seen as paternalistic. In this chapter I will say a little about autonomy and paternalism although I will not be exploring these concepts in depth, but merely saying sufficient to make it more clear what meanings should be attached to my uses of them.[1] After that I will discuss some of the different ways in which one person may intervene in the suicidal self harming act of another, from simple discussion to coercive intervention to change the course of events.

THINKING ABOUT AUTONOMY

Autonomy is frequently held up as an important good for people. Essentially the ability and freedom to be in control of one's life, it is associated with a wide range of other ideas including individual liberty, self determination, freedom of choice, and accepting responsibility for one's moral positions.

In order to be able to act autonomously, a person must be free from constraint by external forces, and from domination by or excessive influence from, the will of others; the autonomous person has a will of her own and pursues goals that she chooses, not goals that are chosen for her. She has a developed self and is aware of that self as the author of actions; she has the capacity to make considered choices and is aware of acting for reasons that are connected to her goals and purposes.

It is interesting to think carefully about when and how children develop the skills, knowledge and awareness that are necessary for autonomy. My guess is that though for most people autonomy

164

develops gradually from the earliest stages of childhood, the way in which this happens and the speed with which it happens depend very much on the way in which we are reared, and in particular on the extent to which we are treated as people. Most children are less autonomous than most adults, though some people with very severe learning disabilities, for example, will fail to develop autonomy to any measurable extent even when they are physically full grown. Inevitably also, as the result of brain damage or disease, severe psychological disturbance or senility, some people who have developed the capacity for autonomy, lose it or lose it to some extent.[2] The capacity for autonomy is not an absolute thing and a person may have phases of her life during which she is, for a time, less autonomous than she is at others.

An autonomous individual is 'her own person' in the sense that she is able to choose what to do without constraints of either an external or an internal kind. Being fully autonomous is something that we may strive for without achieving, not least because each of us carries in our life history constraints of which we are unaware. Using the language of behavioural psychology some people would talk, for example, about constraints that result from both natural and contrived conditioning; in other words they would claim that our capacity for autonomy is influenced both by aspects of our upbringing and by aspects of our physical and social environment. Those who use the language of psychodynamic theory, on the other hand, would refer to constraints arising partly as a result of the influence of the 'super-ego': the internalised parent which directs, coerces or otherwise influences our actions and decisions, and partly as a result of the 'id': that primitive source of desires that socialisation and becoming a person is partly about bringing under control.

So a person's capacity for autonomy may be influenced by her psychological make-up, upbringing and other environmental influences. In addition her ability to exercise her capacity for autonomy can be influenced by a range of other factors. For example, it may be defective because, for the moment, something is interfering with her ability to think straight. A wide variety of things could interfere in this way, most obviously perhaps emotional or psychological disturbance, though other things such as overtiredness, divided loyalties, political pressure and moral confusion could also do so.

It is sometimes argued that in order to be autonomous a person must be in possession of relevant and reliable information; defects in autonomy could thus arise from defects in, or misapprehensions of, information. Thus, for example, Lindley (1988) thinks that when Aegeus jumped to his death because he believed Theseus to be dead, he was not acting autonomously because he was acting on the basis of false information.

A person could thus have the capacity for autonomy and yet act non-autonomously or less autonomously because her ability to exercise this capacity somehow is, or has been, interfered with. For example, a person whose thinking is controlled by others cannot act autonomously; one who acts in accordance with false information that she has been fed by others acts less autonomously as a result; and one who is upset by others, whether deliberately or inadvertently, may also have her capacity for autonomy interfered with.

A person could also act more autonomously as the result of interventions by others. Lindley (1987) talks about the fact that psychotherapy is largely about the attempt to increase people's autonomy: 'Psychotherapy is especially concerned to enable its clients to free themselves from obstacles to autonomy' (p. 227).

So we can restrict or enhance a person's ability to act autonomously by interfering with her mind. We can also do so by interfering with her body. For example, we can restrict a person's autonomy by incarcerating her in a prison, or by restraining her as she is about to jump out of a fast moving train. If it is less obvious that we can increase a person's autonomy by interfering with her body, consider the reasons for performing heart-bypass operations or orthopaedic surgery, or for giving people false limbs, hearing aids, or spectacles. Aren't these moves at least partly about increasing a person's ability to act and decide?

The degree of autonomy necessary before a person can autonomously choose death over life is difficult to determine. However, a person who can make such a decision autonomously will certainly be one who has developed the ability to decide for himself in most other areas of life, though to say this is not to say that he will always be able to do so. There is so much difficulty in deciding just what should count as 'autonomous enough' in the matter of self harm, that I think it is impossible to set out criteria by which it may be determined whether a person who seems to have acted or to be acting suicidally is autonomous enough for his act to count as suicide. This means that it will be very difficult for a person who finds another either in the midst of, or about to engage in, an apparently suicidal act, to determine whether he is in the relevant

166

sense, and in the relevant degree, autonomous. Of course, the problem is likely to be more acute the less knowledge she has of him.

Autonomy and intervention in the lives of others

Autonomy is frequently used in liberal arguments against uninvited intervention in the lives of others. For example, it features in the argument that since no one has the right to interfere in the autonomous act of another, interfering in suicide is something we should not do. More surprisingly perhaps, autonomy is sometimes pointed to not only by suicide conservatives but by those suicide liberals whose views are less than extreme, as a reason for intervening in the suicidal acts of others. The view expressed by such a liberal, which I have already described, would be that since it is in the interests of the suicide that his action be as autonomous as possible, intervention is warranted in order to ensure that he is autonomous in his self harming. On the conservative side of the suicidal fence, there are several ways in which autonomy may be used in arguing in favour of intervention in suicide and in other deliberate and serious self harmings. For example, it might be argued that since a person who was autonomous would not kill himself, anyone who is killing himself cannot be autonomous, and that therefore we should intervene in suicidal acts whenever possible. Or it might be argued that intervention protects the individual's future autonomy interests because if he dies, he will have none.

THINKING ABOUT PATERNALISM

In paternalism there is often a conflict between what the person who is the object of the paternalistic behaviour prefers or wants and what others judge to be in his best interests; as a result, paternalism is often defined in terms of one person's acting in what she takes to be another person's best interests even when that other might wish to act otherwise. I would define paternalism like this:

> *An act, whether of omission or commission, will be paternalistic if, without the intention to harm, it restricts the liberty of some autonomous other or others to act – whether by omission or commission – in ways that they might otherwise act, provided that the agent is aware of the restrictions her*

actions impose or would continue with them regardless, if she was aware.

The central feature of this definition is my claim that paternalistic acts must limit the ability to act of the subject/s in relation to whom they are performed. I have avoided the claim that paternalistic action must be intended to benefit its subject because not all paternalistic actions are intended to benefit him as an individual. For example, if without my agreement, my wife changed my lifestyle by substituting the butter in my diet with some substance based on vegetable oil, she would be acting paternalistically towards me regardless of whether her actions were motivated by concern for my health or because a vegan friend had persuaded her that it was morally wrong to use dairy products, in which case naturally I would also be deprived (at home at least) of a number of other products.

There will be different varieties of paternalism depending on other features of the acts in question. Where the act is carried out with the intention of aiding a person in some way, we might talk of *best interests paternalism*. Where, as is the case with corporate strategies such as lacing a public water supply with some chemical that has been found to be generally beneficial to health, it is carried out to benefit a whole population although individuals of that population might be harmed, we might talk instead of *utilitarian paternalism*. Where the action, though seeming to benefit the subject, is actually intended to benefit the agent, we might refer to *self interested paternalism;* an example of this would be where one person interferes in another's suicide, not for the suicider's benefit but for her own – because she does not want him dead, for example.

Paternalism involves interfering with the ability of others to act autonomously in the sense of taking responsibility for themselves and for their actions or omissions; it is an invasion of privacy, by which the paternalist imposes some plan of her own on others and prevents them living their lives in the way that they wish. Paternalistic actions in relation to another can involve removing his liberty to act in significant areas of his life; but it can also involve taking away his liberty in less significant areas. So, for example, I could interfere paternalistically in your life both by preventing you from swallowing a bottle of sleeping pills and by preventing you from swallowing a piece of chocolate cake. In relation to the second of these my paternalistic action could take different forms, from snatching the cake from your hand as you raise it to your lips, to arranging that what you eat as a sweet after your (healthy high fibre brown bread, low-fat spread, salad and low fat cheese) sandwich, is a healthy apple and not the chocolate cake you would have chosen had I given you the choice; I can arrange this by making sure that you do not have the choice because all I offer is the healthy apple.

Paternalism will often, but not always, result from a feeling on the part of the paternalistic agent or agency that he (or they) are somehow superior. In the case where I change your lunchtime menu because I think I know what is best for you, my paternalism does involve this kind of superior–inferior relationship (our relationship may not in fact be such, but I certainly act as if it is). On the other hand a government could intervene paternalistically in the diet of its citizens by banning chocolate cake (as the USA banned alcohol during the years of prohibition) without such a relationship of superiority–inferiority being implied, because they could ban chocolate cake in the interests of the overall public good rather than because they believed any particular individual citizen to be faulty in his estimation of what is good for him.

The view that paternalism usually results from some agent or agency believing herself (or themselves) to be somehow superior to those over whom they exert paternalistic influence is very common. The arrogance that is often implied by a paternalist believing herself to be superior to another in whose life she interferes is perhaps partly responsible for the distaste with which many people view paternalism. However, it is probably the great emphasis that is placed, within 'liberal' societies such as ours, on the value of autonomy that contributes chiefly to a situation where paternalism is frequently frowned upon. That the main reason paternalism is thought bad is that it is concerned with an invasion of autonomy, is supported by the fact that some actions would be frowned upon when performed in relation to most adults, but not when performed in relation to children and adults who are considered non-autonomous or barely autonomous. It would be unusual to label acts that, performed in relation to an autonomous adult would be considered paternalistic, as paternalistic when performed in relation to those who have not developed autonomy to a measurable extent. Whereas it is often thought objectionable to interfere in the lives of autonomous individuals in ways that deny them opportunities for responsible choice, acting in such ways towards those who are considered incapable of autonomy is accepted because, for example, acting to protect them is considered to be the responsible thing to do.

Lindley (1988) asserts that 'The capacity to choose distinguishes us from the brutes, and to deny someone the chance to exercise the capacity (to act autonomously) is to treat her as less than human' (p. 57). Since paternalism involves taking away a person's possibility for autonomous choice, it is, by Lindley's analysis, to fail to respect her as a person. Lindley is by no means alone in placing such a very high value on autonomy. For example, in their book *Respect for Persons*, Downie and Telfer (1969) assert that impairing a person's abilities to choose and execute his own plan is 'to that extent to destroy him as a person' (p. 21). In discussing interventions in self harming in the next section I address the conflicts that arise for someone who believes in the principle of respect for others and hence wishes both to respect a person's wishes and to care for his welfare. The problem is that respecting a person's wishes will sometimes involve neglecting his physical welfare.

THINKING ABOUT INTERVENTION IN SUICIDE

Intervention in suicidal acts will often be aimed at preventing the death of the suicider. Indeed, what probably comes to mind most readily when one thinks about intervention in suicidal self harming is, in line with what we have seen in the movies or on TV, a range of dramatic actions designed to prevent the suicider taking the fatal step. However, intervention can take a number of forms and intervention will not always be aimed at preventing a suicidal act proceeding. Not only are there a range of different aims that an intervener might have in intervening, there may also be very different reasons for her doing so. For example, she may be motivated to do what is best for the suicider or others; or she may simply wish to do what is best for herself.

I will consider a range of different ways of intervening in suicide, from intervention of an apparently weak kind in which the intervener's intention is simply to talk with the suicider about what he is doing, through persuasion to coercive intervention to prevent a person killing himself. I will argue that the distinctions to be made between the different kinds of intervention are not as clear cut as it might at first seem they are.

Discussion of the suicider's intentions and wishes

Discussing a person's intentions with him is most often thought to be a neutral activity because it is thought possible to discuss something with someone without having an effect either on his views or on the actions he performs as a result of those views. Changes in the suicider's beliefs, hopes and intentions that took place following discussion of them with another person, would usually be considered to have emerged from the suicider's own reflections about his situation rather than as a result of the influence of the other person. Those who believe that discussion with a suicider is a neutral intervention would argue that it simply involves giving him an opportunity to work through his feelings and intentions in order that he may be absolutely sure that he really wants to take his life.

This kind of neutral stance on the part of one person towards the plans, expectations, feelings and so on of another, is at the heart of what has come to be known as 'non-directive counselling' and it has its roots in the early work of the American psychotherapist Carl Rogers. Rogers (1965) himself implies that the therapist should honour his client's right to choose death instead of life:

> But is the therapist willing to give the client the full freedom as to outcomes? Is he genuinely willing for him to choose goals that are social or anti-social, moral or immoral? If not, it seems doubtful that therapy will be a profound experience for the client. Even more difficult, is he willing for the client to choose regression rather than growth or maturity? to choose neuroticism rather than mental health? to choose to reject help rather than accept it? to choose death rather than life?
>
> (p. 48)

But even if those who have trained in counselling of a non-directive kind can avoid influencing their clients, most people who discuss a suicidal person's plans and intentions with him will not be thus trained and it is likely that they will allow their feelings and beliefs to enter into the discussion, perhaps especially if the suicidal person is someone with whom they have a close relationship. It is in any case doubtful how feasible it is to hold a neutral discussion about a topic of such importance as a person's plans to end his life. Even if it is, however, it is worth noting that if discussing a suicider's situation with him is a worthwhile thing to do, those who do it must believe that there is some chance that he will change as a result of the discussion; otherwise there is no point in their discussing things with him. Indeed it is most likely the case that they hope that some change will occur even if the change they hope for amounts only to a growth in the suicider's certainty that what he is doing is what he wants to do and that his reasons for taking this action are sane and sensible. If such a change occurs it will occur because the intervener has given him the opportunity to reconsider and thus the intervener will have influenced his beliefs; what the intervener who feels neutral may be able to claim is that it is not her intention to bring about any particular change in the suicider, that her ends would be served just as well by a strengthening of his resolve as by a change of heart on his part.

Most often discussion would take place during the planning stages or while the suicider is making his preparations, that is, before suicidal steps have actually been taken. However, it could take place afterwards. There is a scene in Michael Winner's film *The Mechanic* (Winner, 1971) in which Charles Bronson, who plays a super cool hit-man, sits quietly watching a young woman bleed from serious, self inflicted wounds to her wrists. As she slowly bleeds to death he discusses with her the likely course of events as the bleeding takes its toll. A suicide intervener in real life (if he had the nerve) could have a similarly calm discussion with a suicider who had taken an overdose or inflicted wounds which would result in his death, which was aimed simply at giving him the opportunity to say something about his intentions, perhaps to reconsider them; the case of hunger strikers is probably the variety of suicidal act where such discussion is most likely to take place.

Persuasion

Secondly, and more strongly, intervention can amount to persuasion where the attempt is made to persuade the suicide to change his mind about killing himself. Persuasion can take place before the suicider has taken his planned suicidal steps. For example, it can take place before the suicide puts the pills in his mouth and classically, in the movies, it takes place as, buffeted by the wind, he perches on a window ledge high on a multi-storey block preparing to jump. However, persuasion can also take place even after a suicide has taken his planned suicidal steps. For example, in the case of a drug overdose or self wounding, an intervener might have the opportunity, even after the suicide has acted, to persuade him to go to hospital to have his stomach pumped or wounds attended to.

Some persuasion, even when it occurs before a suicide has begun in earnest, constitutes an interruption in a suicide; but not all persuasive interventions involve taking action that interrupts the attempt. Consider the situation where someone tries to persuade a friend who has taken an overdose to seek help. If after his intervention the intervener is satisfied that the suicide autonomously wishes to die, he may simply walk away, allowing the pills to take their intended effect.

Coercive intervention

Coercive intervention can take place both before and after the suicidal action is taken and it will take different forms depending on the chosen method of suicide and the point at which it takes place. Before suicidal action is taken, coercive interventions could vary from removing a bottle of pills from a friend who has announced his intention to wash them down with a bottle of Scotch, to rugby tackling (from the side) someone who is about to jump from a cliff. Where it takes place after the suicide has taken steps to procure his death, coercive intervention will usually involve taking steps to undo the work done by the suicide. Such interventions could include, for example, forcibly feeding a hunger striker, having an overdoser's stomach cleaned out, or binding the wounds of someone who has cut his wrists.

The overlap between discussion, persuasion and coercion

Though I have described these varieties of intervention in suicide as if they are discrete, in reality, discussion, persuasion and coercion will often overlap to some extent. Some people who intend merely to discuss a suicider's plans with him will, by their method of discussion, induce him to persuade himself to change his mind (or perhaps to become more definite in his determination to end his life). And some will be so forceful in their persuasion that it will amount to verbal coercion; this might, for example, be the case where a persuader uses religious arguments to persuade an individual not to proceed with his suicide because he becomes fearful of the consequences of dying in sin. In addition, different interveners will have different opinions about what kind of intervention is justifiable. Someone who is basically liberal on the matter of suicide, but who believes that it is in the interests of a suicide to be maximally autonomous in his act, might believe that discussing his plans with him is not only justifiable, but a mark of respect for him as a person.[3] A paternalistic suicide conservative, on the other hand, might believe that persuasion or even coercion of a moral, emotional or physical kind is not only justifiable but required.

And so depending on who a suicide or suicide gesturer is found by, his fate may be very different. A suicide who is discovered by a person who is strongly liberal on suicide may decide that he still really wants to die and redouble his efforts as soon as possible and a suicide gesturer discovered by the same liberal might also decide that whatever his intention when he acted, he really wants to die. On the other hand, if he is discovered by someone who is convinced that suicide is always irrational and is good at persuasion, a suicide might give up his self harming behaviour and return to life chastened and persuaded that there are other and better ways of working at his problems. His fate might also depend, to some extent, on characteristics of the intervener other than her beliefs about whether suicide is a good or a bad thing and whether in general people have the right to arrange their deaths. For example, after talking to an empathic and experienced non-directive counsellor, intent on merely discussing his feelings with him, one person might decide that he really and rationally does want to die, whereas another might come to see that really he wants only to have an effect on others which he could achieve at a cost lower than his life. On the other hand, if they were found by someone who was less committed to the idea that influencing others in their life decisions is to fail to respect their autonomy, or less skilled in avoiding influencing others, the first might unintentionally be persuaded to refrain from killing himself while the second might be induced into killing himself just to show that he can.

Of the three varieties of intervention in another's suicidal action that I have discussed, the first two – discussion and persuasion – both depend upon its being possible for the intervener to communicate with the suicider. This will not always be possible; for example, if the suicider was unconscious following an overdose, discussion of any kind would be impossible unless steps were first taken to intervene in his act. In such a case, coercive intervention is the only course open to the intervener. Even if she believes that autonomous individuals who wish to kill themselves should be

174

permitted to do so, she will have to stop the attempt in order to try to find out whether the suicider has taken his action autonomously intending to be dead. So sometimes coercive intervention may take place in the name of autonomy; in the case of a serious overdose, where a suicider is ill as the result of his actions, it might be several days, even weeks, before attempts at discussion or persuasion can take place, and before any attempt can be made to discover whether death was indeed his aim.

What is at stake when one person intervenes in another's suicidal act?

Apart from the effects of suicide on others, which I will consider later, two things are at stake when it comes to considering whether to intervene in another's suicide:

1 The idea that human lives are generally thought valuable.
2 The idea that for human lives to have maximum value, their bearers must have as much control as it is possible to have over them; in other words, the idea that autonomy matters.

Roughly speaking these may be thought of in terms of concern for a person's welfare and care for her as an autonomous person. The first would lead us to intervene where possible in events that are likely to lead to a human life being prematurely ended. The second would lead us to refrain from intervening in self killings, at least in cases where they seemed to be the result of autonomous acts.

If a person comes on another who appears to have taken suicidal action but is still living, adherence to the notion that human lives are valuable, and thus to be saved where possible, will often conflict with adherence to the idea that autonomy is an important good for human persons. The conflict arises because welfare is often considered primarily in physical terms. A person who adopts such a narrow view of welfare must decide between doing what is in the interests of the suiciding individual, physically speaking, and respecting his wish to die.

But things are more complex than this. First, there may be occasions where a person's autonomy may be best served by preventing a suicide bid from progressing further; this would be the case, for example, where we are sure that the bid will not end in death but rather in a situation where the suicide is worse off in terms of autonomy than he was before he took his suicidal action. Secondly,

175

the conflict between looking out for a person's welfare and respecting his autonomy becomes less clear if it is allowed that a person's welfare is to be considered not only in physical but also in psychological (even spiritual) terms. In that case, it could be argued in relation to at least some suicides, that a person's welfare is best served by allowing him to die.

NOTES

1 I discuss my views of autonomy and paternalism at greater length in Fairbairn (1992d).
2 A physically disabled person (or person with a physical disability – take your pick according to your interpretation of political correctness in this matter) who has developed the capacity for autonomy might find that she is handicapped or disabled (again choose your term according to your view of political correctness) in her expression of it by the social and physical environment in which she lives. And so a disabled person's ability to act autonomously may be reduced as much by moving, geographically, to a place that is less facilitative of her autonomous acts, as it might by her becoming physically less able.
3 This position is adopted by Harris (1985); some problems with this view, and others that Harris holds, are discussed in Chapter 13.

13

JUSTIFYING
INTERVENTION 1
Arguments from autonomy

The problems that arise when a person is faced with suicide or a range of related human acts, including those that I have referred to as 'suicide gestures' and 'cosmic roulette', are both moral and practical in nature. They are practical problems because they involve decisions about how to act. They are moral problems because the reasons that we might have for acting in a particular way in relation to another person's self harming will begin with our beliefs about the value of human life, the value of autonomy, what it is to respect another as a person, and whether intervention in another's life can be justified or even required, and if so under what circumstances. In this chapter and the next I shall say a little about arguments justifying intervention in the suicidal acts of others. In Chapter 14, I shall discuss the argument that intervention is always justified as a way of protecting oneself, or others, from harm. For the moment I want to say something about other grounds that may be put forward to justify intervention, that refer to the autonomy of the self harming individual.

In thinking about how one might react in situations where one is confronted with what is, or looks as though it may be, a suicide, two questions suggest themselves:

1 When is it permissible (i.e. morally right) to intervene in another's attempt (or apparent attempt) to end his life?
2 When is it permissible (i.e. morally right) not to intervene in another's attempt (or apparent attempt) to end his life?

The first question represents the dilemma faced by those who incline towards the liberal end of the liberal/conservative continuum on suicide, but are aware that some apparently self destructive acts are no more than gestures at suicide or gambles with life and death, or who worry about the possibility that some people may attempt to kill themselves irrationally.

The second question represents the dilemma faced by someone who, although inclined towards a secular version of the conservative view, nevertheless accepts that there may be times when an individual might have rational reasons for wishing to be dead, and believes that in such cases allowing him to die might be the caring thing to do.

The reason that these questions present problems for those who are neither committed liberals nor conservatives on suicide is rooted in the view that autonomy is a primary good for human persons. As a result of this emphasis on autonomy, many people think that except in the case of children and of adults who for some reason are incapable of responsible decision making, it is nearly always wrong to take control of the lives of others unless invited to do so.

ARGUMENTS FROM AUTONOMY

Intervention in suicidal acts is most commonly justified by referring to the autonomy of the suicidal individual. For example, it is commonly believed that intervention in the suicidal acts of others is justified where the individual is unable to act autonomously because he has not developed the capacity for autonomy, has lost it to some extent, or because something is interfering with his ability to exercise his capacity for autonomous action. It is because autonomy is commonly thought to be centrally important to being a human person, that intervention may also be thought to be justifiable in cases of suicidal self harm where the suicider's autonomy is threatened. I want to say something about each of these justifications for intervention in suicidal acts. I shall begin with those that hinge upon the individual's ability to act autonomously; then I shall consider arguments in favour of intervention on the grounds that it will protect the autonomy interests of the individual.

Intervention in the suicidal acts of those whose actions are less than fully autonomous

Intervention is commonly believed to be justified in relation to the actions of those who for some reason are thought to be lacking in the capacity for autonomy, whether in the long or short term, because such individuals are thought to be incapable of making reasonable decisions about whether particular courses of action are in their best interests. It is also commonly thought that intervention to prevent harm, including the harm that would be caused by death, would be justifiable where the ability to exercise autonomy is impaired or essential information is lacking.

Immaturity or intellectual impairment

Most people would agree that those who are lacking in the capacity for autonomy because of immaturity or intellectual impairment may justifiably be protected against themselves because they are incapable of thinking through their actions well enough to allow them to reach properly informed and responsible decisions. And so most people would agree that a person who is intellectually impaired because of genetic or congenital factors, or as the result of brain injury or disease, may be prevented from ending his life because though he could kill himself he could not understand what he was doing and hence could not suicide. Though this sounds straightforward, difficulties arise in delineating the level of understanding below which it may be assumed that a person does not understand what he is doing sufficiently to justify intervention.

Most people would also agree that a child could justifiably be prevented from taking his life. The assumption that is being made is that a child, like an adult with a severe intellectual impairment, is not autonomous enough to suicide. But is this always the case? Whereas I guess that no one would allow that a 2 year old could autonomously decide to take his life, some might wonder whether at least some 10 year olds could, or perhaps some 9 year olds, or 8 year olds or 7 year olds? One inclination might be to think that there must be some age at which a person may usually be assumed to be capable of the degree of rational thought necessary for autonomy. But as I argued in Chapter 11, autonomy is not like this. Children mature and become autonomous at different rates; and so age, while offering a guide, does not offer a watertight criterion. Measures of intellect are likewise of little help since intellectual measurement is inexact and in any case, intellectual level does not necessarily go hand in hand with autonomy.

So a child could kill himself, but until he had developed the requisite degree of autonomy, his self killing would not amount to suicide. Whether it did or not, most people would probably agree that intervention to prevent a child (however defined) ending his life would always be justified. It is worth noting a problem for those who maintain the liberal belief that everyone who is autonomous has the right to end his life, unless they are willing to include children of whatever age, who are clearly autonomous in their decision to kill themselves and who have thought about the nature of life and death and have good reason for wishing to be dead, in the category of those who they believe have the right to kill themselves.

Psychological disturbance

Where a person is psychologically disturbed, for example by severe depression or psychosis – such that though he thinks he knows what he is doing, actually he does not – intervention seems reasonable in order to prevent him ending his life. It is, of course, difficult to say what constitutes a sufficient degree of disturbance to justify intervention in the suicidal acts of others. However, I think it is clearly OK to prevent someone who is suffering from delusions or who has a greatly distorted view of things because of deep depression, from harming himself, at least in cases where his delusions or distorted world view underpin his self harming. Attempts at self killing in such cases cannot arise from a rational wish to be dead because the individual is, for a time at least, incapable of rational thought, at least in relation to those aspects of his life that impinge upon his reasons for self killing. Even if capable of rational thought in some sense, at least some of the time, the individual is acting on the basis of false 'information' resulting from his delusional system or distorted world view, rather than reality. So, for example, I believe that it would be in the interests of a deluded person's autonomy that we should prevent him from setting fire to himself because he believed that this was the only way to kill the ants that were infesting his body (if they were infesting his body I think we should try to help him get rid of them rather than allowing him to kill himself).

Although I believe that at least some individuals who have been diagnosed as suffering from a mental illness should be prevented from taking their lives because their ability to think clearly about what they want will be affected by their condition, I do not go along with the idea that a person who has set out on a suicidal path or expressed a wish or intention to do so is, for that reason alone, mentally ill. Nor do I think that we can intervene solely on the grounds that a person who has been diagnosed as suffering from mental illness of some kind is acting or has acted in a life threatening way, so as to end his life, because there will be cases where people are crazy and yet able rationally to suicide. Consider, for example, a person who suffers from encapsulated delusions in relation to a limited part of his life, but is rational the rest of the time. Intervention in such a person's suicide act could be justified on the grounds that his rationality was impaired, if he acted as a result of his encapsulated delusions, but not otherwise, unless there was other evidence that he was generally acting extremely irrationally. Or consider a person who has frightening psychotic episodes interspersed with rational 'windows' during which he is able to reflect on the psychotic parts of his life. Such a person might, in a rational window in the midst of a psychotic illness, decide to suicide rather than face the next psychotic episode. Though intervention on the grounds that he did not know what he was doing would be justifiable if he acted suicidally while floridly psychotic, it would not if his suicidal act was performed while he was not.

Where the individual is badly informed

Another common belief is that it is justifiable and perhaps even morally required of decent people to intervene in the suicidal actions of a person who acts on the basis of false or incomplete information, because actions based on false beliefs are less than autonomous. As a result, even though the suicider has the capacity for autonomy, he may be acting less than autonomously. Or at any rate, many people believe that in a situation where we knew something the suicider did not, which might affect his decision were he to be made aware, regard for his autonomy would lead us to intervene at least in order to share this information with him. Lindley (1988) illustrates this justification for benevolent paternalism in relation to suicidal self harm using the story of Theseus and Aegeus. He argues that had we known of Theseus' success, benevolent concern for Aegeus would at least have led us to try to inform him of this before he leaped because his action in jumping was going to be less than autonomous.

Where the person's autonomy interests are best served by intervention

Those who believe that each person has the right to choose the time

181

of his death would argue that it is in the interests of each person to be allowed to exercise his capacity for autonomy freely and without hindrance, even when that means that he must be allowed to kill himself if he wishes. And so the most important argument against intervention in suicidal acts is that intervention involves acting against the protagonist's autonomy. However, as I have already shown, some instances of intervention may take place in the name of autonomy.[1]

One kind of case where it could be argued that intervention would protect rather than harm autonomy would be where the person's autonomy is threatened by the action he is taking or proposing to take, for example, where a genuine suicide seems likely to fail with the tragic result that the autonomy interests of the individual in question are damaged. Lindley (1988) discusses a case of this kind. John is desperately depressed and about to jump off a bridge. If it was the case, Lindley argues, that we knew that John was likely to survive but that if he did he would probably spend the rest of his life in a hospital bed, non-interference would result in our allowing his autonomy interests to be damaged.

In a case where allowing a suicide to continue is likely to end with the individual alive but horribly handicapped, action in the name of autonomy could take more than one form. Most obviously, one could prevent the suicide progressing to the point at which harm is caused and the protagonist is faced with the tragedy of a life with greatly reduced autonomy; of course, this will only work if we are aware that the suicide is likely to fail with horrible results and things have not already gone so far as to have caused permanent damage. Less obviously, some people might suggest that if the suicide has already reached the point at which irreparable harm has been caused, one could ensure that the suicide act goes beyond that point and ends in death. Against this, of course, it might be argued that life with greatly reduced autonomy is better, in terms of autonomy, than no life, because when we are dead autonomy, like everything else, is not experienced at all.

Another range of cases in which autonomy would be served by intervening in suicide would be those in which the person, though extraordinarily upset with a current situation, would nevertheless be glad to be helped through it because what lies beyond it is worth getting to. This would be like pushing a young person through an exam because she really wants to pass but is worried about sitting the exam itself. In a way what is at question here is the balance between respecting long and short term interests. When Gloria, the blood vomiting client to whom I referred in Chapter 11, woke up after the incident in question, she told me that she had been serious in her intention to die. When I said, 'Yes, I know,' she went on 'But do you know what? I'm glad you stopped me.' I tell this story not as some kind of awful example to persuade those who would have allowed Gloria to die, as I thought seriously about doing, to think again. The details of one case do not constitute an argument. However, this story makes the point that even in the case of someone who really wishes for death, who seriously intends to bring it about and has objectively speaking good reasons for wishing to be dead, wishes can change drastically; it emphasises the fact that long term and short term interests can be quite distinct. Before acting in such circumstances, those for whom the protection of autonomy is of prime importance will have to become clear about whether they believe that long or short term interests are most important.

There is, finally, another range of cases where it might be thought justifiable to interfere in another person's suicidal action in order to protect his autonomy. This line of justification would only be open to those who share my belief that not all that looks like suicide *is* suicide, although I hope I have said enough to persuade even the most unthinking suicide liberal to agree with this. It might, for example, be argued that where it seems likely that an individual has gestured suicide or engaged in a game of cosmic chance rather than having attempted to end his life, anyone who finds him should intervene on the grounds that death will probably not serve his interests. Since they do not intend to die, the autonomy of those who gesture suicide or play cosmic roulette is not protected by allowing them to harm or kill themselves; and so, the argument would go, any caring person should do what she can to prevent him coming to harm regardless of whether she is liberal or conservative in relation to suicide. This would be especially easy to argue when the individual in question had developed a habit of acting in dangerous ways.

OTHER VIEWS OF THE PROPRIETY OF INTERVENTION ON AUTONOMY GROUNDS

Even some writers who incline towards the liberal view of suicide agree that on some occasions intervention is permissible on the grounds that it is in the interests of the person's autonomy to intervene.

Persuasion and limited coercion – Glover's view

Glover (1977) expresses an interesting, though I think over-simplistic, view which rests on the belief that reasoning does not encroach on a suicider's autonomy because it does not prevent him from doing what he wants. He writes:

> Where we think someone bent on suicide has a life worth living, it is always legitimate to reason with him and to try to persuade him to stand back and think again. There is no case against reasoning, as it in no way encroaches on the person's autonomy. There is a strong case in its favour, as where it succeeds it will prevent the loss of a worth-while life. (If the person's life turns out not to be worth-while he can always change his mind again.) And if persuasion fails, the outcome is no worse than it would otherwise have been.
>
> (pp. 176–7)

Glover thus seems to believe that it will be relatively easy for a suicide to return to the business of killing himself after his attempt at self killing has been stopped. This belief is convenient for those who both want to express care for others, and to avoid the charge of unwarranted interference. However, it fails to take account both of the complexity of suicidal self harm and of those who engage in it. Whether reasoning and persuasion encroach on a person's autonomy depends on how susceptible he is to persuasion and how persuasive the persuader is; some people will be persuaded rather easily and in such cases at least, persuasion does interfere with autonomy. Just as we can increase an individual's autonomy by talking with him – as those who engage in psychotherapy and counselling set out to do – it is possible to reduce an individual's autonomy by talking to him. Reasoning with someone whose sense of self and of self direction is well developed and established, may not interfere with his autonomy; however, if he was not a terribly autonomous person in the first place things may be different.

Not only does Glover think that a certain amount of persuasion is legitimate, he also believes that coercion to prevent suicide is sometimes justifiable, and what's more, he is willing to restrain a person from suiciding on more than one occasion: 'Where someone has decided that his life is not worth living and is not deflected from his decision by persuasion, it is legitimate to restrain him by force from his first attempt, or even several attempts' (p. 177). However, there is a limit on the amount of prevention that Glover thinks is acceptable. Although he thinks that we should save as many worthwhile lives as we can, he adds the proviso that we should save only as many as is compatible with the use of paternalistic restrictions of autonomy of only a temporary kind in the case of sane adults, because he believes that 'a persistent policy of forcible prevention is a total denial of . . . autonomy' (p. 177).

So Glover is arguing that where a person has decided to kill himself and cannot be persuaded to reconsider, it is legitimate to restrain him. He believes that this does not deny his autonomy provided that we do not restrain him too often because 'If we prevent him once or a few times this gives him a chance to reconsider, and the decision later is still his own' (p. 177).

Glover does not think that his endorsement of 'limited coercion' should extend, for example, to the forcible feeding of people on hunger strike since they will have plenty of time to reconsider. At first sight this seems a truism. However, it is worth remembering the possibility that those who refuse food with the avowed aim of ending their lives may intend at the beginning of their action to do no more than bring about change in others; they may, in other words, intend to gesture a slow, horrid death rather than to die one. And, as I argued in Chapter 8, though they may have 'plenty of time to reconsider', the effects of malnutrition might creep up on them rendering them incapable of rational decision making. I think, therefore, that Glover's argument against force feeding is untenable because the actions of a hunger striker in refusing food are no more a clear indication that the individual intends to die than the actions of an overdoser in taking a large quantity of drugs are an indication that he intends to die.

Harris and 'maximally autonomous decisions'

Glover is not the only philosopher with liberal leanings who believes that paternalistic intervention in suicidal self harm may at times be permissible. For example, though he believes it is wrong to interfere in suicide attempts which result from maximally autonomous decisions, Harris (1985) believes that it is in the interests of an individual to make a decision of such major importance as that whether to take his own life 'as autonomously as possible' (p. 203) and hence that:

where we come upon an attempted suicide or a would-be suicide, it is the act of someone with respect for others to try to stop the suicide for the purposes of ascertaining the cause of any distress that has prompted the action and attempting to remedy it if possible. And of ensuring that the decision was maximally autonomous.

(p. 203)

Having intervened to assess the suicider's autonomy and to offer help to remedy his distress if possible, Harris thinks that:

if the distress is irremediable or the suicide does not want it remedied, and if the decision was maximally autonomous, then the bystander must allow the agent to control his own destiny, if that is what he wants, and no longer obstruct the attempt.

(p. 203)

Further than this he adds:

And if a bystander has made a further attempt at suicide impossible or very difficult, perhaps by destroying the means of suicide, it may be that he ought to replace what he has destroyed or otherwise assist the would-be-suicide.

(note 7, p. 269)

In practice of course, it is likely to be very difficult to decide whether a self destructive act does result from a maximally autonomous decision. I find it difficult even to decide how I would know a maximally autonomous decision if I came across one. How are we to decide that a person really wants to kill himself?

Faced with a suicide or gestured suicide in the flesh rather than in the mind, it will typically be difficult for the potential intervener to decide whether a person's decision was maximally autonomous. This will be so even if she is fortunate enough to have come across a suicide with whom it is possible to have a sensible discussion, who, for example, has not yet taken the overdose he has prepared, cut his wrists, or put his head in the gas oven. Someone who comes across a suicide before he enacts his death wish will at least have the opportunity to try to ascertain how autonomous his actions are. However, in most instances those who are faced with the problem of deciding whether or not they should intervene in another's suicide will be unable to do this, because most people who come across suicide will encounter a situation where the suicidal individual has already taken the possibly fatal step, is already on the way to death or disaster, and is perhaps already unconscious or otherwise incapable of communicating. In order to try to ascertain a suicider's level of autonomy it will thus often be necessary first of all to arrange his survival – like the good Samaritan (though if he turns out to have been serious in his endeavour the suicide may in the end view the intervener as a bad Samaritan).

I have been critical of Harris' idea that having stopped a suicider in order to ascertain whether he is acting in a maximally autonomous way and discovered that he is, we can then simply leave him to get on with things again; my main reason for this is that ascertaining whether he is autonomous is not a simple matter. However, in my view Harris also seems mistaken on several other grounds.

First of all, he ignores the practical difficulties of the kinds of situation he is discussing; in such situations people become involved emotionally, physically and spiritually. Those who find suiciders will typically intervene without thinking, in a reflex way. This will be just as true, I expect, of most suicide liberals as it will of suicide conservatives. Whether or not they are aware that suicide is what is afoot, most people are likely to intervene (whether directly or by going for help) if they come across another human being who is apparently dying, for whatever reason; most people find death and in particular the idea of allowing another person to die so upsetting that (barring squeamishness) they will do what they can to prevent it. And similar reasons, along perhaps with the failure to comprehend the reasons that could possibly make a person want to take his life, will, I think, lead most to intervene in the actions of someone they come across before he has actually taken suicidal action, in order to prevent him doing so or to attempt to dissuade him from this action.

Secondly, Harris seems to believe that intervening in a suicide is of no more significance than offering someone a cup of tea when he is rushing off to do something; having drunk the tea he can just set about his business as before. And Harris seems to think that after he has chatted calmly to someone who has interrupted his suicide, and passed muster as an autonomous person who does not wish to have his distress remedied or whose distress cannot be remedied, the suicide can just return to the business of killing himself. Glover, as I have already pointed out, also seemed to believe that everyone who has once been persuaded to stop his suiciding behaviour can always begin another attempt, if his life is sufficiently bad.

It is naive to believe that it will always be easy for the agent of an interrupted suicide to begin again. Though a person who has once been prevented from taking his life theoretically has the opportunity to try again (he may indeed seize the first available opportunity to finish the job), in many cases, intervention will be more than a mere interruption from which the suicide may easily recover and some potential suicides, once stopped, will never again attempt to end their lives even though their desire to do so is hardly diminished. There are many reasons why this might be so. For example, it may have taken a suicide considerable time and effort to plan his death and to get over various qualms about procuring it; perhaps he is strongly religious and has had to get over qualms about doing what he thinks is wrong; perhaps he has found difficulty in working out a foolproof (or almost foolproof) method; perhaps he is simply cowardly and has taken weeks to summon the courage. In such a case the effort involved in finally taking the fatal step may have been so considerable that once prevented, the chances of the protagonist taking a similar step again are slim; intervention in such a case would, like suicide, be final. Being prevented once, while theoretically allowing the possibility that he can simply redouble his efforts to achieve his own death, might thus effectively mean the suspension of his chances of suiciding for ever. In such a situation the temporary restriction of autonomy would be no less serious a matter than restricting it in the longer term. Thus, unless a potential intervener knew whether the suicider in whose act he was contemplating intervening was the kind of person who, after intervention, would readily be able to try again, he would run the risk of interfering coercively in a way that had long term, ongoing effects rather than merely short term, temporary ones.[2]

The problems I have described in the last paragraph are common not only to Harris and Glover but to all who entertain the idea that a suicide once interrupted will always be able to begin again, so that interrupting him is not an all or nothing affair. To be fair, Harris takes account of the problem for those whose opportunities for suicide are limited, by his suggestion that it may be incumbent upon those who have intervened to replenish the means of death or otherwise to assist. But he cannot easily take account of the further problem I have outlined, that even those who have easy access to the means of death might be inhibited from trying again by interference because the most difficult element in coming to attempt suicide was, for them, not obtaining the means, but building up the courage (physical, emotional or spiritual) to do so.

There is another problem here. Having prevented a person's suicide once and decided that he really was intent, in an autonomous way on suicide, how is an intervener with liberal leanings going to decide whether to intervene again if she discovers him redoubling his efforts? Say, for example, Harris has prevented Mavis from suiciding, for the purpose of determining whether she was maximally autonomous, and that Mavis has persuaded him that she was. Consider the possibility that however serious she was at the time of her interrupted suicide bid, Mavis does not make another such bid for a few days; will Harris then believe that she is still autonomous, or will he have to intervene again (should he be unfortunate enough to stumble on her once more) in order to ensure that on this occasion Mavis really wants to do it? And what if Mavis leaves it not for a few days but only for a few hours, or even minutes before she acts again? How long must elapse between discovering (or deciding) that a person really is autonomous in his intention to kill himself and his trying again, before we should think it necessary, once more, to intervene to ensure that his act is *maximally autonomous*?

Suicides can change their mind about suiciding. So whereas if Mavis simply pursued the same course of action immediately, as if nothing had happened, Harris may be correct in assuming that she is still maximally autonomous, if she begins again but sets out on a different suicidal trajectory, perhaps using the supplies that Harris has given her to do so, I think Harris would be bound, as one with respect for persons to intervene once again, to ensure that Mavis really was still acting maximally autonomously. And what's more, I think he and everyone else who believed that though suicide is a person's right, it is the mark of someone with respect for persons to interrupt those who are attempting suicide for the purposes of ascertaining whether they are autonomous in their acts, would be obliged to interrupt Mavis each time they found her repeating her act, because none of us can ever be sure from one minute to the next, what another person is thinking or feeling.

Finally, I think that Harris is mistaken in placing so much emphasis on the idea that every person has the right to do what he wants with his life; he wants to protect this right both by refraining from interfering in the suicidal acts of another when he knows what the person wants and by interfering when he is unsure what the person wants. It is not that I disagree with the idea that having freedom and authority over one's life is very important, but rather that I believe there are other things that are also important, so much so that at times gratifying one's desires may have to be sublimated to them, even in the matter of whether one lives or dies. In giving such prominence to the importance of the idea that everyone has the right to direct his own life even down to the decision about whether to live it till he dies, Harris fails adequately to take account of the fact that those who find suiciders and suicide gesturers and cosmic rouletters and other suicidal self harmers whose acts may be dangerous, also need to be considered. I need not respect the wishes of others when to do so would cause me harm; and anyone whose suicide I come across unexpectedly will cause me harm. This is why, as I argue in the next chapter, I believe that in most circumstances intervention in suicide is justified on the grounds of self defence.

NOTES

1 Of course those who are not committed to the idea that to take one's life can be the ultimate expression of autonomy would believe that all intervention in suicidal self harm that prevents death will be positive as regards the individual's autonomy, because an individual who dies has no autonomy at all.

2 It is worth noting that if, as Glover and Harris believe, those who are thwarted in their attempts at suicide could always make another attempt, there would be good reason always to intervene in suicidal acts. Death is such a final thing that in general it would seem better to risk preventing the deaths of those who really want to die, than to risk allowing some people to die who really did not wish to do so. After all, if those who have been prevented from dying and may have been attempting to die will always have the opportunity to try again, there is no harm to be done by preventing them again and again. Indeed given that they are able to learn from their mistakes, they will have the opportunity to refine their approach so that in the end they can be successful with the minimum of fuss.

14

JUSTIFYING
INTERVENTION 2
Self defence and the defence of others

> Those of us who have had experience of actual suicides
> among those who were especially significant to us as relatives,
> friends or callers, will realise how awful the emotional wound-
> ing of death by suicide is.
>
> (Wertheimer, 1991, p. 93)

> It is not possible to take a morally neutral stance on suicide,
> since it is the most significant of all deaths in its impact on
> survivors, causing long-lasting grief and guilt and a high
> suicide-expectancy: in spouses, around one thousand times
> the average according to one study.
>
> (Fox, 1981, p. 46)

> suicide is 'the skeleton left by the deceased in the survivors'
> closet'.
>
> (cited by Fox, 1981, p. 426)

In Chapter 13, I discussed justifications of intervention in the suicidally self harming acts of others that referred to the autonomy of
the protagonist. I want, finally, to address what I consider to be the
strongest justification of all for interference in the suicidal act of
another person, that to do so amounts to self defence. The justification of interference on the grounds that it is necessary to defend
others from harm is closely related and in my view, only marginally
less strong.

What is in question here is paternalism of a kind that many
people would not refer to as paternalism because it neither arises
out of respect and care for the person, nor has as its focus the
welfare of the party in relation to whom the person acts. At first I
thought to refer to acts of this kind as instances of *self interested
pseudo-paternalism* to show that they differed from instances of
paternalism that would usually be recognised as paradigm cases.
Then in developing the definition of paternalism that I put forward

in Chapter 12, I came to realise that such cases are genuine cases of paternalism because they display the central features of paternalism by limiting the ability to act of the subject/s in relation to whom they are performed.

So where a person intervenes in another's suicidal act in order to protect her own welfare rather than the suicider's, she engages in that sub species of paternalism that I now refer to as *self interested paternalism*. There is nothing pseudo about it; this is genuine paternalism. In self interested paternalism the agent acts out of concern, not for the other, but for herself; this is not to say that she has no regard for the other but only that in this instance she is putting herself first.[1] Notwithstanding what paternalistic interveners might say about their reasons for acting as they do, much paternalism is self interested because it is more concerned with its agent's interests than with those of the suicider. I do not intend to sound moralistic here. Protecting one's own interests is always understandable and often morally justified.

Who are the victims of suicide?

It is common to find those who suicide or engage in other forms of suicidal self harm being referred to as *victims* whether they live or die and even when the intended consequences of the act can be construed as somehow beneficial for them. In most cases, it seems to me to be odd to say of a suicide that he was a victim because in general victims do not actively intend to bring about the result of which they are said to be a victim and those who suicide intend to do so. A suicide might be the victim of circumstances as the result of which he decides to suicide but he cannot be a victim of suicide because he was its agent.

However, there are some situations in which talking of victims may make sense. For example, where one person drives another to suicide, or to use Daube's turn of phrase, when one person 'suicides' another, thinking of the deceased individual as a victim does not seem unreasonable. In the case of self harmings not aimed at death that go wrong, so that the individual ends up dead when he expected and intended to end up alive, talking of the deceased as a 'victim' could perhaps also be justified even though the individual is the agent of his own end, because the individual in such a case is a victim in the same way that any accident victim is the victim of circumstances. Some other ways in which it might make sense to say of such an individual that he was a victim would be to say that he was a victim of his own stupidity, impulses or irrational state.

Though most often it does not make sense to refer to those who suicide as victims, in most situations where a person kills himself, there will be victims. The victims (and there may be many of them) will be others: his relations, friends, neighbours, colleagues, the man at the newspaper stand from whom he had bought his *Times* every morning for twenty years, the social worker who had tried hard to help him rebuild his life, the person who finds his body floating in the canal as he walks his dog, or who is driving the underground train that kills him. These victims will suffer the suicide in a way that the suicide, being dead, will not.

The idea that most people who come in contact with suicide, whether directly or in its aftermath, are wounded by their experience is common. For example, Wertheimer (1991), who has made an extensive study of the effects of suicide on those that she refers to as 'victims of suicide' and who others refer to as 'survivors', writes:

> The idea that a person chooses to die creates in us a profound sense of unease. Suicide challenges some of our most deeply held beliefs. It defies the cherished notion that all human life is sacred; it challenges the value of life itself, and places a question mark over the taboos against the taking of life. The suicide of another person forces us to question the value and meaning not only of life in general but of our own individual lives.
>
> (p. 1)

Wertheimer's point here concerns the existential anxiety that contact with suicide may induce. Eldrid (1988) is much more pointed in drawing attention to the bad effects of suicide on survivors. He cites Shneidman's summing up of the psychological effects of suicide:

> I believe that the person who commits suicide puts his psychological skeletons in the survivors' emotional closet – he sentences the survivors to deal with many negative feelings, and, more, to become obsessed with thoughts regarding their own actual or possible role in having precipitated the suicidal act or having failed to abort it. It can be a heavy load.
>
> (p. 272)

The effects of contact with suicide are likely to last for a long time, perhaps years and maybe for ever, especially for a person who has been directly involved. Wertheimer (1991) relates an account by a 29 year old woman who was 4 when her father killed himself:

> [My mother] sensed there was something wrong. She went whipping through the house and got to the foot of the stairs and started to scream and then ran out; and so I followed to see what she was screaming at – and he'd hung himself on the staircase; and I do remember quite vividly; I remember standing there looking; I haven't blotted it out. I haven't been told that either . . . it's a memory that's always been with me.
>
> (p. 37)

But as I have tried to make clear, it is not simply those who have been closely involved with a suicide or who have become closely involved with him in his suiciding who may suffer trauma. An ever widening circle of those who were related to the suicide may be affected. For example, Brock and Barnard (1988) write about the psychological effects of suicide on survivors:

> suicide has a dramatic ripple effect; the lives of relatives and friends are seriously damaged, in the form of emotional and mental disturbances, failure in life tasks, and repetition of suicide and other self-destructive behaviour.
>
> (p. 108)

If a successful suicide did not affect others, no one would be upset because they cared about the person's dying. No one would be upset because they had witnessed the incident, found his body, or otherwise been involved in the suicide or its aftermath. Suicide that did not affect others would result in no questions being asked about standards of care in the case of those who were receiving professional help and in no professionals being forced to question their competence and professionalism.

It is because of the suffering that involvement in another's suicide is likely to cause that I think those who are unwillingly involved may intervene without moral qualms.

Self interest, self defence and intervention in suicidal acts

I think that self interest is most often a sufficient justification for interfering in the suicidal actions of others. I can't avoid being involved in the outcome of a person's action if I find him suiciding, and since whether I act to save him or allow him to die, I am implicated, I think I can stop him because my feelings count, just as his do. Unless he has obtained their agreement to his suicide or has given them forewarning about what he intends to do and shared with them his reasons for acting as he does, a person who suicides offends grievously against friends and others who care about him; in addition he offends against anyone who is inadvertently involved in his dying. He offends against them because in acting as he does, he fails to respect them as people. And this offence is not offensive in the same sense that it is offensive to pick one's nose or make love in public; such acts on the part of others offend against the dignity or good taste of those who are offended against but in general they do not harm them. Suicide, however, is an offence in the much stronger sense that it harms those who are offended against. Those who have had close personal contact with suicide are likely to understand what I mean here. I am referring, for example, to the psychological and at times physical distress that may be caused by, for example, recurrent visions of the sight which met one's eyes when one discovered a suicide or suicide gesture; I am referring also to the persistent doubts that may plague those who punish themselves with the thought that perhaps they could have done something to help a suicide before he acted, if they had only been more empathic and caring.

In Chapter 13, I discussed Harris' views about intervention in suicide (Harris, 1985). You will recall that Harris uses the expression 'bystanders' to refer to those who find suicides. This term seems inappropriate to me because it kind of neutralises their part in the event, as if they are not involved in the human tragedy in which, in truth and however unintentionally, they have become involved. In practice most people who suicide are found either by relatives or friends or by people with public responsibilities: social workers, nurses, doctors, policewomen and the like. But even if they are not, everyone who finds a suicider, dead or alive, has feelings and moral beliefs, and is vulnerable to the harm that involvement in a suicide can cause. To call those who find a person suiciding or suicide gesturing or gambling with his life 'bystanders' denies that they have any real connection to the event. In contrast to this I guess that most people who have had direct experiences with suicide and other serious self harming will have felt intimately and inextricably bound up emotionally, intellectually and morally with what was going on, hardly able just to stand by passive and uninvolved.

It might be thought that those who come across a person who

intends to take his life will be affected in different ways depending, for example, on the extent to which they are related to him. Thus it might be thought, for example, that close friends and relatives are likely to be most badly affected. Though this seems to make sense initially, I think that other factors are likely to be more significant in shaping the extent to which others are affected by contact with another person's self inflicted death. For example, I think that the most significant factor affecting the degree and extent of upset caused to those that Harris refers to as 'bystanders' is likely to be the nature of the suicide act; my guess is that those that involve shooting, hanging, jumping in front of moving vehicles, the ingestion of corrosive poisons and other violent suicides will be more difficult to stomach than those that are relatively genteel – such as straightforward overdosing with prescribed medication.

I have discussed the liberal position on suicide which gives rise to the view that those who find others in the middle of a suicidal act ought to allow those others to get on with ending their lives because they have the right to do so. To adopt the view that many people who lean towards the liberal position do, that intervention in self harmings is wrong except where the person is (or may be) acting non-autonomously, is to fail to take account of the feelings of others who are, and will be, involved. This is true even of those whose liberal views are what we might describe as being of a *reformed* kind, because they would claim as Harris and Glover do, that there are occasions on which it would be legitimate to prevent a suicide proceeding, for whatever reason. Even reformed liberals have a narrow focus when it comes to thinking about intervention in suicidal acts, because in them they look only at the significance of the possible death in the life (or death) of the suicider and not at its significance in the lives of others. So, for example, as I have already pointed out, Harris claims that where a suicide does not want his distress remedied or it is irremediable, and his decision is found to be maximally autonomous (whatever that means and however it is to be ascertained), those who come across a suicider must allow him 'to control his own destiny . . . and no longer obstruct the attempt' (1985, p. 203). And as we have seen, although Glover believes that limited intervention is permissible in order to save as many worthwhile lives as possible, he believes that persisting with coercive prevention where a person attempts to kill himself on more than one occasion 'is a total denial of . . . autonomy' (1977, p. 177).

In contrast to the views not only of extreme liberals, but even of reformed liberals like Harris and Glover, I think that it will nearly always be legitimate to intervene in suicide, to prevent it proceeding even where one is aware that the suicider really is a *suicide* because he really does want to die and is autonomous in his wish to do so. It is not just that I think that intervention in suicidal acts will most often be justifiable because the likelihood of a suicidal act's being a suicide is rather small (though I do believe this), it is also that I believe those who come across a suicidal act have a right to defend themselves against the harm that they might suffer as a result of being involved[2] in another's death, if death is the result. It does not seem right that those who stumble inadvertently upon suicide must suffer the consequences of allowing another to die if they do not wish to do so. And so I believe strongly that a person who attempts suicide in such a way that others may discover him before he dies cannot expect them to stand by and allow him to die. He cannot expect someone who loves him or cares for him and/or who does not share his views of the rightness and wrongness or rationality of suicide, to act against her moral or rational beliefs in order to facilitate his demise by her omissions.

Nor can a suicide realistically expect to be allowed to die by a person with public responsibilities, such as a member of the caring professions or a police officer, who discovers his self harming, even when that other believes that everyone has the right to take his own life if he wishes, because to do so would put the career of the professional in jeopardy. Even if such a person had good reason to believe that an individual who had caused himself harm intended to kill himself and wished to die, it would be unwise of her to allow him to die, at least while she was about her professional duties, for fear of recriminations, because such an action is likely to meet with disapproval from others – both those in authority and those who control the media. Other writers recognise the problems that face practitioners of the caring professions in such situations. For example, Haley (1980) writes: 'The therapist . . . not only does not want the tragedy of a suicide, but is also vulnerable in the professional community if he does not take the accepted steps to prevent it' (p. 138).

Autonomy is important. However, I think it can be overridden where its exercise involves harming others. So to my mind, intervention in another person's suicide can be justified on the grounds that if one does not, one will be harmed: by the feelings or nightmares one might have afterwards, or by the effects on one's career if one works in one of the caring or other public services. I think intervention can also be justified on the grounds that one is concerned to prevent harm to others – to the relatives and friends of the suiciding individual, though it is perhaps harder to do this because of the difficulty in knowing how others will be affected. There might even be times when it was wrong to intervene because others were involved and would be harmed if one prevented someone they loved from suiciding. Consider, for example, a situation in which a couple, each dying with AIDS, had made a suicide pact and had satisfied their friends that the best and most fulfilling end both of the relationship and of their lives, would be to die together. In such a case, though intervention on the grounds of self defence would still be possible, it would be difficult to justify intervention in order to protect these others.

In most circumstances, then, I think it will be possible to justify intervention in another's suicide simply in order to protect oneself or others. This does not mean, however, that I believe that we are morally obliged to intervene, only that we may intervene in order to prevent harm.

Exceptions to the justification of intervention on the grounds of self defence

I have argued that most often it is permissible for one person to prevent another killing himself on the grounds that to do so constitutes self defence or the defence of others. However, there are exceptions to this. For example, there are cases where it seems clear that it would be morally wrong to intervene and where concern for another would lead one to refrain from intervention even if this meant that another was allowed, or perhaps by omission *enabled*, to die. There are a number of such circumstances.

One case where it seems clear to me that intervention would be wrong would be where a suicidal individual had entered into an agreement with another to the effect that this other would not interfere with his suicide. This might, for example, occur in circumstances where the 'suicide' could be viewed as self administered euthanasia. It would be wrong to go back on one's word in relation to an agreement concerning a matter of such importance to the suicide. On the other hand it would be understandable if an individual who had made such an agreement developed cold feet when she was actually watching a loved one die by his own hand.

A second instance in which it is difficult to justify intervention in a suicidal act by reference to the harm that will be experienced by oneself or others as a result of the death, would be where that harm is likely to be small relative to the suffering the person will undergo if he is prevented from killing himself. Consider, for example, the following story.

Daniel is suffering from terminal cancer. He is in dreadful pain and his family has suffered for a long time because of his illness; his anguish and pain is so great before his suiciding action that anything others might suffer as a result of his suicide would be small by comparison. No one will suffer materially as a result of Daniel's death and everyone close to him is unanimous in believing that death would be a merciful release.

It seems reasonable to think of suicide in a case like this as a kind of self administered euthanasia because it is motivated by the intention to bring about a peaceful death and to avoid a horrid one rather than the intention to avoid a horrid life. And it seems clear to me that we would be best not to interfere with Daniel's attempt should we find him. Of course, if we were uninvolved in his plans to die, we may be unaware of them and intervene because we cared for him or believed that he was not acting autonomously. This just goes to show how important it is for a person who wishes to end his life to share his plans with others.

There is another type of case where I think it could be best to let a suiciding person die and perhaps wrong to prevent him. This is where, because of the nature of the suicide attempt and the point it has reached, intervention will mean that the suicide is left in a state so bad as to make any suffering that might have been caused to others had the attempt been allowed to succeed small by comparison. Stopping a serious suicide attempt after it is well under way could mean that although we prevent the individual from dying, we do not prevent him from being badly damaged so that our good intentions produce a state of affairs just as horrible as, or even more horrible than, that which we were trying to prevent. Indeed it could be argued that by stopping such an attempt we actually harm the suiciding person. Anyone who comes across a serious self harming situation is in a double bind because of the lack of certainty about the outcome of intervention, about whether, for example, it will save the person from a fate worse than death or rather condemn him to such a fate.

Postscript

In any situation in which one person finds another person suiciding there are likely to be difficulties in making an accurate prediction about the likely after effects both of the suicide attempt if it is allowed to proceed and of intervention in it. To return to Gloria, the blood vomiting client to whom I have already referred, it was difficult to tell what her state might have been afterwards; indeed after being in a coma for many days she was told by the doctors that she was lucky not to have damaged her liver permanently. Perhaps if her liver had been dreadfully damaged, my stopping her suicide attempt could have been viewed as morally wrong because my suffering and the suffering of her family and friends had she died might have been less than hers had she survived in a dreadful state. But accurately predicting the future is beyond most of us. And so perhaps had this been the outcome I would have been able to avoid moral condemnation on the grounds that I had acted to avoid harm that was more certain rather than harm that was less certain; and surely that is not something for which a person may be ostracised.

NOTES

1   There is a hybrid form of paternalism in which the paternalist acts with both her own and the other's interests in mind. A paternalistic intervener in suicidal self harm may, for example, save another's life partly because she believes it to be in that other's best interests to remain alive and partly because for her own reasons she would not want him to be dead. In reality there will be a continuum between cases that are dominantly motivated by care for oneself and others that are dominantly motivated by concern for the other. It is also worth noting the distinction between instances of self interested paternalism in which the paternalist, while acting in her own interests, claims that she was acting in the other's best interests and others where she makes no claim to be doing so.

2   And what's more, being causally involved, because by refraining from intervention, they have omitted to do what they could have done to save the person.

REFERENCES

Alvarez, A. (1972) *The Savage God*, London, Weidenfeld and Nicolson.

Barrington, M.R. (1969) 'The Case for Rational Suicide', in Downing, A.B. and Smoker, B. (eds) (1986) *Voluntary Euthanasia: Experts Debate the Right to Die*, revised, updated and enlarged edition, London, Peter Owen.

BBC, *Omnibus*, Tuesday 7 December, 1993.

Beauchamp, T. and Childress, J. (1983) *Principles of Biomedical Ethics*, second edition, New York, Oxford University Press.

Berne, E. (1979) *What Do You Say After You Say Hello?* London, Corgi.

Brazier, M. (1987) *Medicine, Patients and the Law*, Harmondsworth, Penguin.

Brock, G.W. and Barnard, C.P. (1988) *Procedure in Family Therapy*, Boston, Allyn and Bacon Inc.

Campbell, R. and Collinson, D. (1988) *Ending Lives*, Oxford, Basil Blackwell.

Camus, A. (1975) *The Myth of Sisyphus*, tr. O'Brian, J., Harmondsworth, Penguin.

Chapman, A.H. (1970) *Put-Offs and Come-Ons*, London, Corgi, Transworld Publishers Ltd, Corgi Edition.

Clare, A. (1975) *Psychiatry in Dissent*, London, Tavistock.

Curran, D. et al (1980) *Psychological Medicine: An Introduction to Psychiatry*, ninth edition, Edinburgh, Churchill Livingstone.

Daube, D. (1972) 'The Linguistics of Suicide', *Philosophy and Public Affairs*, Vol. 1, No. 4. pp. 387–437.

Douglas, J. (1970) *The Social Meanings of Suicide*, Princeton, Princeton University Press.

Downie, R.S. and Telfer, E. (1969) *Respect for Persons*, London, Allen and Unwin.

Durkheim, E. (1897) *Suicide: A Study in Sociology*, tr. Spaulding, J.A. and Simpson, G. (1952), London, RKP.

Dyck, A. (1980) 'Beneficent Euthanasia and Benemortasia: Alternative Views of Mercy', in Horan, D.J. and Mall, D. (eds) *Death, Dying and Euthanasia*, Frederick, Maryland, Aletheia Books.

Dyer, C. (1993) 'Lords Lift Last Bar to Mercy Death', *Guardian*, 4 March, p. 1.

Eldrid, J. (1988) *Caring for the Suicidal*, London, Constable.

Ellis, R. (Director) (1982) Film: *Reuben, Reuben*.

Fairbairn, G.J. (1991a) 'Enforced Death: Enforced Life', *Journal of Medical Ethics*, Vol. 17, pp. 144–9.

—— (1991b) 'Suicide and Justified Paternalism', in Brazier, M. and Lobjoit, M. (eds) *Protecting the Vulnerable*, London: Routledge.

—— (1992a) 'Integration, Values and Society', in Fairbairn, G.J. and Fairbairn, S.A. (eds) *Integrating Special Children: Some Ethical Issues*, Aldershot, Avebury.

—— (1992b) 'Small People, Disability and Values', paper presented at a conference at the Centre for Social Ethics and Research, University of Manchester, March; forthcoming in *Disability, Handicap and Society*.

—— (1992c) 'Enforced Death: Enforced Life: A reply to Saunders and Singh', Letter to the Editor, *Journal of Medical Ethics*, Sept.

—— (1992d) *Suicide: Some Conceptual and Ethical Issues*, PhD thesis, University of Manchester.

—— and Mead, D. (1990) 'Therapeutic Storytelling, Ethics and the Loss of Innocence', parts 1 and 2, *Paediatric Nursing*, June, pp. 22–3, July, pp. 11–12.

—— and Mead, D. (1993a) 'Working With the Stories Nurses Tell', *Nursing Standard*, Vol. 7, No. 31, pp. 37–40.

—— and Mead, D. (1993b) 'Storytelling and Ethics', *Nursing Standard*, Vol. 7, No. 32, pp. 32–6.

—— and Winch, C. (1991) *Reading, Writing and Reasoning*, Milton Keynes, Open University Press.

Fleming, D.L. (1980) *The Spiritual Exercises of St Ignatius: A Literal Translation and a Contemporary Reading*, St Louis, Institute of Jesuit Sources.

Flew, A. (1986) 'The Principle of Euthanasia', in Downing, A.B. and Smoker, B. (eds) *Voluntary Euthanasia: Experts Debate the Right to Die*, revised, updated and enlarged edition, London, Peter Owen.

Fox, R. (1981) 'Suicide', in *Dictionary of Medical Ethics*, revised and enlarged edition, London, Darton, Longman and Todd.

Frey, R. (1981) 'Did Socrates Commit Suicide?', in Battin, M.P. and Mayo, J.D. (eds) *Suicide: The Philosophical Issues*, London, Peter Owen.

Galloway, K. (1988) *Imagining the Gospels*, London, SPCK.

Glover, J. (1977) *Causing Death and Saving Lives*, Harmondsworth, Penguin.

Haley, J. (1980) *Leaving Home: The Therapy of Disturbed Young People*, New York, McGraw-Hill.

Hardy, T. (1957) *Jude the Obscure*, London, Macmillan.

Haring, B. (1972) *Medical Ethics*, Slough, St Paul Publications.

Harré, R. and Secord, P. (1972) *The Explanation of Social Behaviour*, Oxford, Basil Blackwell.

Harris, J. (1980) *Violence and Responsibility*, London, RKP.

—— (1985) *The Value of Life*, London, RKP.

—— (1991) Personal communication.

Holland, R. (1969) 'Suicide', in Vesey, G. (ed.) *Talk of God*, London, Macmillan.

Hume, D. (1784) 'Of Suicide', repr. in Singer, P. (1986) *Applied Ethics*, Oxford, Oxford University Press.

Humphry, D. (1991) *Final Exit: The Practicalities of Self-deliverance and Assisted Suicide for the Dying*, Eugene, Oregon, Hemlock Society.

Iga, M. and Tatai, K. (1975) 'Characteristics of Suicides and Attitudes toward Suicide in Japan', in Farberow, N.L. (ed.) *Suicide in Different Cultures*, Baltimore, University Park Press.

Kamisar, Yale (1980) 'Some Non-Religious Views Against Proposed "Mercy-Killing" Legislation', in Horan, D.J. and Mall, D. (eds) *Death, Dying and Euthanasia*, Frederick, Maryland, Aletheia Books.

Kelly, G. (1955) *The Psychology of Personal Constructs*, Vols 1 and 2, New York, Norton.

Kessel, N. (1965) *Milroy Lectures*, Roy. Coll. Phys. London, 1 and 3 February.

Kirwan, P. (1991) 'Suicide in a Rural Irish Population', *Irish Medical Journal*, Vol. 84, No. 1, pp. 14–15.

Kreitman, N. (ed.) (1977) *Parasuicide*, London, John Wiley.

—— and Dyer, J. 'Suicide in Relation to Parasuicide', *Medicine*, Vol. 36, p. 1827, cited in Eldrid, J. (1988) *Caring for the Suicidal*, London, Constable.

Lebacqz, K. and Englehardt Jr, H.T. (1980) 'Suicide', in Horan, D.J. and Mall, D. (eds) *Death, Dying and Euthanasia*, Frederick, Maryland, Aletheia Books.

Lee, L. (1959) *Cider with Rosie*, Harmondsworth, Penguin.

Lester, D. (1990) 'A Classification of Acts of Attempted Suicide', *Perceptual and Motor Skills*, Vol. 70, pp. 1245–6.

Linacre Centre (1982) *Euthanasia and Clinical Practice: Trends, Principles and Alternatives. The Report of a Working Party*, London, Linacre Centre.

Lindley, R. (1987) 'Psychotherapy as Essential Care' in Fairbairn, S. and Fairbairn, G. (eds) *Psychology, Ethics and Change*, London, RKP.

—— (1988) 'Paternalism and Caring', in Fairbairn, G. and Fairbairn, S. (eds) *Ethical Issues in Caring*, Aldershot, Gower.

Louisell, D.W. (1980) 'Euthanasia and Biathanasia: On Dying and Killing', in Horan, D.J. and Mall, D. (eds) *Death, Dying and Euthanasia*, Frederick, Maryland, Aletheia Books.

Lyttle, J. (1991) *Mental Disorder*, London, Baillière Tindall.

McLuhan, M. (1969) *Understanding Media*, Aylesbury, Sphere.

Martin, R.M. (1981) 'Suicide and Self-Sacrifice', in Battin, M.P. and Mayo, D.J. (eds) *Suicide: The Philosophical Issues*, London, Peter Owen.

Mill, J.S. (1859) *On Liberty*, in Dent edition (1976) *Utilitarianism, On Liberty and Representative Government*.

Mitchell, A.R.K. (1971) *Psychological Medicine in Family Practice*, London, Baillière Tindall.

Moreno, J.L. (1948) *Psychodrama*, New York, Beacon House.

Rachels, J. (1986) *The End of Life*, Oxford, Oxford University Press.

Ringel, E. (1981) 'Suicide Prevention and the Value of Human Life', in Battin, M.P. and Mayo, D.J. (eds) *Suicide: The Philosophical Issues*, London, Peter Owen.

Rogers, C. (1965) *Client-Centred Therapy*, Boston, Houghton Mifflin.

Saunders, J.B. (1970) *Mozley and Whitley's Law Dictionary*, eighth edition,

London, Butterworth.

Scott, R.F. (1935) *Scott's Last Expedition*, Vol. 1, London, John Murray.

Smoker, B. (1983) cited in 'Arthur Koestler and Suicide', abstracted from the *Voluntary Euthanasia Newsletter*, reprinted in Downing, A.B. and Smoker, B. (eds) (1986) *Voluntary Euthanasia: Experts Debate the Right to Die*, London, Peter Owen.

Soya (1992) Personal communication.

Szasz, T. (1971) 'The Ethics of Suicide', *Antioch Review*, Vol. XXXI, No. 1, reprinted in Battin, M.P. and Mayo, D.J. (eds) (1981) *Suicide: The Philosophical Issues*, London, Peter Owen.

Taylor, S. (1988) *Suicide*, London, Longman.

Tredennick, H. (trans.) (1959) *The Last Days of Socrates*, Harmondsworth, Penguin.

Wertheimer, A. (1991) *A Special Scar: The Experiences of People Bereaved by Suicide*, London, Routledge.

Windt, P. (1981) 'The Concept of Suicide', in Battin, M.P. and Mayo, D.J. (eds) *Suicide: The Philosophical Issues*, London, Peter Owen.

Winner, M. (Director) (1971) Film: *The Mechanic*.

Wittgenstein, L. (1961) *Notebooks 1914–16*, edited by von Wright, G.H. and Anscombe, G.E.M., English translation by G.E.M. Anscombe, Oxford, Basil Blackwell.

—— (1974) *Philosophical Investigations*, tr. Anscombe, G.E.M., Oxford, Basil Blackwell.

Wolfensberger, W. (1987) *The New Genocide of Handicapped and Afflicted People*, New York, Syracuse University Training Institute (available in Britain from CMH Publications, 5 Kentings, Comberton, Cambridge, CB3 7DT).

INDEX

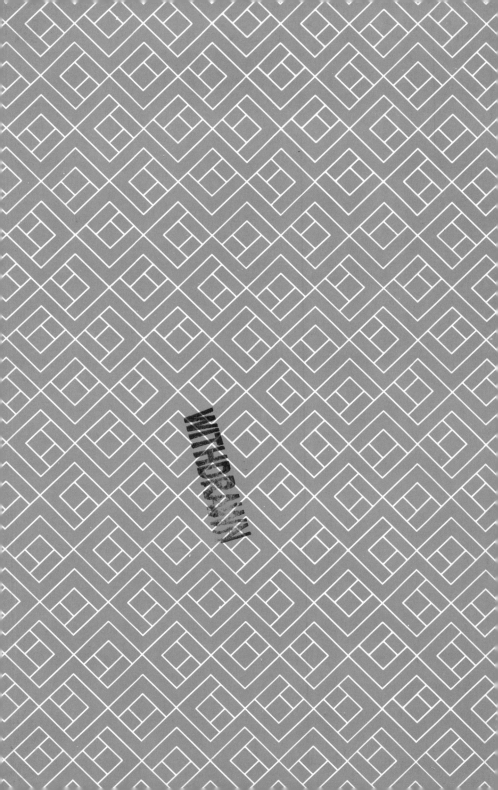